I0559514

BREAKING
THE
CYCLE OF SIN!

Lessons Gleaned from the Judges
A Wake Up Call for Today's Christians.

DR. MARIO A. BRUNI

Copyright © 2024 Dr. Mario A. Bruni.

All rights reserved. This book or any portion thereof may not be reproduced or used in any manner whatsoever without the express written permission of the publisher except for the use of brief quotation in a book review.

Unless marked otherwise, all Scripture quotations are taken from the New King James Version®. Copyright © 1982 by Thomas Nelson. Used by permission. All rights reserved.

Scripture quotations marked KJV are taken from the King James Version.

Scripture quotations marked AMP are taken from the Amplified® Bible, Copyright © 2015 by The Lockman Foundation. Used by permission.

Scripture quotations marked CEB are taken from the Common English Bible, Copyright © 2011 by the Common English Bible Committee. All rights reserved.

Scripture quotations marked CEV are taken from the Contemporary English Version®, Copyright © 1995 American Bible Society. All rights reserved.

Scripture quotations marked ISV are taken from The Holy Bible: International Standard Version. Release 2.0, Build 2015.02.09. Copyright © 1995-2014 by ISV Foundation. ALL RIGHTS RESERVED INTERNATIONALLY. Used by permission of Davidson Press, LLC.

Scripture quotations marked GNT are taken from the Good News Translation® (Today's English Version, Second Edition). Copyright © 1992 American Bible Society. All rights reserved.

ISBN: 978-1-965679-01-2 (sc)
ISBN: 978-1-965679-02-9 (e)

Rev. date: 09/10/2024

CONTENTS

DEDICATION

I am dedicating this book is to my wife of 49 years Maria J. Bruni who for the last three years insisted that I continue with my writing as she went to work each day in order to pay the bills, and buy the food necessary to sustain our family. Without her there would be no True Light Ministry Int. Inc., internet teachings, or books that God can in some way help the Church of God grow and become a greater presence in the world today. For after all, that should be the desire of all Christian ministries! May all Christian men who are unmarried find a Proverbs 31 woman like my dear wife; and may all the Christian women who read this dedication strive to give this type of love, faith and dedication towards the man that they love.

KNOW GOD KNOW PEACE — NO GOD NO PEACE

Any person who has been around Christianity for any length of time has come to realize that Christians are not perfect. Christians continuously fall into sin either by omission or commission. The "Cycle of Sin," referred to as this recurring pattern of sinning and repentance, permeates our Christianity like pollution does our atmosphere. We can't avoid it, we can't always live apart from it, and we can't ever conquer it without God's almighty power and His methods. It is part of our world, our lives, and our very nature, for that matter. This "Cycle of Sin" is distasteful, destructive, and devastating to our witness, our families, friends, and, more importantly, our fellowship with Jesus. Despite our best efforts to conceal this cycle's effects, it too often reveals our vulnerabilities and sinfulness openly to a cruel, unbending, and evil world. Those imperfections are used by our enemies as a weapon to humiliate and destroy us and our faith. These recurrent failures produce a severe blow to our pride until we deal with the sin. Repetitive sin causes emotional upheaval and distress and at times, forces us to circumvent our ministries. The devil uses these times to his advantage. He steals our joy and victory and takes back any advancement we may have made in the times between the cessation of one cycle and the onset of another.

These times of failure force us to see our wretchedness up close and at times, way too personally. They bring us face to face with defeat in spite of our God-given promise of victory, and to some of our brethren, these recurrent failures drive them to doubt their salvation and calling. The best we can do is to take the lessons gleaned from those experiences, learn from them, and apply what we have learned to our lives. This knowledge will help us to minimize the number of times we fall into the "Cycle of Sin," which consists primarily of 4 steps, failure, bondage repentance, and deliverance. It will also shorten the time in which we spend going through each phase of the sin cycle and extend the amount of time between the start of another period.

Each time the "Cycle of Sin" begins, the Book of Judges records the same information. Seven times we see this phrase; *So the children of Israel did evil in the sight of the Lord. They forgot the Lord their God and served the Baals and Asherah's."* (Ref. Judges 3:7 NKJV) Below is an illustration adapted from the Ryrie Study Bible, of the "Cycle of Sin." The verses listed show the beginning of each cycle, and next to them are the judges God used to deliver His people from the "cycle of sin."

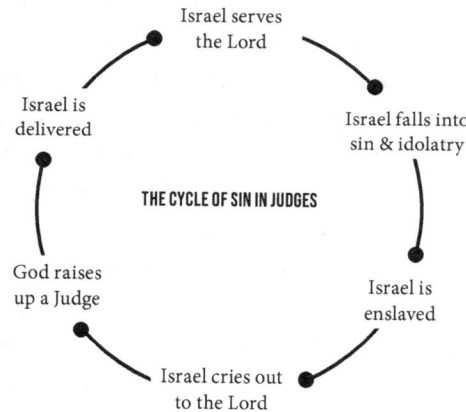

Israel serves the Lord

Israel is delivered

Israel falls into sin & idolatry

THE CYCLE OF SIN IN JUDGES

God raises up a Judge

Israel is enslaved

Israel cries out to the Lord

Judges 2:11-19 Declaration of Israel's sin and the description of the cycle revealed.

Judges 3:7 Othniel

Judges 3:12 Ehud

Judges 4:1 Deborah

Judges 6:1 Gibeon

Judges 10:6 Jephthah

Judges 13:1 Samson

This illustration found on page 283 of The Ryrie Study Bible NASB (9780802484635)

Brethren, we will all continue to experience this "Cycle of Sin" as long as we live. Even the Apostle Paul went through it, notice what he said;

"For we know that the law is spiritual, but I am carnal, sold under sin. (15) For what I am doing, I do not understand. For what I will to do, that I do not practice; but what I hate, that I do. (16) If then, I do what I will not to do, I agree with the law that it is good. (17) But now, it is no longer I who do it, but sin that dwells in me. (18) For I know that in me (that is, in my flesh) nothing good dwells for to will is present with me, but how to perform what is good I do not find. (19) For the good that I will to do, I do not do; but the evil I will not to do, that I practice. (20) Now if I do what I will not to do, it is no longer I who do it, but sin that dwells in me. (21) I find then a law, that evil is present with me, the one who wills to do good. (22) For I delight in the law of God according to the inward man. (23) But I see another law in my members, warring against the law of my mind, and bringing me into captivity to the law of sin which is in my members. (24) O wretched man that I am! Who will deliver me from this body of death? (25) I thank God—through Jesus Christ, our Lord! So then, with the mind, I myself serve the law of God, but with the flesh the law of sin."

Romans 7:19-25 NKJV

Paul is not the only one who has experienced this "Cycle of Sin," it has been around since Adam and Eve ate the fruit in the Garden of Eden. Anyone who has ever read God's Word can see it. God did not hide the shame caused by Disobedience; He openly declared it! Why? So, man could see it, examine it, and learn from it. To that end, I write this book, not on the "Book of Judges," but on the Judges themselves! Those men, some well-known others not, those that God called and gave the ability to lift His people out of this "Cycle of Sin." By the lessons gleaned from their experiences, God's people will possess valuable keys essential in minimizing the occurrences, depth, duration, and utterly devastating effects of the "Cycle of Sin."

Now you might be saying to yourself, "why has it been around so long without being defeated? "How can this continue to happen?" "Why could they not recognize it so that they could avoid it?" If you are proud of your righteousness, you might even think that "this could never happen to me!" And as naive as it would be for me to say that this is a message only of history, one that only applies to them and not to us, because Jesus has made us "more than conquerors" (c.f. Romans 8:37) It would not be the truth. The truth of the matter is that Christians today go through this same "Cycle of Sin" that the people of God did in the time of the Judges. All of us have failed God in one form or another, and it has affected us in ways that sometimes are momentary and at other times, long-lasting. These failures can stem from an enemy attack in an area of weakness caused by our tainted past, compromise, an overwhelming desire for something, or even from taking action without the Lord's instruction. Even outside activities can create it by permitting deceptively innocent activities far too high an influence in our lives. And maybe the most common way we fall into sin is through the enemy attacking us in an area we thought we had already conquered. And suddenly, the same temptation rears its ugly head, and we find ourselves back amid failure. There is not one Christian that cannot relate to one or more of these subtle deceptions. That is why all of us can learn from a study of the character, situations and actions taken by God's Judges.

Have you seen this cycle in your own life? Has your Christian walk been a cycle of victory and defeat? Does it bother you that your walk with God is not what you desire it to be? Do you recognize that your periodical failures seem to set you back from your walk with God? Do you see the cycle occurring right now in your life? Brethren, the lessons gleaned from the Judges are a wake-up call for each of us. It is a warning of what can happen once we become comfortable in our Christianity, and begin to compromise our commitment to God and His precepts. Complacency, compromise, and Disobedience are things that we cannot tolerate or afford in our lives; it will, at least, hurt us, and eventually, if not corrected, destroy us.

Do you remember the story of the unnamed young prophet whom God sent to confront Jeroboam at an altar at Bethel? You can find the story in 1st Kings 13. God told the young prophet not to stop for anything, (verse 9) only deliver his message and return without hesitation; even though he understood God clearly, he disobeyed; as a result, a lion ate him. In other words, whom God calls have no time to relax from following the Lord's instructions. We must continue to fight and work until the Lord comes. Run the race with all diligence, running as to win the prize of the high calling in Christ. Paul saw and declared to us the importance of not resting in the war in which we are now engaged.

> "Do you not know that those who run in a race all run, but one receives the prize? Run in such a way that you may obtain it. (25) And everyone who competes for the prize is temperate in all things. Now they do it to obtain a perishable crown, but we for an imperishable crown. (26) Therefore, I run thus: not with uncertainty. Thus, I fight: not as one who beats the air. (27) But I discipline my body and bring it into subjection, lest, when I have preached to others, I should become disqualified."
>
> 1 Corinthians 9:24-27 NKJV

> "Brethren, I do not count myself to have apprehended; but one thing I do, forgetting those things which are behind and reaching forward to those things which are ahead, (14) I press toward the goal for the prize of the upward call of God in Christ Jesus."
>
> Philippians 3:13-14 NKJV

The writer of the book of Hebrews agrees.

> "Therefore, we also, since so great a cloud of witnesses surrounds us, let us lay aside every weight, and the sin which so easily ensnares us, and let us run with endurance the race that is set before us, (2) looking unto Jesus, the author, and finisher of our faith, who for the joy that was set before Him endured the cross, despising the shame, and has sat down at the right hand of the throne of God. (3) Let us consider Him who endured such hostility from sinners against Himself, lest you become weary and discouraged in your souls. (4) You have not yet resisted to bloodshed, striving against sin."
>
> Hebrews 12:1-4 NKJV

If we become complacent, or disobedient to the least of God's instructions, we inevitably fall into the "Cycle of Sin," and perhaps never escape, just like the young prophet in 1st Kings 13:26.

So far, in this introduction, I may have presented the book of Judges as unfavorable, one of recurrent failure. But I have great news! Judges is not just a negative book, it does not only show us the temptations and reasons why we fall, but the message of the judges is also a very glorious and positive one. Though there is a consistent "Cycle of Sin," failure and bondage that permeates the book of Judges, we should also recognize that the Judges teach us by what means God uses to give His children victory over their slavery. How they were able to maintain a period of peace lasting longer in most cases than the period of bondage; it also demonstrates God's faithfulness toward his children. The methods of victory over this "Cycle of Sin" are beautiful truths to comprehend. You can prevent the "Cycle of Sin" only by God's grace, power, and the guidance of the Holy Spirit who leads us to all truth and by God's word, which is the lamp to our feet and the light unto our path (Ref. Psalm 119:105). Through God's word, we can learn how to minimize the amount of times we fall into this "Cycle of Sin, and how to shorten the time it takes for this cycle of failure and bondage to come to an end.

Each judge's actions teach us a slightly different and essential lesson for overcoming our enemy. You can learn many vital lessons from Israel's enemies, as well. By understanding our enemy's abilities, and subtle trickery and recognizing the snares Satan places before us, we possess strategic, powerful, and intelligent foresight to avoid any attacks Satan may throw at us (c.f. Matthew 12:22; 2nd Corinthians 2:11). Here is a historical example that precisely makes this point.

From January 16, 1991, through February 28, 1991, a coalition of 28 nations led by the United States was at war with Iraq, which was under the leadership of Saddam Hussein. A dispute over a shared oil field caused Iraq to invade Kuwait on August 2, 1990. This invasion and subsequent annexation of Kuwait by Iraq provoked a massive buildup of United Nations troops in Saudi Arabia.

In December 1990, the United Nations authorized the use of force if Iraq did not withdraw before January 15, 1991. Within 24 hours of the deadline, the United States and Allied forces in an unprecedented show of unity and force launched a massive air bombardment against Baghdad, hitting strategic targets such as military air bases and communications systems. This air offensive lasted six weeks, in which it destroyed about one-third of Iraqi equipment and inflicted massive casualties. A one-hundred-hour ground war followed, which effectively destroyed the remnants of the 500,000 strong Iraqi army in or near Kuwait.

This war, known as "The Gulf War" and referred to by the Americans as "Desert Storm," it was the first large-scale demonstration of modern technological warfare. This technology included the use of Satellite imaging, which gave the Allied forces superior intelligence and understanding concerning the enemy's numbers, locations, weapons, and movements. As a result of this intelligence, the outcome of the war was never in question. The ground war started on February 24, 1991, and the superior range of the US artillery soon devastated the retreating Iraqi forces: and by the end of February, the war was over.[1]

At the end of the Gulf War, General Norman Schwarzkopf, who was the commander and chief of the UN forces, in an interview, said "he thought such a quick and decisive victory came because *we had the best and most reliable, up to date intelligence on the enemy. We knew what their positions were, their movements, weapons, supplies, and numbers. Then we just positioned our troops in the best strategic locations, positions we knew that they could not defend. Then we hit them hard and fast, right where it hurt the most, giving them no ability to regroup or mount any offensive.*" [2]

Christians, we need to learn this lesson, get it deep down in our souls. We should take General Schwarzkopf's response and apply it to the war against Satan. If we knew all the vital information about Satan, his whiles, his troops, their positions, movements, numbers, and what weapons are at his disposal, then we could position ourselves and our families in the best strategic location we knew that Satan could not defend against, then we could easily thwart his attacks and be the conquerors God has called us to be. God commands us to put on all the armor that God supplies. In this way, you can take a stand against the devil's strategies. We must realize that our intelligence and spiritual weapons come from an all-powerful and all-knowing God whose weapons are much more powerful, long-ranging, and destructive, and His intelligence is perfect and all-inclusive. God is very much aware of the enemy's plans, devices, and strength. For God knows where Satan's deploys his forces, and what actions it will take to obtain victory over them. He has in His arsenal the exact weapon, tool, and plan not only to stop the enemy's offensive but to destroy his ability to inflict harm. God is well aware that this is not a wrestling match against a human opponent. We are wrestling against rulers, authorities, the powers who govern this world of darkness, and spiritual forces that control evil. When will we realize that even though we cannot sense or see the war we are in – it still exists? This undefeatable tandem of perfect intelligence and all-powerful weaponry, coupled with our obedience to God's commands, along with our determination, ability, and diligence, will give us all we need to avoid and overcome Satan, defeat him and gain the ultimate victory!

Using the information found in these pages along with prayerful hope and their application means we can-go on to greater heights in God, free ourselves our families and all we come into contact with to live a more productive, happy, victorious and peaceable life

Oh Lord, let the same blessing You gave to Peter, (Ref. Matthew 16:18-19; Luke 22:31-32) become a reality in our lives. Satan has had his way for too long; it is now time to take back that which he has stolen. Let us allow him no quarter. Help us, Lord, to clearly and poignantly declare Your truths so that they will have the same powerful effect on all who will listen. In Jesus' name, Amen!

> (18) Moreover, I also say unto thee, thou art Peter, and upon this rock, I will build my church; and the gates of hell shall not prevail against it. (19) And I will give unto thee the keys of the kingdom of heaven: and whatsoever thou shalt bind on earth shall be bound in heaven: and whatsoever thou shalt loose on earth shall be loosed in heaven."
>
> Matthew 16:18-19 (KJV)

BACKGROUND — THE JUDGES

Judges is a record of seven apostasies, seven servitudes, seven cries for help, and seven deliverances. Judges as a whole takes its name from the history of 15 Judges raised to rescue and rule Israel. This sad and solemn book has a two-fold message; one is the perpetual proneness of the human heart to wander from God, and two; God's unceasing desire and mercy to restore His backslidden people to fellowship with Himself.

Judges is a sad contrast to the book of Joshua which chronicles Israel's victory and the blessings God bestowed on His children for their obedience in conquering the land God had given them; note the phrase "the land had rest from war" (Ref. Joshua 11:23, 14:15; 21:44). Judges, on the other hand, chronicles Israel's failure due to their Disobedience and disregard for God's covenant. Their failure was not driving out the enemies of God as commanded, but the fact that they made agreements with them so that they could remain in the land. Israel not driving their enemies out of their land is what spelled Israel's doom! The corrupting influences of these idolatrous nations led Israel into idolatry. As a result of Israel's willful Disobedience and their failure to conquer their enemies and claim their rightful inheritance, God's chosen people experienced devastating tragedies in their lives, families, country, and most importantly, in their relationship with Jehovah God. Israel became morally, spiritually, and physically weakened, resulting in them becoming the conquered instead of the conquerors. When we as children of God do not remove all corrupting influences in our lives, the results are inevitably the same as these Israelites.

Each time Israel's people recognized their pitiful plight, they called upon God, who graciously sent a deliverer who delivered them and set them on the path of righteousness again. The term "Judge" was not, regarded only to the ordinary judicial functions of the time. Instead, these judges were leaders or rulers chosen and anointed by God to be Israel's representatives, and they were to represent Israel's faith and its hopes. Whatever these Judges were able to achieve was only by their faith. The time of peace brought by these Judges only lasted as long as the judge lived; for shortly after their death the stiff-necked and idolatrous children of God would once again fall headlong into wickedness. They would turn their backs on God, and the "Cycle of Sin" would begin again. 4 words can easily describe This "Cycle of Sin": Sin, Servitude, Sorrow, and Salvation, or Rebellion, Rejection, Repentance, and Restoration. This repetition of Sin, Servitude, Sorrow, and Salvation continued until Israel went into captivity by the Babylonians approximately 870 years later.

It appears that Joshua's last address, deepened Israel's hearts, For Israel began to conquer and occupy the Promised Land as God-ordained. For God said that the measure of the sin of the nations who occupied Palestine was now full (Genesis 15:13-16), and God's declared judgment was to take place and sweep these heathen nations away. On the ruins of what was the kingdom of Satan, Israel was to build a theocracy dedicated to Jehovah God. God used his sword (Word) for creating this theocracy. but only as long as their purpose was to dedicate the land to Him. Instead, heathenism overspread Palestine and, eventually, the world. What thwarted the kingdom of God was their rebellion and their incomplete mission to spread the light of truth to the remotest parts of the earth. Any thorough study of history will reveal that Canaan was not only the focus of ancient heathenism in its worst abominations but the hub in which it spread. Historians and theologians strongly believed that much of the mythology and most of the vileness of Greek and Roman heathenism originated in Canaan.

For the 25 years (approximately) after the death of Joshua, Israel stayed relatively loyal to Jehovah, then their memories of God, His mighty works, and His precepts that gave Israel their victories soon faded. As Israel lost sight of their purpose and goal, they began to serve Baal, Ashtoreth, and many other false gods. God allowed the Israelites to suffer the consequences of worshipping these false gods. As a result of this exceedingly poor choice, the people of God became enslaved, and then that they would cry out to Jehovah God for help. God in His infinite and unbounded mercy sent His children judges to deliver them from their bondage and gave them a time of peace, which demonstrated to His people the superiority Jehovah had over all false gods the way He did in Egypt. Christians should always be aware of God's mercy; for when we do not, we tend to forget His mercies, and as a result our love wanes; frustration, anger, and doubt come alive and we tend to fall away from God like the Israelites did (Ref. Deuteronomy 4:9, 23; Proverbs 2:17; Jeremiah 3:21-22; Hebrews 2:1). That is why we must praise him all day long. We must Praise Him for His wonderful works. We must meditate upon his wonderful works (Psalm 77:12). We must relate his wonderful works to our children (Psalm 78:4). Again; Because we cannot remember all of them, for there are too many (Psalm 40:5). (c.f. Psalms 35:28, 44:8, 78:4, 111:4, 119:27); We are to speak of His wonderful works (Psalm 78:4) throughout each generation.

God does His work so that anyone that forgets them forgets the mercies that God has shown them, and if a man ignores the work of God in his soul, he loses his love for God. It is not sufficient to lay up divine things in one's memory alone, but in the heart as well. "Your word have I hidden in my heart," David tells us, "that I might not sin against you" (Psalm 119:11 NKJV).

After spending seventy years in captivity, the Jews returned to the land of promise and no longer served foreign Gods! However, the "Cycle of Sin" continued. Its cause was not the worship of foreign gods like Baal or Ashtoreth as it once was, but they still served other gods. This verse *"Then the sons of Israel again did evil in the sight of the Lord."* recurs in each of the scriptures listed next to illustration # 1; Add this statement with Judges 17:6 "everyone did that which was right in his own eyes," and you discover that the God Israel served was their evil hearts (Ref. Genesis 6:5; 8:21; Proverbs 6:16-18, 23:7; Jeremiah 4:14; Matthew 15:18-20; Hebrews 3:12; 2 Peter 2:14-15). Man's evil heart is the reason why the "Cycle of sin" continues today and will not cease until Jesus comes and finally does away with all evil.

In Judges 2:18-19, we see the pattern of the entire book of Judges.

"The Lord raised judges who delivered Isreal out of the hand of their enemies all the days of the judge's life. The Lord was moved to pity by His people's groaning, (19) And it came to pass when the judge died, Israel reverted and behaved more corruptly than their fathers, by following other gods, to serve them and bow down to them. They did not cease from their doings nor from their stubborn way."

Judges 2:18-19

Below is a chart that will help us to recognize the events better as they unfolded during the time of the judges.

Illustration # 2 taken from *Webster's Gold Encyclopedia*, Topics Entertainment, 1997

Israel's Enemy	Years of Bondage	Judges	Years of Rest	Approximate Dates of Deliverance and Rest***	Scripture References
Time of Conquest		Joshua		1451 – 1390	Joshua 1 – Judges 3
Mesopotamia	8	Othniel	40	1389 – 1346	Judges 3:7 - 11
Eglon King of Moab	18	Ehud	80	1345 – 1313	3:12 - 30
Philistines	?	Shamgar*	?	1313 – 1312	3:31 & 5:6
Jabin King of Canaan	20	Deborah	40	1312 – 1257	4:4 – 5:31
Midian	7	Gibeon	40	1256 - 1214	6:1 – 8:28
Not named	?	Abimelech	3	1213 – 1211	9:22
Not named	?	Tola*	23	1210 – 1190	10:2
Not named	?	Jair*	22	1189 - 1170	10:3-5
Philistines and Amorites	18	Jephthah	6	1169 - 1147	10:6 – 12:7
Not named	?	Ibzan*	7	1146 – 1141	12:8 – 10
Not named	?	Elon*	10	1140 – 1131	12:11 – 12

Not named	?	Abdon*	8	1130 – 1123	12:13 – 15
Philistines	40	Samson	20	1122 – 1105	13:1 – 16:31
Philistines**	30	Eli	40	1104 – 1068	1st Samuel 1 – 4:18
Philistines**	20	Samuel	86	1067 – 1013	1st Samuel 4:18 – 25:1

*These Judges have little said about them, and their histories are vague and limited at best. These Judges are what Bible scholars have dubbed "the Minor Judges." But they also deserve the title "God's unsung heroes."

** Israel was battling the Philistine oppression on and off throughout the time of Samson, Eli, Samuel, and David. By the time of Solomon, Israel knew peace from all oppressors, along with abundant prosperity. You can find all of Eli, Samuel, David as well as Solomon's histories in the books of 1st and 2nd Samuel.

*** The Chronological dates given above are approximate, and they vary widely depending on the references used. The King's Calendar, by R. P. BenDedek, modified the dates used above in the chart.

Israel's obligation within God's covenant was to give loyalty and unwavering obedience to the Lord, who had shown them many mighty works and abundant grace and mercy in their deliverance from Egypt throughout the wilderness journeys and their initial conquest of the land of Canaan. It is also important to note that God kept His side of the Sinai Covenant without fail. He fulfilled all the promises He had made to the patriarchs concerning the Promised Land (Ref. Joshua 23:14). Israel's Disobedience to this covenant was the determining factor that inevitably led to the divine discipline of God (Ref. Joshua 23:15). Obedience to God's covenant brings abundant blessings while Disobedience brings disasters.

To the modern reader, it seems somewhat inconceivable why a loving God would leave evil within Israel's borders as a test to the faithfulness of His people. But to the Israelite historians, who had a much deeper and genuine understanding of God's sovereignty, the reasons were obvious. The first reason was for their protection and preservation. The land was too large, there were too many enemies, and as a result, if God had removed them all at one time, the beasts of the field would overrun them and destroy them (Ref. Exodus 23:30-31; Deuteronomy 7:22). The second reason was to examine the hearts of His people, which God in His sovereignty, mercy, and grace allowed so His people could see their evil hearts (Ref. Judges 2:22-23; 3:4). God did so with the hope that this purifying revelation would result in change, and lead to infinite blessings and salvation.

Judges 2:7 says, "So the people served the Lord all the days of Joshua and all the days of the elders who outlived Joshua." The reason for Israel's failure comes to light four verses later.

> "When all that generation had gone to their fathers, another generation arose after them who did not know the Lord or the work which He had done for Israel. (11) Then the children of Israel did evil in the sight of the Lord, and served the Baals."
>
> Judges 2:10-11

Israel forgot their God, His blessings, and His mercies that He had shown them and by personal choice eliminated Him from their thinking. They started to replace the Lord Jehovah with false idols more suited to their desired way of thinking and moral conduct (Ref. verse 13). Verse 14-17 reveals the result of this action.

> "And the anger of the Lord was hot against Israel. So, He delivered them into the hands of plunderers who despoiled them; and He sold them into the hands of their enemies all around, so that they could no longer stand before their enemies. (15) Wherever they went out, the hand of the Lord was against them for calamity, as the Lord had said, And they became greatly distressed. (16) Nevertheless, the Lord raised judges who delivered them out of the hand of those who plundered them. (17)

They would not listen to their judges, but they played the harlot with other gods and bowed down to them. They turned quickly from how their fathers walked, in obeying the commandments of the Lord; they did not do so."

Judges 2:14-17

In Judges 2:17, you can see the incentive that fueled their need for deliverance. In Judges, 2:16 salvation came purely from God's pity and tender compassion. It came from within God Himself, and there was no other source of this deliverance outside of God's mercy and grace. Notice, however, it does not say, "It repented them because of their iniquities," but it does say, "Nevertheless, the Lord raised judges who delivered them." (Ref. Judges 2:16) Notice also that it was not the burden of sin they were groaning about, but the difficulties of affliction. For if it was the burden of sin, they would have listened to the Judges that God sent, but no! They did not want to listen to the Judges; all they wanted was to play the harlot with their preferred gods and bow down to them (Ref. Judges 2:17). It is also true they deserved every bit of what they were getting and more, but God in His abundant mercy and patience did not bring it all upon them. God's love and sympathy overshadowed His justice and judgment He withheld His mercy and judgment temporarily, and God delivered them.

The instruments God used to bring about their deliverance were judges. God did not send angels from heaven to rescue them, or bring in any foreign power to their aid, but raised judges from among their nation; men to whom God gave extraordinary qualifications and abilities for an exceptional purpose. But God's mercy did not end there – he crowned them with incredible success, because: "The Lord was with the judges" (Judges 2:18).

There is another important fact I would like to present regarding the judges of Israel. The Lord is our judge (Ref Judges 11:27) in the context of the Philistine and Amorite oppression; the (shâphaṭ or judge is the same Hebrew word used for those God rose up). The idea derived from the use of this particular word and the Lord being their judge form the foundation of the book of Judges. The Lord is the real judge of His people; it is He who gives them into the hands of their oppressors, and it is He who raises their deliverers. It is also His Spirit that comes upon them and equips them for the task of deliverance (Ref. Judges 3:10; 6:34; 11:29; 14:6, 19; 15:14).

The men who God raised to be their saviors had peculiar qualities, which were the manifestation of a unique endowment from the Lord. The people could recognize this quality once revealed in the judge's life and actions, the most spectacular of which would be deliverance. But mighty exploits or one's success in battle, though highly regarded, was not the only significant endowment given by the Lord and recognized by the people, though it was the determining factor in the establishment of the Davidic dynasty. Even though David was the man God called a "Man of War" (1st Chronicles 28:3), it was not until Solomon a man of great wisdom and discernment that the attributes of wisdom and discernment received recognition and esteem from man.

Samuel, probably the greatest judge of Israel, is not known for his warlike exploits. His position as a judge, as well as a prophet, never once involved taking military action. He delivered the nation from the Philistines by acting as a magistrate (Ref. 1 Samuel 7:3-14; cf. 7:15-17). Eli another high priest, judged Israel by the authority of his position. Both men possessed varied but still outstanding qualities of leadership, which were the result of God's calling and anointing not their military abilities

The Priesthood, as presented in the Old Testament is hereditary, and the Priests were of the tribe of Levi and while Kings were, ideally at least, hereditary and legitimately from the line of David, the judges, on the other hand, were raised up by God with no regard to tribe or family background. They vary significantly in personal characteristics, but they all have one thing in common, the calling and anointing of God. The most spectacular evidence of the Holy Spirit's calling and anointing was Israel's deliverance from the yoke of their oppressors. It is also essential to note that when national emergencies were no longer a problem, other qualities assumed prominence, such as leadership, wisdom, courage, commitment, and obedience to God and faith. Those who manifested these "other qualities" drew the recognition of those in need of advice or direction. These men and women, by the attributes and actions taken while under the influence of God's Spirit, made this group of individuals unique in all of ancient history.

The book of Judges forms an essential link in the history of God's people. It furnishes us with a clear look at an unsettled nation caught between a true Theocracy and false religious practices, which was the desire of its people's hearts. This battle between true religion and superstition; demonstrates the beneficial effects that flow from the former, and the miseries and evil consequences that flow from the later. Judges is a striking picture of the disorders and dangers which prevailed in a nation without a godly leader; when few prophets came to control the people and "everyone did that which was right in his own eyes" (Judges 17:6). What is most remarkable is the justice, grace, and mercy of God, His long-suffering towards His people, which we see vividly repeated over and over again in these "Cycles of sin."

In the days of our greatest immorality, distress, and need there shall be people whom God will raise, empower, and in whom He will work with, to set things right. Therefore, we must give all honor and recognition to God because it is He who bestows on men wisdom and courage, and gives them courage to accomplish their appointed tasks. All that they are, and in everything they do for God are gifts from God. In other words, those whom God calls He gives His presence, whom He raises, He will accompany. When God comes to the aid of His children, He does not hold anything back. God was present with, directing, and involved in all the actions of the judges to assure success and victory.

The lessons we can glean from the judges can only expand our understanding of God and His abundant grace and mercy. These lessons will allow us to walk with God more closely, with more clarity, assurance, confidence, and authority. Our battle for holiness will become more comfortable, and our love for God will noticeably increase. Let us all take a glorious trip down the road to this blessed enlightenment, with the characteristics, aptitudes, personalities, and actions of the Judges guiding our way.

In the upcoming chapters, we will examine who these men of God were, what they faced, how God used them, the victory they brought, and what it all means to us. For all of us who desire a deeper, more fulfilling relationship with Almighty God, this information is critical and helpful. Do not read these pages to learn the facts contained therein but read this book with the desire to implement the lessons taught and demonstrated by these men and women of God, to learn to go beyond your comfort zone. If you do, your walk with God will never be the same!

A. Joel Osteen
B. Greg Laurie Daily Devotion - April 1, 2008
C. lao tzu
D. Smith Bible Dictionary

OTHNIEL — THE LION OF JUDAH VS. MAN'S PRIDE AND ARROGANCE

Judges chapter 3 gives us a list of evil nations, God used to test His people, and it describes just how wicked Israel's abominations were at the time of God's testing. God's people not only forgot God, but they eliminated Him from their culture by following their evil desires. They shared God's promised land with nations that God wanted removed, and, they intermarried with them and adopted their religious customs and beliefs (Ref. Judges 3:1-11). God, due to His people's outright disobedience and continuous acts of wickedness, allowed Israel to experience evil oppression and bondage.

God's people learned by experience that "there is a way which seems right to a man, but its end is death" (Proverbs 14:12; 16:25). How foolish man must be to adopt the worship of false gods to prosper. Did not Jehovah promise fertility, prosperity, protection, safety, and security to His people when they obeyed His commands (Deuteronomy 28:1-12)? Did He not deliver on His promise by giving them a land filled with milk and honey, with prosperity,and peace all around (Ref. Joshua 24)? All God's people had to do was continue to obey God's commands and eliminate all foreign gods from their land along with the people who worshiped them. But the children of God decided instead to forgo God's commandments and dwell among the evil and idolatrous nations that had possessed their land. Now think, our country is doing the same thing, and our nation and its people are suffering the same ills as the children of God did.

Entering into a relationship with anyone who does not share the same beliefs and strength of conviction is severely destructive (ref. Amos

3:3). Eventually, they will draw you away from God and back into their system of false and deadly beliefs; God put it like this, So I have this to say, 'I will not force them out of your way. They will be as thorns in your sides, and their gods will become a trap for you.'" In Psalm 106:36-38, God declares the results of their disobedience. God commanded His people not to allow the nations around them to influence them to do evil.,. we are special and "set apart" unto Jehovah (Ref. 1ˢᵗ Peter 2:9). 2ⁿᵈ Corinthians 6:17 says, "Come out from among them and be separate, says the Lord." Remember the last warning of Joshua to the people of God. "Therefore, it shall come to pass, that as all the good things have come upon you which the LORD your God promised you, so the LORD will bring upon you all harmful things until He has destroyed you from this good land which the LORD your God has given you. (16) When you have transgressed the covenant of the LORD your God, which He commanded you, and have gone and served other gods, and bowed down to them, then the anger of the LORD will burn against you, and you shall perish quickly from the good land which He has given you" (Joshua 23:15-16).

God's people chose not to serve Jehovah; instead, they decided to serve gods who are not gods, Jehovah therefore, gave them into the hands of a "doubly wicked" pagan king. God sometimes gives us what we want if we persist in rebelling against His loving leadership. Charles Spurgeon once said that "God never allows His people to sin successfully! Their sin will either destroy them or invite the chastening hand of God" (cf. Hebrews 12:5-11). Proverbs 14:34 says that "Righteousness exalts a nation, but sin is a reproach to any people."

The first hand of tyranny which came upon Israel was by Cushan-Rishathaim king of Mesopotamia. The children of Israel served him eight years. The exact meaning of "Cushan-Rishathaim" is not absolute is translated "Dark one of double evil;" "Cushan of Double Wickedness,"; or "Doubly-wicked Cushan." The word Cushan comes from the root word Cushi, which means "darkness" hence, another translation is "doubly-wicked darkness." The only part of this translation universally accepted is the "two-fold" aspect of the name, the rest, as you can see, is not. One thing of significance to keep in mind is who the Bible refers to as the "Power of Darkness" and the "Ruler of Darkness." Satan is to both (Ref. Colossians 1:13; Ephesians 6:12)!

Scholars are not sure of the exact identity of this ruler. Some identify Cushan as one of the Kassites who governed Mesopotamia between the 16th and 12th centuries B.C. He was to live in the desert region south of Othniel's tribe of Judah. Cushan was to have conquered the Israelites around 1200 B.C. as his army moved across their territory in conquest of Egypt. Others believe that Cushan-Rishathaim was King Hammurabi, and the name Cushan-Rishathaim is more of a description of his character than his actual name. He ruled parts of Southern Syria for eight years. The two-fold wickedness attributed to his reign was because:

1. He brought Babylon a small growing city at the time, to prominence over the more ancient cities of Mesopotamia.
2. He also brought the Babylonian God Marduk into prominence by identifying him with the God Bel.[1]

Another aspect that stems from the name Cushan-Rishathaim is that when it is associated with the prominence of the land of Aram-naharaim or Mesopotamia, it gives us a picture of a man who was doubly wicked due to his immense pride and arrogance. The Hebrew name Aram-naharaim is translated in Judges 3:8 and means "exalted one of the two rivers. The area between the two rivers is known as Mesopotamia. That is why many believe that the name Cushan-Rishathaim is a description of His extreme pride and arrogance.

What is very interesting about this aspect of his name is the relationship between Jehovah being Lord, which means "master," and Israel's first conqueror, who was a man of exalted pride and arrogance. Israel lost their way by dismissing the lordship of Jehovah and exalting themselves to the position of being their masters, by believing they were Kings of exalted pride and arrogance due to their accomplishments! Having lofty pride and arrogance is extremely meaningful for us because it happens to us all the time. At the very core of our sinful fleshly nature is pride and self-exaltation. These sins, when embraced, leave no room for someone to accept a master; "For it is I who live, not the Lord who lives within me," which is the mantra of all such individuals. It may be well at this point to remember man's first temptation and failure. Was it not one of self-exaltation? Notice;

> "Then the serpent said to the woman, "You will not surely die. (5) For God knows that in the day you eat of it, your eyes will open and you will be like God, knowing good and evil."
>
> Genesis 3:4:5

Why do you think, pride and arrogance are 'doubly-wicked'? Could it be that God can do nothing with a man who does not see the need for Him? "God resists the proud but gives grace to the humble" (Ref. James 4:6; 1st Peter 5:5). Why? Because the proud man questions God, resist His commands, and is convinced that his ways are superior to God's. Pride and arrogance see only their wisdom, achievements and independence, in other words, their lordship. They have no conception of their wretchedness, and therefore, they see no need for a master. This type of person believes that God is weighing their good deeds against their evil ones and their exoneration will come based on that scale. This belief is based solely on one's actions, and the arrogant assumption that their works and not God's is the catalyst of their salvation. These individuals, God cannot help.

On the other hand, people who are humble and see their need for salvation from such evils see their wickedness and the desperate inescapable situation in which they are living. That revelation produces humility; they then cry out to God because of their helplessness, and the dire need for forgiveness, along with God's grace, wisdom, and power to help them live above sin. These individuals, God can and will help escape the 'cycle of sin."

Israel was under the dominion of this doubly wicked monarch for eight years before they cried out for God's help. What took so long? Could it be that they initially thought they could quickly shake off the yoke of bondage by their worship of Baal and Ashtoreth? However, when all their efforts and devotion failed and when their arduous slavery continued for eight years, the sting of it became so bitter they realized the vanity and utter uselessness of these false gods to deliver them. These same people who, due to their pride and arrogance, laughed at their bondage earlier, now cried out to Jehovah from whom they had revolted and rejected.

Let us look at what happened to God's people when they recognized their need for a Lord and a Savior.

"When the children of Israel cried out to the Lord, the Lord raised a deliverer for the children of Israel, who delivered them: Othniel, the son of Kenaz, Caleb's younger brother."

Judges 3:9

Before we look at the lessons, we can learn from Othniel, let us take a close look at the word "cried." Cried "za'aq" in Hebrew refers to a cry of distress in response to suffering or impending doom. It is essentially a cry of pain, often accompanied by a lament over one's condition or by request for divine help. It is important to note that when "zaaq" is used, it indicates that the cry does not include a confession of sin or repentance; the only logical interpretation then is that it came with no change of heart concerning their belief system. All we can safely assume is that Israel's cry for help in the context of Judges 3:9 did not include repentance from there idolatry or for doing what was right in their own eyes. Israel was crying out in sorrow, not for their sin, but the removal of their punishment and deliverance.

Is this not true of many Christians today? When we are in the middle of a severe trial, we find ourselves praying, "God take this trial away," or "deliver me Lord" or some such prayer. But that prayer is self-centered; it has no bearing on what God wishes to do for you through those trials. Remember what James 1:3-4 and Romans 8:28-29 says;

"James 1:3 knowing that the testing of your faith produces patience. (4) But let patience have its perfect work, that you may be perfect and complete, lacking nothing.

"(28) And we know that all things work together for good to them that love God, to them who are the called according to his purpose. (29) For whom he did foreknow, he also did predestinate to be conformed to the image of his Son, that he might be the firstborn among many brethren. (Ref. Romans 8:28-29).

Notice what these verses say, especially Romans 8:29. Everything we go through is for our good. Why, because God predestined us and wants us conformed into the image of His Son. That is, God's ultimate design for His children is to make us like Jesus. Recreating man like he initially was in the Garden of Eden; in His image! Everything we experience God has ordained for that very purpose!

We must step out in faith, looking to move forward by trusting God. We cannot just ask God to remove us from our bondages, without knowing why God put them there in the first place. Sometimes God leaves the Canaanites in our path because He knows our needs (cf. Exodus 23:29-30; Deuteronomy 7:22). Notice that God did not drive out His children's enemies right away, but little by little. The Canaanites kept possession of the land till Israel had grown strong enough to displace them and occupy the whole land in peace and safety. We as Christians should understand that God leaves our enemies in our midst until we grow dependent, and strong enough on God to conquer them so that we can live our lives in peace and security. God is crucifying our old man slowly. God, in His never-ceasing mercy and grace which He exerts in and over all His works, often delays His mercies, because we are not ready for them. Christians have room enough to receive God and all His mercies, but Christians are not strong enough, nor are we dedicated or experienced enough to rule His kingdom.

So, when we pray, we should first ask God for wisdom on what to ask for during the trial. Should the prayer be one of deliverance or one of repentance and self-purification? For example, note King David's heart as he prayed the following prayer after his sin with Bathsheba and the murder of her husband Uriah, which caused King David unbearable testing and trials and the death of David and Bathsheba's firstborn Son. His first response to this trial was not one of deliverance – but of repentance and cleansing. Notice his prayer in Psalm 51:1-10.

"Have mercy upon me, O God, According to Your lovingkindness; According to the multitude of Your tender mercies, Blot out my transgressions. (2) Wash me thoroughly from my iniquity and cleanse me from my sin. (3) For I acknowledge my transgressions, and my sin is always before me. (4) Against You, and You only, have I sinned, and done this evil in Your sight. When you speak, you may be found just and blameless when You judge. (5) Behold, I was brought forth in iniquity, and in sin, my mother conceived me. (6) Behold, you desire truth in the inward parts, and in the hidden part, you will make me to know wisdom. (7) Purge me with hyssop, and I shall be clean; Wash me, and I shall be whiter than snow. (8) Make me hear joy and gladness, That the bones You have broken may rejoice. (9) Hide Your face from my sins and blot out all my iniquities. (10) Create in me a clean heart, O God, and renew a steadfast spirit within me."

Psalm 51:1-10

Are you tired of testing and trials? Maybe they are ongoing because you haven't seen the sin in your life that is causing them. Ask God about them then cast them out! Ask yourself, do you like some of the freedoms and blessings they offer. Are you unhappy, sure! Do you want the burdens gone! Yes! But the real question is, are you completely ready to renounce, conquer, and eliminate all the Canaanites (sins) from your life? Or do you want the testing to stop without any repentance, purification or change; The latter will never happen so, don't seek it!

God left the "Canaanites" in the land until His people were strong enough to eliminate them. They were left to test His people, for "the testing of your faith produces patience. (4) But let patience have its perfect work, that you may be perfect and complete, lacking nothing James 1:3-4 says. God allows testing for three reasons.

1. To strengthen God's children both physically and spiritually
2. To see if they will follow God's way, or their fleshly wisdom and desires
3. To allow them to see what is in their evil hearts

God does not allow temptation to go beyond our abilities to withstand them. (Ref. 1st Corinthians 10:13). God wants His people conformed into His image (Ref. Romans 8:29). He knows that physical and spiritual strengthening comes through the testing of our faith, much like weightlifters gain strength by testing the limits of their abilities. They continually add more weight to their workouts, and by doing so, their power increases. So, it was with the Israelites in the age of the judges, and so it is today with God's children.

One last point about testing; the testing of our willingness to follow the Lord will not only come in church, or when we are around other Christians. The measurement of our willingness to follow the Lord will also come when we are in the world or when we are alone at the computer or watching T.V., or alone in a different city. The actual test of a Christian's walk is when no one else is around when no one can see or hear us. True testing comes when we think no one will ever find out what we are doing or even thinking for "Character is what you are in the dark!" (c.f. 1st Chronicles 28:9; Psalm 94:11, 139:23; Matthew 12:25; 1st Corinthians 3:20; Hebrews 4:12).

It was when the children of God cried ("za'aq") out to God that God raised Othniel, the Son of Kenaz, Caleb's younger brother, a deliverer (yaw-shah') (Judges 3:9). The primitive root of that Hebrew word means to be open, or free, that is, (by implication) to be safe. It also means an assistant, an avenger, defender, Helper, preserver, and rescuer, one who brings salvation or victory, a savior. Othniel was such a man. Othniel was a man who came from a good lineage. He was a warrior, a man of courage, unafraid, brave, and true to his word. Othniel was the only judge chosen from the tribe of Judah. His name means "power, or strength, or "lion of God;" [i] in other words, Othniel was "God's lion from the tribe of Judah filled with God's power and strength," To bring salvation to his people. It is interesting to note the implication made when we compare the meaning of the names of the two main characters in this story. God's people fall under the power of a doubly wicked dark individual (Cushan-rishathaim) due to their arrogant and deliberate disobedience. And as we discovered earlier, Satan is the ruler and power of darkness, the prince of darkness whose pride and arrogance got him cast out of God's presence. Then after realizing the dreadful state

BREAKING THE CYCLE OF SIN!

God's children were in, God's people cried out desperately to God for deliverance, and God graciously complies by setting them free by the hands of Othniel, the power, and strength of God, God's lion from the tribe of Judah. Hallelujah!

We first hear of Othniel, the Son of Kenaz, the brother of Caleb in Joshua 15:17; Judges 1:13-15, when he, according to Josephus was about 35 to 45 years of age, and took a city by the name of Debir, which was formally known as Kirjath Sepher. As a result of this victory, Caleb gave Othniel his daughter Achsah to wife. Then, as a result of his prompting, she requested Caleb to give them land to the south of the city along with springs of water to the north and south. Now some 35 to 40 years later, God called Othniel to be a deliverer, at the ripe young age of 70-85, only this time, not of a city but of a nation. Please learn this simple lesson; when God wants to use you, age is not an issue. Moses was 80 when he was called to deliver a nation. Othniel was about 85 when he was called to do the same. Age is a frivolous and unusable excuse!

We can see by Othniel's strength, power, and life that the meaning of his name seems to describe him perfectly.

First, he belonged to the tribe of Judah, the tribe from which our Lord Jesus Christ came. Judah was the tribe that was to ultimately and eternally reign; "The scepter shall not depart from Judah" (Ref. Genesis 49:10).

Second, he was a man prepared for war, a man ready and willing to overcome the enemy.

Third, he was not afraid, nor was he willing to compromise his faith in God.

Fourth; The Spirit of God filled and governed Othniel, and his obedience allowed him to achieve great things for God and His people.

Fifth, Othniel was a man committed to accomplishing anything that God set before him.

Othniel was a perfect type of Christ and what God expects His people to be. We must ask ourselves how many of these traits we possess. And how ready we are to lead God's people and set them free.

In Ephesians 6, we have an appeal of unwavering dependability and encouragement in our Christian walk. We, as God's children are in a warfare, we can neither avoid nor escape. Is not our Christian life one of constant warfare? Yes, of course! No one who reads Ephesians 6:10-12; can escape the inevitability of war. We all struggle with the common calamities of human life. Our life of faith is not our religion but much more a spiritual warfare, for we strive in opposition to the powers of darkness, enemies fleshly and spiritual, which would keep us from God and heaven. We have enemies to fight against, a captain to fight for, a banner to fight under, and specific rules by which we must fight. Ephesians 6:10 starts with the words, "Finally, my brethren." In other words, the last thing I have to say to you is this; apply yourselves to the work and duty of a Christian soldier. For it is vital that a soldier be both stout-hearted and well-armed; "For we do not wrestle against flesh and blood, but against principalities, against powers, against the rulers of the darkness of this age, against spiritual hosts of wickedness in the heavenly places" (Ephesians 6:12). "Christians, we have no choice; we must fight!"

Let us, therefore, be warriors, strong, prepared, committed, and determined, up for any challenge that God sets before us, just like Othniel. When God needed a particular man for a great work, Othniel was the man God chose. We must be like him, a man prepared for war, a man ready and willing to overcome the enemy — a man who was not willing to compromise his faith in God. A man filled, governed, and obedient to the Spirit of God, ready to achieve great things for God and for His people, a man prepared for any challenge, and a man committed to accomplishing anything that God set before him.

Let us now take a close look at Judges 3:10.

"The Spirit of the Lord came upon him, and he judged Israel. He went out to war, and the Lord delivered Cushan-Rishathaim king of Mesopotamia into his hand, and his hand prevailed over Cushan-Rishathaim." Judges 3:10

From this verse, an interesting two-step approach to deliverance appears. Othniel received his marching orders. These orders did not come from man, or by man. This commission came when "the Spirit of the Lord came upon him." Remember, no man can do a lasting work for God without the Spirit of God overshadowing and accompanying him. Othniel, after he received his marching orders and before he went out to battle the enemy, took step one and proceeded to "judge Israel, which means He reviewed, evaluated, and appraised Israel's lifestyles." Othniel reproved them, called them to account for their sins, and reformed them, only after this cleansing they went out to war. Self-examination and repentance are essential for us to understand! It reminds us of our constant need to first judge ourselves. 1st Corinthians 11:31 tells us that "if we judge ourselves, we would not be judged." Think back to the battle of Ai (Joshua 7, 8). God's people just conquered an impenetrable great and mighty walled city, Jericho. Now they would go up against a small town called Ai. Ai means "heap of ruins." Sounds like no contest, right? Wrong! Israel sinned by directly disobeying God's commands. This disobedience defeated Israel, and thirty-six men died.

Israel has sinned, and they have also transgressed My covenant which I commanded them. For they have taken some of the accursed things, and have both stolen and deceived; and they have also put it among their stuff. (Ref. Joshua 7:11).

Once Othniel judged Israel, which included himself, making everyone aware of the precepts and judgments of Jehovah, he proceeded to step two, which was to go out to war against Cushan-Rishathaim king of Mesopotamia. This two-step approach to deliverance is the right method. Let us conquer our sins first, and remove them, and then go to war with our enemies. It is only through this two-step approach that victory came, "For the Lord is our Judge, The Lord is our Lawgiver, The Lord is our King; He will save us" (Isaiah 33:22). This verse is talking about the discipline that our Heavenly Father applies to all of His children. If God's children, while forgetting the Lord their God and serving the Baals and Asherahs, would have first judged the condition of their heart and cried out to the Lord in repentance. God would have rushed on the scene, and Cushan Rishathaim would have never taken dominion over their lives.

This teaching is not new. Knowing our need for righteousness, and holiness, and standing firm on God's love, grace and power is critical if we are to be effective Christians. Notice: What Ephesians 1:18-19 tells us; along with Ephesians 3:16-21 and Ephesians 6:10

"The eyes of your understanding being enlightened; that you may know what is the hope of His calling, what are the riches of the glory of His inheritance in the saints, (19) and what is the exceeding greatness of His power toward us who believe, according to the working of His mighty power." Ephesians 3:16-21

"That He would grant you, according to the riches of His glory, to be strengthened with might through His Spirit in the inner man, (17) that Christ may dwell in your hearts through faith; that you, being rooted and grounded in love, (18) may be able to comprehend with all the saints what is the width and length and depth and height (19) to know the love of Christ which passes knowledge; that you may be filled with all the fullness of God. (20) Now to Him who is able to do exceedingly abundantly above all that we ask or think, according to the power that works in us, (21) to Him be glory in the church by Christ Jesus to all generations, forever and ever Amen." Ephesians 3:16-21

"Finally, my brethren be strong in the Lord and the power of His might." Ephesians 6:10

Now getting back to God's lion from the tribe of Judah, we see that God raised Othniel, who was a visible sign of His power, and as a result, defeat came to Israel's enemies. In doing so, we read that the "land had rest for 40 years" (Judges 3:11). This rest or peace continued as long as Othniel lived. Once Othniel died, however, the children of Israel did evil in the sight of the Lord once again (Judges 3:11-12). Is this not a good picture of what happens in our own heart once we come to know and trust in the power of God? We rest! Read Hebrews 4, and you will notice how many times we find peace in Christ. Just like in Othniel's Reign, they found peace for 40 years as long as Othniel lived. The Israelites lost their peace because they "forgot the Lord their God." who is their peace. But those that keep in their remembrance, Jesus our "Prince of Peace" find rest (Ref. Exodus 33:14; Psalms 23:2; 37:1-11; 116:7; Isaiah 14:3; Matthew 11:28-29; Hebrews 4:1-11, etc.). This rest comes to us by our eternal savior and will last as long as He lives. The difference is that Jesus, our judge, and savior defeated death when He resurrected from the dead and He now lives forever. If our peace lasts as long as He lives, there will be no end to that peace. No man can despair who remembers that his Helper is omnipotent and eternal. Therefore, "I will lift my eyes to the hills from whence comes my help? (2) My help comes from the Lord, who made heaven and earth." (Psalm 121:1-2).

Children of God may we learn from this lesson gleaned from the first judge, Othniel, the lion of God from the tribe of Judah. Let us be careful and keep watch for evidences of exalted pride and arrogance in our own lives; it is the first enemy to conquer God's people completely. Let us also remember first to judge our hearts and cry out in repentance and purification when we discover our sin, then fight our enemies by relying upon the power, presence, and plan of God. Self-examination is what Othniel did, and the land had rest for 40 years. Oppression and bondage were over, and the peace of God reigned! Peace will remain as long as Christ lives, and we keep Him in our remembrance.

[i] Smith's Bible Dictionary; Cyclopedia of Biblical, Theological and Ecclesiastical literature

EHUD — THE POWER OF PRAISE

After Othniel led God's people to victory over the tyranny of Cushan-Rishathaim king of Mesopotamia, they had rest for 40 years until Othniel died (Judges 3:11). Those 40 years of rest or "shâqaṭ" pronounced shaw-kat' in the Hebrew, means to appease, to be still, idleness, quietness, or inactivity; this Hebrew word shows that Israel, meaning the people of God, were idle or in a state of inactivity. The implication is that though the people of Israel had no war, they were not actively pursuing any improvement in their relationship with or participation in the worship of Jehovah. Their idleness prevented them from gaining any knowledge and experience presented to them by God. They were just satisfied. Does that not describe the state of most Christians today? They are satisfied in their relationship with Christ and in the way their lives are going. They are idle and apathetic in their pursuit of those critical things that God requires and offers. Their idleness deprived them of the exercises and conflicts necessary for learning about God, His ways, and the fellowship God desires to have with them. They are not wanting any knowledge of weaknesses or areas of repair that their hearts were needing. They were sitting back, enjoying the peace and prosperity of everyday life. This type of rest requires nothing, as long as no problems come along that they could not overcome, by their natural ability, so, therefore, you can understand why they were not pursuing a deeper relationship with the Lord.

Self-contentment and pride were a problem that the children of God never seemed to overcome. Approximately seven hundred and ninety-two years later, they still had the same problem. Zephaniah speaking to the "oppressing city" ((3:1) Jerusalem) in verse two says: "She (the oppressing city – Jerusalem) has not obeyed His voice, nor did it received correction; She has not trusted in the LORD, she has not drawn near to her God." Did you notice the four things that idleness or satisfaction breeds?

1. She has not obeyed His voice
2. She has not received correction
3. She has not trusted in the LORD
4. She has not drawn near to her God

In the time of Christ, these same symptoms were still prevalent throughout the Jewish nation. Even though they were under the rule of the Romans, the Jewish nation was secure and relatively free to live as they would. It was by no means a hostile, oppressive, and toxic environment. Here breeds the problem – outward prosperity, comfort, contentment in one's natural state does not cure unbelief; it breeds it; it does not incite faithfulness to God; it produces faith and dependence in oneself. Ask yourself, why should I ask God for financial help and guidance if I have enough money in the bank to handle any significant problem? Why did only a total of 50,000 men women and children out of over 2.5 million return to Jerusalem with Ezra after 70 years of living in bondage? Could it be that even though they were in bondage, life was not bad, they had their hoses, lands, and vineyards? (Ref. 2nd Kings 18:31-32). Was life comfortable and unrestricted? I would say so! Open your eyes, and you will see the same thing today. Americans have a life of relative ease and contentment, so why ask any more from God. We do not need him, because we are content, so, let us not bother him or even acknowledge him. (Ref. Jeremiah 44:17-19). Let us take a moment and look a little closer at these four deadly symptoms of an idle heart.

1. **We do not obey God's voice** – Neither through conscience nor the Law of God's or God's holy prophets. As previously stated, the same pattern of passivity existed 2,000 years later. Inhabitants of Jerusalem and Israel hearkened not to the voice of John the Baptist, the forerunner of Christ, who gave notice of the Messiah coming. Nor to the voice of Christ Himself, who stretched out His hand and heart to a disobedient and prideful

people, nor to the voice of God's apostles, whose doctrines they contradicted and blasphemed; thereby judging themselves unworthy of eternal life.

2. **We do not receive correction** – the change produced by God's correction was, at best, temporary. For soon after being saved, Israel fell back into the same evils that God's chastisements were to remove. Like many today who have not received God's loving hand of correction, they blamed God and fled to the foot of foreign God's philosophies, mysticism, and prosperity messengers and their doctrines and formulas for success. The Targum interprets Zephaniah 3:2, "she received not doctrine." What doctrines? You know the ones our pulpits speak of rarely. The doctrine of baptism, repentance, and remission of sins. The same ones preached by John the Baptist. The ministers rejected them, and so did the people (Ref. Luke 7:30). It was the same with the doctrine and instructions of Christ and His apostles; they were worth so much more than gold and silver, yet belittled, despised, and rejected.

3. **We do not trust in the LORD** – They did not consider Christ as the Fountain from where all help comes; instead, man sought support from himself, others, his government, social services, or ill-gotten gains, not to mention a multitude of other sources. Man has ignored the fact that "All blessings shall come upon you and overtake you because you obey the voice of the Lord your God" (Deuteronomy 28:2). But instead, they despised Him, and would not submit to the righteousness of Christ. They did not trust Him even though they understood that disobeying Him would cause them death for their sins.

4. **We do not draw near to God** – We did not worship Him; We did not walk in His ways; we did not make prayer and supplication to Him. Even in trouble, when many call on Him, they did not draw nearby Him through repentance, by faith hope or love, or by works worthy of repentance, but in their hearts, they remained far from Him (Ref. Isaiah 29:11). He was still their God, and as He had shown Himself in times past, He changes not, even though we are ever-changing. He remains

faithful even though we are unfaithful to Him. He is still our God who "waits, to show mercy," even though we forget Him. God's people, for the most part, refuse to meet him where He has appointed and where He has promised to meet us. God's people stand at a distance and say to the Almighty, "Depart – we will call you when we need you."

Notice these verses;

"My brethren, count it all joy when you fall into various trials, (3) knowing that the testing of your faith produces patience. (4) But let patience have its perfect work, that you may be perfect and complete, lacking nothing."

James 1:2-4

"I will bring the third part through the fire, and will refine them as silver is refined, and will try them as gold is tried: they shall call on my name, and I will hear them: I will say, it is my people: and they shall say; The Lord is my God."

Zechariah 13:9

"That the trial of your faith, being much more precious than of gold that perishes, though it be tried with fire, might be found unto praise and honor and glory at the appearing of Jesus Christ."

1st Peter 1:7

God requires and provides times of rest for us but not to remain inactive or idle. Idleness is something condemned throughout scripture. Idleness is, "Lost time which is never found again," said Rev. John Hill Aughey, a 19th-century Presbyterian minister. Socrates described one who is idle like this "He is not only idle who does nothing, but he is idle who might be better employed." Isaac Watts warned us about idleness when he said: "For Satan finds some mischief still for idle hands to do." Most importantly, however, here is what the Bible tells us about idleness.

1. Do not act that way (Ref. Romans 12:11; Hebrews 6:11-12).
2. It produces apathy (Proverbs 12:27; 26:15).
3. It is associated with being wasteful (Proverbs 18:9).
4. Conceit accompanies laziness (Proverbs 26:16).
5. It leads to Poverty (Proverbs 10:4; 20:13).
6. It leads to Wantonness (Proverbs 20:4; 24:34).
7. It leads to Hunger (Proverbs 19:15; 20:13).
8. It leads to Bondage (Proverbs 12:24).
9. It leads to Disappointment (Proverbs 13:4; 21:25).
10. It leads to Ruin (Proverbs 24:30, 31; Ecclesiastics 10:18).
11. It leads to Gossip and interfering in the affairs of others (2nd Thessalonians 3:11; 1st Timothy 5:13).
12. It is void of understanding (Proverbs 24:30).
13. It will keep you from your rightful inheritance (Hebrews 6;12)

Do not get me wrong; there is a time for rest, but not for idleness or inactivity. God required and instituted a short period of rest for His people from the very beginning. He rested on the seventh day! That seventh day God called the Sabbath, and we are to keep it holy.

> "Remember the Sabbath day to keep it holy. (9) Six days you shall labor and do all your work, (10), but the seventh day is the Sabbath of the Lord your God. In it, you shall do no work: you, or your son, or your daughter, nor your male servant, nor your female servant, nor your cattle, nor your stranger who is within your gates. (11) For in six days, the Lord made the heavens and the earth, the sea, and all that is in them, and rested the seventh day. Therefore, the Lord blessed the Sabbath day and hallowed (consecrated it, made it sacred) it."
>
> Exodus 20 8-11

The Hebrew word for "rested" used herein Exodus 20:11, is entirely different than that of Judges 3:11. The Hebrew word used in Exodus 20:11 is "noo'-akh;" compared with "shâqaṭ" which is used in Judges 3:11. Both words "shaqat - and "noo'-akh" are used in the sense of settling down, or withdrawing from work, in order to receive rest. Shaqat however, means to be idle, where "Nooakh" means to cease from work. God called this restful day the "Sabbath day." It is a day we give voluntarily of ourselves to Him. We are to consecrate (declare, appoint, make, or present) it to God for His desires and His will in our lives. We are to do only that which He deems necessary for our wellbeing. "Shâqat" is much more dangerous.

When God commanded us to be still, to relax or refrain from work, it came linked with another commandment, keep the Sabbath. God blessed the seventh day and hallowed it because He rested upon it. The significance of the Sabbath is found in God sanctifying the seventh day after the work of creation. God blessed and hallowed the created world, filling it with the powers of peace and goodness which belonged to His blessed rest, and raising it to a participation in the pure light of His holy nature. For this reason, Israel was to keep the Sabbath. So that on the Sabbath, they might rest from their work, which was no longer the work appointed to man at first, but from the hard work as a result of the fall. Our times of stillness is to get to know God. It is just like the battery in your cell phone. We work it so much until it runs down. It is then that we rest our phones and connect it to a charger that adds power back into the battery for further use. That is what the word "noo'-akh" means. Unlike the type of rest meant by the word "shâqat." God commanded us to take a Sabbatical to recharge our spirits by resting, in the God of rest, will renew our spirits and our very souls for the continuation of our work for him.

"Be still and know that I am God" (Psalm 46:10). This verse is perfect in the context of our discussion of Judges 3:11 notice:

"Come; behold the works of the Lord, who has made desolations in the earth. (9) He makes wars cease to the end of the earth; He breaks the bow and cuts the spear in two; He burns the chariot in the fire. (10) Be still, and know that I am God; I will be exalted among the nations, I will be exalted in the earth! (11) The Lord of hosts is with us; The God of Jacob is our refuge. Selah"
Psalm 46:8-11

Do you notice the pattern in Psalm 46:8-11? God gives His children victory over their enemies, the wars cease, peace reigns, and they are commanded to be still and know (yaw-dah') (meaning to ascertain by seeing or to acquaint oneself with) that He is God. It does not mean to rest on your laurels or be at rest/satisfied because of your situation. Our God is the God of peace/rest (cf. Philippians 4:7; Colossians 3:15). His rest we must enter (Ref. Matthew 11:28). Because there is no rest outside of Him, let us be still; let us be calm, and tremble no more, but let us rest assured knowing, that the Lord alone is God, He is our comfort and peace our resting place. Our enemies will flee before Him, and we will exalt our God above all.

Though we may be depressed, let us not be miserable, for we may rest assured that God will be exalted and that He will deliver and satisfy us. He will work to establish His great name, and then no matter what becomes of us, when we pray "Father, glorify thy name," God will answer "I have both glorified it, and I will glorify it again." (Ref. John 12:28). Does this sound good to you? Then do what Job instructed us to do while he was going through the worst trial of his life.

> "Now acquaint yourself with Him, and be at peace/rest; thereby goodwill comes to you. (22) Receive, please, instruction from His mouth, and lay up His words in your heart. (23) If you return to the Almighty, you will be built up; you will remove iniquity far from your tents. (24) Then you will lay your gold in the dust, and the gold of Ophir among the stones of the brooks. (25) Yes, the Almighty will be your gold and your precious silver; (26) for then you will have your delight in the Almighty, and lift your face to God. (27) You will make your prayer to Him, He will hear you, and you will pay your vows. (28) You will also declare a thing, and it will be established for you; so, light will shine on your ways. (29) When they cast you down, and you say, 'Exaltation will come!' Then He will save the humble person. (30) He will even deliver one who is not innocent; yes, he will be delivered by the purity of your hands."
>
> Job 22:21-30

Now, look at Hebrews 4:1-11. The word "rest" appears nine times in the first 11 verses. Seven times the word is "katapausis," which is a noun which means a resting place or abode or a place of calm. This rest is our heavenly blessedness in which God dwells, and of which he has promised to make persevering believers in Christ, partakers after the toils and trials of life have temporarily subsided. In verse 8, the verb form of the word "katapausis" appears. Which is "katapauo," it means "to cause or to grant one a restful abode. In verse 9, the word translated rest is "sabbatismos," which is a noun which means Sabbath. It refers to a place provided by God ever available for God's people to find and abide, for that is where Christ is. This place of Sabbath is to be our eternal sanctuary, which is available to all who believe. All three of these Greek words, when taken in the context of Hebrews 4, refer to a permanent resting place only God can give and a place of restful bliss only found in the presence of Christ. It is here that we are to abide forever once we have discovered and learned of Him.

Does this sound like something you need? With troubles and worries all around? Do you feel that no matter what you do, you can't escape the problems of life? Then let Christ be your resting place! Remember, God told us to "Be still and know that I am God" (Psalm 46:10; ref. Matthew 11:28; John 14:27, 16:33; 2nd Thessalonians 1:7). The Amplified Bible puts it like this: "Let be and be still, and know (recognize and understand) that I am God, exalted among the nations! I am exalted in the earth!" (Ref. Psalm 46:10) And the Contemporary English Bible says, "Our God says, "Calm down, and learn that I am God! All nations on earth will honor me." (Ref Psalm 46:10) The only effort that should manifest during trials is the effort of finding, abiding, and learning about God.

Israel rejected God's rest in the time when the Judges ruled. Indeed, the people of God did rest, but they rested upon their successes, upon the period of truce that God had provided. But they did not rest, nor did they seek after God who by His loving mercy and unlimited grace had provided rest. They took no steps to know their God, and the result was another "Cycle of Sin." In which, Eglon, the King of Moab, defeated Israel and placed the children of God under subjection and oppressed them for 18 years.

"And the children of Israel again did evil in the sight of the Lord. So, the Lord strengthened Eglon king of Moab against Israel, because they had done evil in the sight of the Lord. (13) Then he gathered to himself the people of Ammon and Amalek, went and defeated Israel, and took possession of the City of Palms (Jericho). (14) So, the children of Israel served Eglon king of Moab eighteen years."

Judges 3:12-14

The same statement found in verse 12 is identical to that in Judges 3:7. This statement shows the direct cause of their oppression. "And the children of Israel again did evil in the sight of the Lord." One thing that is important to note about this statement is that it follows directly upon the statement in verse 11, which says, "So the land had rest (quietness, idleness, stillness) for forty years…" Even though these two statements follow one another, it does not suggest that during the reign of Othniel, the people of God lived righteously, and then at the very moment, Othniel died they began to do evil in the sight of the Lord. No! Once Othniel died the Israelites, were without the moral and political compass he offered. Israel followed their ways all along, but Othniel was the vessel and voice of God; he extended God's judgment and wisdom to a people who were not long in following after their natural desire for idolatry.

With Othniel now dead and His people doing evil in God's sight, God once again brought judgment upon His people. God strengthened another oppressor, Eglon, the King of Moab, in the hopes that God's people would compare their lives under His rule with the rule of an earthly monarch. God was hoping that once and for all, Israel would choose the favorable life God offers. Unfortunately, they did not choose wisely, and the "Cycle of Sin" started again.

Moab lay immediately across the Dead Sea from Judah, south of the Trans-Jordan valley. It was Moab's king, Balak, who years before hired Balaam to curse Israel (Ref. Numbers 22-24). Now the Moabites, assisted by the Ammonites and Amalekites, crossed the Jordan defeated portions of the eastern tribes and then moved down the Jordon Valley and occupied Jericho. Jericho's description in verse 13 describes her as the "city of palm trees." Sixty years had passed since Joshua burnt Jericho and pronounced a curse on any who should rebuild her (Joshua 6:26). 1st Kings 16:34 tells us that Hiel the Bethelite many years later built Jericho again, it is not likely that the Moabites had to dislodge many inhabitants at the time. The Moabites moved on to the bare, unoccupied mound, erected a minimum of buildings, and used Jericho as their temporary headquarters. Once Eglon established his headquarters he proceeded to bring the Israelites on the east bank of the Jordan and in the Jordan Valley under his control.

The fact that Eglon dominated Israel eighteen years again begs the question, why did it take Israel so long to reach the realization that crying out to God was their only salvation? Did they not remember one generation ago, the servitude under a doubly wicked man, the King of Mesopotamia? Could it be that their hearts were callused, and they thought that further faith, devotion, and sacrifice to their false gods, along with paying tribute to Eglon, which was rightfully due to Jehovah, would set them free of their oppression? Did they perhaps feel that their newly chosen Canaanite gods and goddesses were more powerful and benevolent than Jehovah? Or was it that they felt that Life under Jehovah with all His rules and regulations was too much to bear, and even though their oppression was terrible, it wasn't as bad as obeying what they thought were God's obsessive demands? Maybe it was just as simple as God knowing that fewer trials do not cause repentance and faithfulness, but chastisements cause repentance and correction, and leads us to faithfulness? God knew the last to be true and sent a severe punishment on them for their relapse into idolatry. What we know for sure is after being oppressed so long, and continually groaning under their burdens, they finally realized that their humiliation was a direct result of their idolatry. That's when they cried (za'aq – same Hebrew word found in Judges 3:9) out to God for forgiveness, and deliverance once again was sent by God's unlimited grace.

As many of you know, the Moabites are descendants of Moab. He was the son of Abraham's nephew Lot, who, through an incestuous relationship with his eldest daughter, bore Moab (Ref. Genesis 19:30-38). As a spiritual type, Moab speaks to us of a relative in name only. One who goes by the name Christian but has nothing in common spiritually.

Even though they were related, they were enemies of God's people. So, it is also today with these "Christians by name only." They attend Church and outwardly look 'Christian,' yet their lifestyles, vocabulary, dress, and demeanor, demonstrate openly that they never came to know Jesus as their Lord and Savior. We must be careful here not to judge too harshly because even true Christian at times look like they are just going through the motions. Moab is a symbol of those that have departed from their first love, who claim that they are "good Christians," yet have no inner reality of being a Christian, nor do they have a real relationship with God. Let us all guard against the Moabs we come across in our daily lives.

Along this same line, it is also interesting to note that Eglon's name means "a bull calf, heifer, or calf-like." The meaning of his name shows us two important things. One, his name could refer to his size, for he was an obese man (Judges 3:17) hence the meaning "calf-like" referring to his heifer like size. Or, two; it could be referring to his chosen form of worship, a bull calf (Ref. Exodus 32:4-8). Either way, this man would be as a man who got fat off the tribute of others while claiming to be a "Christian," but in reality, he was an idolatrous heathen. Do not think I am stretching the point here. We hear and see men and women like this all the time. So, called ministers who if you send them money, they will send you an anointed cloth guaranteed to heal whatever ails you. Many years ago, we called them snake oil salesmen. These men are charismatic, they can play the crowd with professionalism, but what they deliver with all their rhetoric and incredible charisma is bondage and death, all the while they get rich on poor gullible Christians. The Bible warns us of these men coming into prominence in the last days; (Refer 1ST Timothy 4:1; 2ND Timothy 3:1-7, 4:3-4; 2ND Peter 3:3; Jude 17-19).

> "But know this, that in the last days perilous times will come: (2) For men will be lovers of themselves, lovers of money, boasters, proud, blasphemers, disobedient to parents, unthankful, unholy, (3) unloving, unforgiving, slanderers, without self-control, brutal, despisers of good, (4) traitors, headstrong, haughty, lovers of pleasure rather than lovers of God, (5) having a form of godliness

but denying its power. And from such people turn away! (6) For of this sort are those who creep into households and make captives of gullible women loaded down with sins, led away by various lusts, (7) always learning and never able to come to the knowledge of the truth."

2nd Timothy 3:1-7

The Children of God once again cried out for deliverance, and God raised another deliverer for them; Ehud the Son of Gera the Benjamite. Ehud, a left-handed man, who by the Lord's choice was to deliver the Children of Israel from the yoke of King Eglon (Judges 3:15). Having made a special double-edged dagger a cubit in length [approximately 18 inches long] (Judges 3:16), Ehud went to the king, bringing Israel's tribute (Judges 3:17). Ehud gained admittance to the king's private chamber by pretending to be the bearer of a secret message. Once they were alone, Ehud told the king the message was from God, and as Eglon rose in respect (Judges 3:20), Ehud thrust the dagger into his belly, killing Eglon (Judges 3:21). He then escaped by locking the doors of the porch behind him to prevent the discovery of the body right away. Ehud escaped to the mountains of Ephraim, blew the trumpet as a signal to the Children of Israel to arise, and fight, and he then led them to victory over Moab (Judges 3:26-29) ending the Moabite oppression. Ehud judged Israel and the people of God for 80 years, and the land was at rest (shaqat) again means to appease, to be still idleness, quietness, or inactivity.

The ploy used by Ehud is not strange behavior; we often see it in the modern-day Church. Many men come with special messages from God, and when you give them your attention without asking God first, failure is the result (Ref. 1st Corinthians 14:29). Remember what John tells us in 1st John 4:1; "Beloved, do not believe every spirit, but test the spirits, whether they are of God; because many false prophets have gone out into the world." Also, remember the warning Peter gives us;

> "But there were also false prophets among the people, even as there will be false teachers among you, who will secretly bring in destructive heresies, even denying the Lord who bought them and bring on themselves

swift destruction. (2) And many will follow their destructive ways, because of whom the way of truth will be blasphemed."

2nd Peter 2:1-2

Ehud means "I will give praise," or "I will give thanks." The lesson we can glean from this is that no matter how long and arduous our oppression, praise, and thanksgiving will gain us the victory. Think back to the moving of God's tabernacle while Israel was in the wilderness. God gave His children a specific pattern of movement when the tribes moved God's house (Refer Numbers 2; and 10:14-28). Judah was always to go first leading the way. Judah, in Hebrew, means "the praise of the Lord" (Ref. Genesis 29:35). Praise and thanksgiving when offered with a whole heart (Psalms 9:1; 111:1; 138:1) always brings deliverance and victory (Psalms 28:6-7; 40:1-3; 59:17; 71:6-8; 103:3; 106:47; 118:21; 124:6; Isaiah 61:3). Numbers 10:35 shows us that whenever the Children of God moved forward, Moses started them out with a prayer of praise. "Rise, O Lord! Let Your enemies be scattered, and let those who hate You flee before You." And when they rested, Moses gave another prayer of praise "Return, O Lord, to the many thousands of Israel."

(Numbers 10:36).

The meaning of Ehud's name according to Hitchcock's Bible Names Dictionary is"

I will – give praise; I will – give thanks." Note, the words "I will" (meaning self-imposed, Colossians 2:23 NKJV or will-worship KJV). It shows that we must make a conscious decision to give praise. "I will give praise!" God testes all of us, and He will continue this testing to affirm and strengthen our faith in God and learn more about Him. God wants to see if we will consciously choose to give Him our whole-hearted praise and thanks in all situations, no matter how arduous they may be!

There will always be times when trials and darkness surround us, and praise is slow in coming. It is then, at that very moment, that we need to make a conscious decision to praise God despite how depressing and dangerous our circumstances seem. Not because we know that there is power in praise, not because we are going through depressing and hazardous situations, and we know that there is victory and abundant blessings in our praise. No brethren! We praise and give Him thanks because He is worthy of it. For it matters not if I am on the top of a mountain or in a deep dark valley, I must consciously choose to give God praise! I will glorify His name! I will lift my hands in praise and surrender to His Lordship! I will dance before Him for the joy of His salvation! Why? For no other reason than God is worthy of it!

There is another important lesson that comes from the name "Ehud." According to the International Standard Bible Encyclopedia, Naves, and Easton's Bible Dictionary, the meaning of the Hebrew name "Ehud" is "united" or "strong." If we take this meaning and combine it with the meaning given by Hitchcock, a doctrinal truth appears. God's people are at their best when they are united in purpose, firm in their resolve, and march forth with praise and thanksgiving. No enemy, no matter how strong or well-armed, and wise, can stand before us when we cry out to God for help. Especially when we consciously employ these principles against all our adversaries.

Now let us look at verses 16-21.

> "Now Ehud made himself a dagger (it was double-edged and a cubit in length) and fastened it under his clothes on his right thigh. So, he brought the tribute to Eglon king of Moab (Now Eglon was an obese man). (18) And when he had finished presenting the tribute, he sent away the people who had carried the tribute. (19) But he turned back from the stone images that were at Gilgal, and said, "I have a secret message for you, O king." He said, "Keep silence!" And all who attended him went out from him. (20) So, Ehud came to him (now he was sitting upstairs in his cool private chamber). Then Ehud said, "I have a message from God for you." So, he arose

from his seat. (21) Then Ehud reached with his left hand, took the dagger from his right thigh, and thrust it into his belly."

Judges 3:16-21

We have spoken about Eglon and how he oppressed Israel. We have also discussed Ehud, the man God raised to defeat the tyranny of Eglon and the Moabites. Now let us examine the methodology used by Ehud and God's people to depose this evil ruler and come out from under his influence. We must first remember that Ehud was God's chosen and anointed vessel, and no victory is possible unless God fights the battle with us and through us. Once Ehud felt the calling of God, he took steps to accomplish that goal. We must learn those steps to employ the same measures to perform something for God.

1. Know your calling and objective is from God
2. Ehud in unison with his brethren devised a plan of attack
3. Confirmed an attack signal so that they could attack in unity and with a singular purpose
4. Made preparations
5. Got everyone in position
6. He made sure everyone had a full understanding of the plan and their part in it
7. They executed the plan

No matter what the objective, this is a good pattern to follow when we want to break the cycle of sin. We need to know that the objective is from God. We need the unity and wisdom of our brethren to devise a good plan; all the preparations need to be available if we are to carry out the plan. We need everyone to know what their duties are and when to carry them out. Finally, we need to execute each step as planned. When all these factors come together, the objective is easily obtainable. And so, it was with Ehud. Judges 3:16 mentions that "Ehud had a plan in which he made himself a dagger (it was double-edged and a cubit in length)," which at the right time he plunged it into the belly of Eglon King of Moab, the enemy of God's people, killing him instantly. He then escaped. Once he joined his brethren, he sounded the alarm, and his brethren began to attack the armies of Moab in unison, and the combined force of God's people brought Moab's oppression to an end.

Now let us take a look at what we can learn from the tool used by Ehud to slay Eglon? The 18-inch dagger represents a type of warfare that, if employed, will be of tremendous help when we are in a war with our enemy. Notice, Ehud prepared an 18-inch double-edged blade. He used that blade to destroy his enemy. In the New Testament, our double-edged blade/sword is not man-made but is God-given. Remember our spiritual weapons.

> "Take the helmet of salvation and the "sword of the Spirit, which is the word of God;" (18) praying always with all prayer and supplication in the Spirit, being watchful to this end with all perseverance and supplication for all the saints."
>
> Ephesians 6:17-18

> "For the word of God is living and powerful, and sharper than any two-edged sword, piercing even to the division of soul and spirit, and joints and marrow, and is a discerner of the thoughts and intents of the heart. (13) And there is no creature hidden from His sight, but all things are naked and open to the eyes of Him to whom we must give account."
>
> Hebrews 4:12-13

Christians, what does all this mean? Let me summarize; when the enemy comes in like a flood, the Lord will build a standard against him (Ref. Isaiah 59:19). The enemy's defeat is inevitable and predetermined if we learn and execute the lessons gleaned from this study. Victory came first through men and women called and anointed by God. Christians, we are such people! Then with unity, cooperation, and the wisdom gained from several judicious counselors, we devise a wise Godly plan (Ref. Proverbs 11:14, 15:22, 24:6). We then execute the plan with hearts filled with praise and minds willing to do all for the Lord and His people. Our mouths should be overflowing with praise and thanksgiving and using the all-powerful sword of the word – a double-edged blade. When we thrust that blade into the enemy's belly, we gain the inevitable victory.

Our double-edged sword is the Word of God, and we must use it in the same manner that Jesus used it in defeating the enemy in the wilderness (Ref Matthew 4). If we are instant in season and out, to declare it openly in the face of enemy attacks; if we fear not to voice the truth and proclaim the promises of God; if we use His promises as the firm foundation of our praise and thankfulness; if we continue to renew our mind daily with His truth especially when the arrows of doubt come, and we submit ourselves to God, and resist the enemy, then using all these things we become more than conquerors through Him that loved us" (Romans 8:37). Only in this manner will the cycle of sin brake and the enemy destroyed. Brethren, rest assured if God is with us, nothing and no one can stand against us; for greater is He that is in me than he that is in the world (Romans 8:31; 1st John 4:4).

Here are some scriptures to comfort and strengthen you:

1. Genesis 9:3
2. Psalm 23:1~; Psalm 91:1~; 104:14
3. Matthew 6:8, 25-26; 10:22
4. John 16:33
5. Romans 8:37; 12:21
6. 1st Corinthians 15:57-58
7. 2nd Corinthians 9:8
8. Philippians 4:6, 7, 19
9. Hebrews 4:16
10. 1st Peter 5:6-7
11. James 1:12
12. 1st John 3:4, 5:4-5
13. Revelation 21:7

SHAMGAR — ALL IT TAKES IS A SINGLE STEP OF FAITH

Shamgar the son of Anath, unlike other Biblical Judges, appears and disappears on the scene of Israel's history with no fanfare, no introduction or beginning, no conclusion, or reference to his length of reign. There are virtually no details given about him whatsoever. His name means "stranger, cupbearer or sword," and it only occurs twice in Scripture; the first time in Judges 3:31 and again in Judges 5:6. Judges 3:31 tells us he is the son of Anath, leaving much speculation about who Shamgar was. Many speculate he was not an Israelite because his name is not Hebrew. Others believe that he was a Canaanite of Hittite origin. And others think he was Hurrian, an ancient group of travelers that entered Mesopotamia and continued to migrate westward early in the second millennium BC. They joined the Israelites seeking to repel the Philistines who were arch-enemies, for the Philistines caused continual disruption throughout the eastern Mediterranean area.

The term "Son of Anath" gives little help in pinning down Shamgar's lineage as well. The Hebrew word "son" is "bên" a word that encompasses many facets, from a child (male or female), sons of God (for angels), people (of a nation, or a class, it can even mean grandfather or father. So, as you can see, to take the words "son of Anath" literally is to make a false assumption, which could lead to false facts.

Anath could also be a reference to Beth-Anath, a town in Galilee, or the name of his father, grandfather, or people. Beth-ānath which means "house of repose or affliction" is a fenced city in the territory of Naphtali, (Joshua 19:38; Judges 1:33). It was a place that was associated with the "house" or "temple" of Anath, a goddess of the Canaanites. All we trully know about Shamgar is thatHe was a man called by God as a deliverer who repelled the Philistine incursions and slaughtered 600 soldiers with an ox goad.

The other mention of Shamgar is in the Song of Deborah found in Judges 5. The description of Shamgar a prior ruler, who God rose up in a time of fear, devastation, and vulnerability. The Song of Deborah records that in the days of Shamgar, Israel consisted of abandoned highways, with travelers taking winding byways, not the main roads, probably due to the fear of death by their foreign oppressors. Village life ceased, war was in the gates of the cities Israel was serving foreign gods, and there was not a shield or a single weapon of war found throughout all Israel. In other words, Israel was in a helpless chaotic and oppressed state.

Let's now take a moment and recap the historical events of Judges 3:12-30. These verses record the second oppression and slavery of God's people, which lasted for eighteen years under Eglon, the King of Moab. Then when Israel cried out to the Lord for help, God raised Ehud, son of Gera, of the tribe of Benjamin, who was left-handed, to deliver them. The deliverance and subsequent peace lasted for eighty years. If you also recall, the Moabites lived east of the Dead Sea, and they attacked Israelite territory by crossing over the Jordon, turning south following the Jordon valley and ultimately established their headquarters, though temporary as it was, in Jericho. Ehud, through a well-devised and executed assassination and battle plan, gained the victory over Moab and reigned, bringing peace for 80 years (Judges 3:30). Then according to the very next verse, "after him (Ehud) was Shamgar." Moab was not the only threat to Israel at this time. The Philistines, who lived along the Mediterranean Sea coast, now tried to conquer Israel from the West.

The Philistines must have seen something about the state of Israel and its people that gave them a strategic advantage and belief that they had an excellent chance of victory over Israel, or they would not have invaded Israel at this time. The Bible tells us that this invasion came at the end of Ehud's reign, after "the land had rest for eighty years" (Judges 3:30). So, what was it about Israel that the Philistines saw and caused them to believe they had a strategic advantage and an excellent chance of success?

Could it be that

> "In the days of Shamgar, son of Anath, in the days of Jael, deserted, highways were commonplace and for the travelers walked along the byways. (7) Village life ceased. Until I, Deborah, arose, Arose, a mother in Israel. (8) *They chose new gods*; then there was war in the gates; Not a shield or spear was seen among forty thousand in Israel."
>
> Judges 5:6-8

When we compare the description of the state of Israel, given by Deborah in Judges 5, to the statement made in Judges 3:30-31, it begs a serious question. What was going on after Ehud secured the victory over Moab and brought peace to Israel that would leave Israel in such a state of desolation? One possible answer could be that this period of rest (shâqat) was of the same character as the 40 years of rest mentioned under the reign of Othniel. It was a time of Idleness, contentment, apathy without godly gain. As a result of this, contentment and apathy verse 8 tells us that "they chose new gods," and then there was war in the gates!

Israel lost the understanding of who they were and the sense of their divine purpose. They, as we have a divine heritage and destiny, and when we are idle, we cannot experience or realize its effect on our situation. Notice:

> "Beloved, now we are children of God; and it has not yet been revealed what we shall be, but we know that when He is revealed, we shall be like Him, for we shall see Him as He is. (3) And everyone who has this hope in Him purifies himself, just as He is pure. (4) Whoever sins also commits lawlessness, and sin is lawlessness. (5) And you know that He came to take away our sins, and in Him, there is no sin. (6) Whoever abides in Him does not sin.
>
> 1st John 3:2-6a

We, the children of God, believe in the finished work of Calvary; we become new creations made in the likeness of God. We have a glory bestowed upon us by God that the world does not understand or recognize, and therefore, the world does not know us – they do not know what to make of us. We are a mystery to them — mysteries' birth curiosity. Curiosity's fruit is questions. Questions are opportunities to share the love of God. Sharing the love of God with others is our divine calling. Oh, but brethren, the glory that Christians now see and experience is nothing compared to what it shall be. Why? For what we shall be is not known as yet (1st John 3:2). What a priceless heritage, what a glorious hope, and unfathomable destiny. Are you part of this invaluable heritage? Do you have this hope? Are you holding on to someday receiving this eternal destiny? If so, you must purify yourself. For everyone that has this hope, that is, the hope of seeing and enjoying Christ in glory must purify himself, according to the pattern and copy which Christ hath set before him. They must continually labor to reproduce it in their own lives. Idleness cannot produce it! Every Christian that has the hope of obtaining His glorious destiny must never be idle. Because the author of this hope is God and the object of His work is us, and our future glory, which He promised and all who believe can expect to receive. Christ's atonement purchased this future hope. Christ's free future hope is our glorious destiny; to be like Jesus, now and forever! All that is necessary to inherit this glorious destiny is for you to ask Jesus for forgiveness and to come into your life and be Lord and master of it. This simple prayer sets you on the path that leads you to a life of joy, peace and contentment and a glorious eternal future.

Israel's Idleness, however, prevented them from gaining any knowledge and experience about their God, His ways, or government. They were just satisfied with the way things were. They were sitting back happy with their lives without any concern for what God wanted or their present state, or the situation taking place in the nations around them. This lack of effort or interest and their lack of faithfulness to God brought on the state of affairs described in Judges 5:6-8.

Shamgar lived during the latter days of Ehud and the early days of Deborah and Barak. Many theologians believe the events described in Judges 3:31 happened within 20 years after the death of Ehud. During the days of Shamgar, the country was in shambles and desolate – Refer Judges 5:6-8.

1. There was no trade. There were no weapons or soldiers to protect commercial endeavors.
2. There was no traveling. To do any trading, one must be able to travel to a place where he would be able to sell his goods. Traveling was impossible out of fear because of many attacks, robberies, and killings along the roads. The only traveling attempted was via the back roads and by stealth.
3. There was no farming. Villages were unoccupied for fear of plunderers. Walled cities were their only protection.
4. No capability of administering justice. There was war in the gates where they held their courts. The continual attacks by the enemy deprived the magistrates of their dignity and the people of the benefit of a government.
5. There was no peace to anyone coming or going. The gates of these fortified cities in which travelers must pass had war taking place in them. Verse 11 tells us that even the people who had to go out to draw water were afraid of death at the hands of enemy archers.
6. Israel had no weapons of war. Not one shield or spear to defend them. Either they were all taken by their oppressors, or they neglected them along with the art of war; either way, they lost all weapons along with the skill or will to use them.
7. They had lost their awareness of God's covenant.

So again, the question is, why did all this happen? Deborah gives us the answer in one clear and precise statement (Ref, Judges 5:8). *"They chose new gods, and then there was war in the gates."* (Ref. Judges 5:8) It was their idolatry that provoked God to give them up into the hands of their enemies. The Lord, their God, was one Lord, but having only one God did not make them content, they needed more. Their God was the Ancient of days, and they grew weary of Him, they wanted something new. Israel's fathers chose the Lord for their God (Joshua 24:21), but now their children would not abide by that choice, they chose to have new gods, gods of their choosing. God, therefore, brought this desolation and destruction and sent the Philistines as another wake-up call for Israel to see their ways and repent. Once they started to cry out to God in repentance, Shamgar became the hero God raised to repel the Philistine invasion and set them free once again.

Many consider heroes to be: smart, possessing great physical attributes, strong, and brave with excellent warlike skills that are battle-hardened. But as we read God's word, we discover that God does not always adhere to this man-made standard. The Christian heritage does not have room for superheroes, because there is only one superhero if you will: God Himself! Shamgar, on the other hand, might be eligible for the position of the most obscure Biblical character found in Scripture: for as stated earlier, there are only two verses ascribed to his complete story. We find no information whatsoever about his birth, childhood, youth, family, education, or career. The author of Judges does not assign any particulars about Shamgar's life or his death. Deborah only mentions him once in the process of describing the historical background, which defined the circumstances at the time of his call.

However, Shamgar-ben-Anath appears to be a local farmer, fought against the Philistine occupation forces, and won a tremendous victory. He had no army, military support, or training, no military weaponry. His weapon was of no military value, nor did it possess any powerful advantage over the weapons of the enemy soldiers. It was a farm tool that was a wooden stick approximately 6-8 feet long, about 2 inches in diameter. The ox goad had a rounded point on one end, which was used for poking the oxen when their movements become intolerably slow. The other end had a broad chisel-like blade sometimes in the shape of a shovel, which was to clear the plowshare of roots and thorns which impede it or stiff clay which adheres to it.

The ox goad was an instrument used for agriculture, not for fighting, especially against seasoned battle hardened warriors. But in Shamgar's anointed hands, God transformed the ox goad into a lethal weapon that killed 600 soldiers and turned back the Philistine invasion. Shamgar's contribution to the history of Israel was significantly important because the writer of the book of Judges, under God's anointed hand, bestowed upon Shamgar the title of "deliverer" (yaw-shah') a word implying "savior."

God used Shamgar for the purpose God assigned to him. Shamgar was ready when God needed him! And that is the main lesson we must glean from him. He was an ordinary man who saw an extraordinary threat from one of God's enemies. He did not wait for a spiritual leader to deal with the threat. He did not go and tell the leaders so they could do something about it; Shamgar became the leader! Interesting enough today, while eating lunch with my family, I saw a military-type T-shirt with writing on the back. It said, "I need no weapon. I am the weapon" Shamgar could have wrote this T-shirt. God sent His spirit out to find someone who would respond to the needs of His people. He found that man in Shamgar. Shamgar recognized sin and its dangers, he was willing to stand for God despite the dangers, he had compassion for Israel and was available for God to use, and he showed up when God called him. Brethren, we must show these same attributes every day, and we must be immediately available when God calls.

In some very striking ways, the spirit of Christian faith and victory is in this man. Here we have a man engaged in the ordinary tasks of life, a man who was available to God when God needed Him and who, because of his faith, was not afraid of the daunting task God set before him. Shamgar met this danger head-on as it came to him. He did not meet the challenge by shirking in his responsibility, nor did he step aside from the path of his ordinary duties. He just obeyed his creator and became a symbol of victory and deliverance. He did not go out of his way to find a place where God could use him; he just responded to God's calling in everything that came his way during his everyday tasks. Shamgar stands as a person who found countless opportunities for fighting the battle of the Lord, even amid the weighty burden of everyday life. He is a symbol of a true warrior of God.

Shamgar did not have to wait till he had a sword or spear or battle-bow, he took whatever lay close at hand, and he turned it against the enemy. God wants you to use whatever resources you have on hand. That is why God asked Moses, "What is that in your hand? (Exodus 4:2) "Like Moses' rod, Dorcas' needle, David's sling, and stone, Joshua's ram's horn, the lad's five loaves and two fishes, the widow's little bottle of oil. And Samson's Jawbone. God uses what we have on hand to gain glory for himself and bring victory to His people. Do not withhold anything from God, and you will see what he can do with what little you have. Just give God what you have on hand and be willing to use it for His glory! That is all God requires for His mightiest victories and His grandest ministries.

No matter where you are or what you are doing, be available when God calls; "I charge you therefore before God and the Lord Jesus Christ, who will judge the living and the dead at His appearing and His kingdom, Preach the word! "Be instant in season Be ready in season and out of season. Convince, rebuke, exhort, with all longsuffering and teaching" (2nd Timothy 4:1-2). Do you notice anywhere in the Bible where it says: "ministerial degree required? No! There is an old Christian saying I am sure you have heard before. It says: God does not begin by asking our ability, only our availability, and if we prove our dependability, He will increase our capability.![1]

Read more at https://www.brainyquote.com/topics/availability-quotes
Be available when God calls you.

Although we are not to seek to be heroes, we can be witnesses and vessels that God can use for dramatic and unbelievable actions because our God is Omnipotent – meaning all-powerful. Get ready for His mighty deeds. No Christian should belittle him-or-herself as insignificant. Challenges and offenses will come (Ref Luke 17:1). God assures us of victory and his glory in all challenges. Not everyone can be an Isaiah or John the Baptist. Still, all Christians can be a "Shamgar" if they are available, and they respond to all potentially overwhelming challenges with faith and courage. And will confront those who aggressively and powerfully threaten God's people, God's ways, or God's Word.

I heard the voice of the Lord, saying: "Whom shall I send, and who will go for us?" Then I said, "Here am I! Send me." Isaiah 6:8

DEBORAH — HUMBLE OBEDIENCE BRINGS VICTORY AND EXALTATION

In Judges 4:1, we once again see the statement, "the children of Israel again did evil in the sight of the Lord." this phrase often appears in Judges. It seems to be the only unchanging fact in Israel's history; Is this true of your history as well. Ask yourself when they write your autobiography how frequently will this phrase occur. These words show us one inevitable human truth, that is that the human heart has a perpetual proneness to wander from God a truth the children of God must recognize and face head-on. The truth of the matter is, even when the removal of God's restraints occurs. In spite of all God's divine favors, men will continue to sin and often be guilty of committing the worst imaginable wickedness. That was the case here with the people of God. The third major oppression came upon God's children from the Canaanites who lived within the land of Palestine, the same Canaanites, Israel was to drive out of the land many years before.

God had warned Israel of impending disaster if they did not eliminate all unholy nations from the land (Ref. Exodus 22:31; 23:33; 34:12; Numbers 33:55-56; Deuteronomy 7:3-4, 16; Judges. 2:3). Let us look at just one of the warnings.

> (55) "But if you do not drive out the inhabitants of the land from before you, then it shall be that those whom you let remain shall be irritants in your eyes and thorns in your sides, and they shall harass you in the land

where you dwell. (56) Moreover, it shall be that I will do to you as I thought to do to them."

Numbers 33:55-56

Instead of heeding God's command and eliminating the inhabitants of the land, Israel made a covenant with them and their gods, demonstrating their recognition and acceptance. This exact attitude is common in Christians today! God wants us to remove all of our iniquities and evil associations (Ref. 2nd Corinthians 6:17). We, like the Israelites, are not obeying God's command. Instead of eliminating all our sins, we tolerate them and accept them as insignificant or as having little value, limited as it may be. Could it be that we have the wrong idea of grace, and as a result, we are over-dependent on it? God forbid (Romans 6:1)! This disobedience added to man's natural sinful tendencies will inevitably lead us away from giving God due recognition and worship; eventually, it will lead to the worship of idols. As we know, any intimate relationship with the ungodly is expressly forbidden (Ref. Genesis 35:2; Exodus 20:4, 34:17: Leviticus 26:1; Deuteronomy 7:25-26, 11:16; 16:22; Psalm 81:9; Isaiah 42:8; 1st John 5:21).

Sin's contamination due to our tolerance has done more damage to the Church than anything else. It is the wolf that is devouring the sheep. It is like cancer in the Body of Christ, and it eventually leads to death. Any sin in our hearts which we do not purposefully drive out will become our plague and scourge, and will ultimately lead to destruction. No man can have real peace while he is content with his sins, no matter how large or small they may be.

God uses the metaphor of irritants in the eye and thorns in the side when referring to the harm caused by tolerating sin in our lives (Ref. Judges 2:3). In this verse, God vividly points out the continual pain God's people would experience at the hand of these idolatrous nations if they would continue to dwell with them. What can be more of an annoyance than a continual goading on every side? Or what can be more painful than a constant pricking in the eye. Will it not harass the mind, torment the body, and hinder the sight? A continual pricking of the eye was the warning God gave His children, but they chose to avoid it. It was simpler to leave the evil nations alone and hope for the best, and then it was to face them in battle and eradicate them. In other words, ignore them, and they will go away. Not going to happen!

These Canaanites, left in the land, can easily represent emblems of indwelling sin. What those un-removed Canaanites were to the people of Israel, is what indwelling sin is to Christians. We must allow the blood of Jesus to cleanse us from all unrighteousness (Ref. 1st John 1:9). It is natural for any Christian, especially while their conscience is tender, to feel restricted in their desires, hindered by their religious services, distressed and overwhelmed because of the power of sin warring in their members. This warring can lead one to feel helpless, powerless, and confused by the constant piercing and combatting of sin. Often these Christians, just like the Israelites, would finally give up or become persuaded that sin must dwell in them as long as they live. Once they accepted that lie, their minds rationalize it as truth, they make up Biblical proof or natural proof to justify it, and as a result, their conscience ceased to be tender. At this point, these precious souls become content to expect the lie that full sanctification and redemption can only take place beyond the grave! How important is it, therefore, for us to understand and accept that our standing before God does not rest on promises, but on *accomplished redemption*! Redemption comes at the moment we accept God's atonement with a committed heart. Christ's omnipotent power, grace, and mercy permit us to live above the power of sin. Living above the power of sin is God's intention for us. Absolutely! (c.f. Matt. 5:48; Romans 6:12-14; 1st Corinthians 15:34; 1st Peter 2:21-22, 4:1-2; 1st John 3:3-9).

Child of God do not feel that you are the only one wrestling with the problem of warring in the inner man, because all of us do; even the Apostle Paul struggled with this same problem. Notice;

> "For what I am doing, I do not understand. For what I will to do, that I do not practice; but what I hate, that I do. (16) If then, I do what I will not to do, I agree with the law that it is good. (17) But now, it is no longer I who do it, but sin that dwells in me. (18) For I know that in me (that is, in my flesh) nothing good dwells; for to will is present with me, but how to perform what is good I

do not find. (19) For the good that I will to do, I do not do; but the evil I will not to do, that I practice. (20) Now if I do what I will not to do, it is no longer I who do it, but sin that dwells in me. (21) I find then a law, that evil is present with me, the One who wills to do good. (22) For I delight in the law of God according to the inward man. (23) But I see another law in my members, warring against the law of my mind, and bringing me into captivity to the law of sin which is in my members. (24) O wretched man that I am! Who will deliver me from this body of death? (25) I thank God – through Jesus Christ, our Lord! So then, with the mind, I myself serve the law of God, but with the flesh the law of sin."

Romans 7:15-25

Christians, if you find yourself in the same circumstance and wrestling with the same dilemma, rest assured Jesus Christ is your answer, just as He was for Paul.

Now that we have seen the reason for Israel's falling back into the "Cycle of Sin," let us look at Deborah, whose name means "a Bee or a word." Now ask yourself, what is the significance of her name? The Hebrew word for bee is "Devorah" (Deborah). "Devorah" is also the feminine form of the word "Davar" (literally: Word). Another derivative from this Hebrew root is "midbar" or wilderness. Jeff Benner has this to say about our root word: The root word is "Davar," frequently translated as a thing or a word. The original picture painted by this word to the Hebrews is the proper arrangement of things to create order. Speech is an ordered arrangement of words. Bees are a community of insects that live in a perfectly ordered arrangement. Therefore, the significance of the meaning of her name is easily understood, Deborah, a prophetess of God, only spoke words that were perfectly ordered and arranged by God to bring order and coherency back to a lost, enslaved, suffering nation lost in the wilderness of their sin. That is why she obtained the title of "mother of Israel" (Ref. Judges 5:7).

The Bible tells us little to nothing about the history of this remarkable woman, and she was the only prophetess used as a judge in the book of

Judges. The Old Testament records only three other women who were God's prophetess; Miriam (Exodus 15:20), Huldah (2nd Kings 22:14), and the unnamed wife of Isaiah (Isaiah 8:3). We usually think of a prophet as one who has divine insight into future events, but this is only a small part of a prophet's function. Old Testament prophets were God's mouthpieces, who God positioned in three important locations.

1. On the walls of the city (Isaiah 62:6-7). Prophets who were placed on the walls of the city had an elevated perspective. That position enables them to see both outside and inside the city. These men were trained to recognize both the enemy and their brethren from great distances,

2. Walking about in the city (Song of Solomon 3:3). The watchman appointed to walk about inside the city could observe activity within the walls more intimately. They were specifically trained to make a way for the king or the nobility who were passing through or to recognize and confront disorder or unlawful behavior.

3. On the hills or countryside (Jeremiah 31:6). The watchmen on the hills patrolled the borders and countryside. They could see either the enemy or nobility long before they arrived in the city. They, too, were specially trained to distinguish their countrymen from foreigners or from their enemies who came as traders or ambassadors,

Deborah's position as a prophetess was one on whom the Spirit of God descended, and an instrument of conveying to God's people the knowledge of God's Divine will. Deborah was more than a wise judge. She is an inspired judge used by God to guide the development of the young Hebrew nation in accordance with God's law.

Deborah's genealogy is a mystery. The only personal information we have is that she was "the wife of Lapidoth" (Judges 4:4), whose name means "lamp or enlightened." Their home was between Bethel and Ramah in the hill country of Ephraim, about 50 miles from the site of this decisive battle. She lived under a palm tree from which she ruled. Deborah seems to have been the utmost authority in both civil and religious affairs. We can deduce this by a statement made in Judges 4:5

"as she sat in her tent under the palm tree… the children of Israel came up to her for judgment." This particular palm tree became a landmark. Her palm tree, in honor of her works, for it became known as "The Palm of Deborah" (Judges 4:5). Though it is probably true that other judges operated in the prophetic, the Bible does not call them prophets or prophetesses.

Occasionally, a strong-minded and unique woman breaks in upon human history and by her exploits, leaves the impact of her personality upon events and secures for herself an imperishable honor. For example, in France, Joan of Arc, the patron saint of her country, professed to have divine visions as to her destiny to restore peace to her troubled nation by the crowning of Charles. From there youth French school teachers teach French children how she led 10,000 troops against the English at Orleans and compelled them to retreat, and of how other victories followed as her banner struck terror into the hearts of her enemies. Another such woman was Mother Teresa. Who from 1931 to 1948 taught at St. Mary's High School in Calcutta, but the suffering and poverty she saw outside the convent walls made such a deep impression on her that in 1948 she received permission from her superiors to leave the convent and devote herself to working among the poorest of the poor in the slums of Calcutta. Throughout the world, everyone recognizes Mother Teresa's work, and she has received several awards and distinctions, including the Pope John XXIII Peace Prize (1971) and the Nehru Prize for her promotion of international peace and understanding (1972).

God gifted Deborah as a judge and prophetess with superior spiritual, mental, and physical powers, God raised her and endowed her with a remarkable personality and a variety of gifts. God used her to deliver the distressed and defeated Israelite people, and by doing so, she left her mark upon the annals of time in precisely the same way as Joan of Arc and Mother Teresa.

Let us now look at what she did to win the day and how it applies to Christians today. If one wishes to have a complete detailed account of the cause, effect, and the military strategies found in this story, look to chapters 4 and 5. But seeing that our aim here is to show what we can learn from Deborah and how we can apply this information to aid in our

Christian walk, all I will do is give you a general outline of the events, then discuss the attitudes and actions taken by this great woman of God.

1. The cause of Israel's distress (Judges 4:1)
2. The Military oppression and strength of Jabin King of Canaan (Judges 4:2-3)
3. The cure for Israel's distress named; Deborah (Judges 4:4-5)
4. The preparations made and instructions for battle given by Deborah (Judges 4:4-13)
5. The nature of the battle and the absolute and total defeat of Jabin's army (Judges 4:14-16)
6. Sisera escapes and flees (Judges 4:17)
7. The death of Sisera (Judges 4:18-24)
8. Deborah's song of praise (Judges 5:1-31)

Now let us look at some essential traits we see in Deborah.

1. Loved God
2. Available
3. Wise
4. Virtuous
5. Spiritually discerning
6. She knew the times and seasons
7. Humble
8. Courageous
9. Level headed
10. Used of God

First and foremost, Deborah loved God. Notice how she demonstrated her love for God in her song of praise in Judges 5.

> "Then Deborah and Barak the son of Abinoam sang on that day, saying: (2) "When leaders lead in Israel, when the people willingly offer themselves, Bless the Lord! (3) "Hear, O kings! Give ear, O princes! I, even I, will sing to the Lord; I will sing praise to the Lord God of Israel."
> Judges 5:1-3

God used Deborah because of Her love for Him and because she made herself available for Him to use. Loving God and being available for Him to use is the "cause and effect" that makes one a useful and cherished vessel in the hands of God. She was a prophetess who judged Israel in both civil and religious affairs. She was available to those who needed her at any time (Judges 4:5). The fact that Israel respected her judgments and those judgments demonstrated her Divine wisdom because all Israel came to her for judgment. Even leaders and men of great respect and authority like Barak (Hebrews 12:29) came to her when called. Ancient Israel was a patriarchal society, whose priesthood was handed down from father to son and all religious roles men oversaw. Women did not fill the role of leaders; their gifts and talents were for social, not governmental functions. However, in the case of Deborah's godly authority, all Israel, men and women alike recognized and respected her wisdom and calling as a judge and prophetess. This fact was extremely remarkable, if not miraculous. The Bible tells that all the people of Israel submitted to her leadership (Ref. Judges 4:5-6).

Let us now look at this excerpt from the Book of Judges, which alludes to Deborah's wisdom.

> "Then she sent and called for Barak the son of Abinoam from Kedesh in Naphtali, and said to him, "Has not the LORD God of Israel commanded, 'Go and deploy troops at Mount Tabor; take with you ten thousand men of the sons of Naphtali and of the sons of Zebulun; (7) and against you I will deploy Sisera, the commander of Jabin's army, with his chariots and his multitude at the River Kishon; and I will deliver him into your hand'?""
>
> Judges 4:6-7

Deborah prepared all the battle plans. She summoned Barak from Kadesh to take the command of 10,000 men of Zebulun and Naphtali, and lead them to Mount Tabor on the Plain of Esdraelon at its north-east end. With his aid, Deborah organized the army. She gave the signal for attack, and the army of God's people rushed down immediately and in haste upon the army of Jabin, and gained a great and decisive victory.

Israel's army under the direction of Deborah and Barak utterly defeated the Canaanite army, and it became a great and ever-memorable day in Israel.

Other prominent attitudes possessed by Deborah were that she was a virtuous and spiritually discerning woman who knew the times and seasons, and one who possessed great humility. Notice this passage.

"And Barak said to her, "If you go with me, then I will go; but if you do not go with me, I will not go!" (9) So, she said, "I will surely go with you; nevertheless, there will be no glory for you in the journey you are taking, for the Lord will sell (into slavery or to surrender) Sisera into the hand of a woman." Judges 4:8-9

Deborah being well aware of the Jewish male patriarchal society, called for Barak, a judge in his own right and a great leader in Israel to take charge. She did not say, prepare the men and I will lead, or for Barak to go before her in battle. She specifically directed Barak to "take charge." She was content in her role as prophetess. She gave Barak the Lord's instructions and was content to stay where she was, taking no credit for herself. It was Barak that broke the traditional societal roles and requested her to go with him. He went as far as to give her an ultimatum "If you go with me, then I will go; but if you do not go with me, I will not go" (verse 8)! Deborah demonstrates her virtue, spiritual discernment, and humility by informing Barak of the consequences of his request. Notice what the consequences were. One, Barak would receive no glory in the victory; two, "a woman," not her, but an unnamed woman would be the instrument that would bring forth the Lord's victory. Barak accepted these consequences with humility, and therefore "Deborah arose and went with Barak to Kedesh."

The decision of Deborah to go with Barak to battle shows she had two other amazing attributes. She was courageous and level headed. Deborah, who was not a warrior or a military leader or strategist, arose to face the battle with the armies of Israel without fear, only relying on her faith in Jehovah God. She accessed the situation, and when the time was right, Deborah gave the command to attack. Barak and Israel obeyed, and the battle ensued; so great was the victory that Sisera, the commander of Jabin's army, leaped down from his chariot and fled. The story concludes with the fulfillment of Deborah's prophetic words to Barak.

A woman by the name of Jael, having hammered a tent peg through the temple of Sisera while he was hiding in her tent, wrought the final victory. God brought Israel deliverance through the efforts of two brave and level-headed women. Proof positive to the men of this male-dominated society that God uses those who are available for use and not always those who we think are qualified for use (Judges 4.4-5). The Bible is full of examples of God calling unqualified people (unqualified by human standards) to do His work. Often God chooses people who will allow Him to use them, and then God glorifies Himself through them (Ref. 1st Corinthians 1:27-29). A perfect example of this is the twelve apostles, none of which were qualified or educated; they were just ordinary fishermen. Matthew was the only One thought educated, and he was a tax collector.

Where Deborah demonstrated great faith and courage, Barak, on the other hand, showed the opposite. Extraordinary courage belongs to those who believe in God (Judges 4.6-10). Fear belongs to those who know, not God. How often do we find ourselves afraid to follow through with God's leading because of fear, doubt, or unbelief? We see fear in Barak. He was willing to obey God **"if"** Deborah went with him. Deborah possessed great courage because she believed God even when she faced Barak's ultimatum, based on his fear, she chose to believe God, accepted the challenge and went forth without fear but in faith. Barak did not believe God. If Barak had believed God, he would have obeyed God. Deborah chastised Barak for his lack of faith, telling him that he would receive no honor because God would give the victory to a woman. And in this male-dominated society, giving honor to a woman would be a total humiliation to Barak, but his fear took control, and he wholeheartedly agreed to this provision.

God waits when giving blessings and answering prayer until people believe He will answer (Judges 4:12-16). Deborah reminds Barak, "Has not the Lord gone out before you" (4:14)? The overwhelming might of the Canaanite army could not stand against the Israelites because Jehovah God fought for them; "If God be for us who can be against us" (Romans 8:31). God waits until someone takes Him at His word before helping. It is faith that pleases God. Deborah believed God. Barak did not. Deborah pleased God. Barak did not.

Notice also that honor belongs to those who obey God (Judges 4.17-24). Jael exhibited tremendous courage, more courage than Barak! She killed Sisera, the commander of Jabin's army, while he hid in her tent by hammering a stake through his temple (4:21-22). It took a lot of courage to kill someone who was a great warrior and much stronger. She showed total commitment to her course of action; for she hammered the stake clear through him into the ground, without regard for her safety or security. For Jael knew that if Sisera awoke for any reason and her plan discovered, death would follow. Her obedience earned her the name of the "most blessed among women" and given honorable mention in God's timeless record (Ref. Judges 5:24-27).

Here are some more lessons we can learn from Deborah, God's faithful, courageous servant.

1. God Himself chooses those whom society considered and weakest and makes them strong.
2. God wants His people to know that they are precious vessels created by God to use when He chooses.
3. Women are not inferior. God chooses the vessel He wishes to use when He prefers to use it; no matter the gender, color, creed, size, or ability.
4. In a strongly patriarchal society that recognized only men as leaders, Deborah and Jael's contributions due to their humbleness, virtue, hard work, and restraint brought them recognition as equal to those of a man.

Being considered equal to men is not a bad thing because society during this era was in great need of order and control, much in the same way as it is today. A woman's duties are endless, necessary, and essential for the survival and wellbeing of the family, recognition and virtue are the rewards of her diligence. Notice Proverbs 31:25-31.

> Strength and honor are her clothing; She shall rejoice in time to come. (26) She opens her mouth with wisdom, and on her tongue is the law of kindness. (27) She watches over the ways of her household and does not

eat the bread of idleness. (28) Her children arise and call her blessed; her husband also, and he praises her: (29) "Many daughters have done well, but you excel them all." (30) Charm is deceitful, and beauty is passing, but a woman who fears the Lord, she shall be praised. (31) Give her of the fruit of her hands and let her works praise her in the gates.

Proverbs 31: 25-31

Here are some of the lessons we can learn from Jael.

A. in the face of our enemy, what is needed is total courage when we have a job to do for God.
B. Total commitment to finish the job despite the apparent dangers and long odds we face.
C. Total self-sacrifice. We know that our lives are in God's hands. If He wishes to call us home, our attitude must be "not my will Lord, but thine be done." "Greater love has no one than this than to lay down one's life for his friends." (Ref John 15:13).
D. God honors those who honor Him. God's Holy Word immortalized Jael's name.

The life of Deborah is a celebration of believing God despite the circumstances we find ourselves facing. You can always trust God to deliver what He promises.

In conclusion, I would like to point out that Deborah was more than a judge and a prophetess. She was a woman who occupied many positions and a woman who personifies Proverbs 31:25-31. Let me show you.

1. **She Was a Wife** – While her husband had nothing said of him, we know that she was married and had the duties associated with being a wife. Many theologians believe that Lapidoth was not a great, charismatic leader who was influential in stature and personality; he was a man who, like Moses, was meek but not weak. Many notable men have testified to the help and

inspiration they received from their wives. Perhaps the shoe was on the other foot in Deborah and Lipidoth's life. Perhaps, Deborah would never have become this amazing character in Biblical history if she had not had the love, sympathy, advice, and encouragement of a husband who was happy to be an enabler rather than the traditional leader.

2. **She was a Voice of one crying in the wilderness and a Light in the time of darkness** – Deborah was one who stirred up Israel's concern about its low spiritual condition. The land was dissolute and in a state of devastation and poverty. Under the rule of the Canaanites. Discouraged, depressed, disheartened, and afraid, was Israel's spirits, and all hope of deliverance had vanished. But Deborah did more than prophecy; she lifted the nation from its horrid condition and brought hope, encouragement, meaning, courage, and freedom. Her anointed words stirred and motivated God's people and allowed them to see their destitute state. Her words gave them the strength and determination to free themselves from their overwhelming bondage and degradation.

3. **She Was a Ruler** – Deborah was the fifth "Judge" of Israel. God raised her to deliver His people from the bondage their idolatry had caused. By her words and deeds, she fulfilled her role as God's "Judge," at a time when men tried to do what was right in their own eyes. From the palm tree bearing her name, she dispensed righteousness, justice, and mercy. Her wisdom guided them along a path that led them to victory and 40 years of peace.

4. **She Was a Warrior** – Deborah sent for Barak, the son of Abinoam of Naphtali, and told him that it was God's will that he should lead Israel's forces and deliver the country. But perhaps due to his repeated failures, Barak feared that calling and responsibility and hesitated. He then presented Deborah with an ultimatum, and the brave-hearted woman became a warrior and went with him to battle. The odds against Deborah and Barak were incredibly long at best, for their army consisted of only 10,000 men who were to face Sisera, who commanded

100,000 fighters and had 900 iron chariots. When the eventful moment of combat came, this brave and faithful woman stood courageous and level headed. She knew that she had God as her ally, and He would fight for her. God, who is always faithful to His word, gave His people the victory; and Deborah gained never-ending fame as the female warrior who rescued her people from their enemy.

5. **She Was a Poet** – "The style and poem found in Judges 4 and 5 reveals that Deborah could not only prophesy, rule and fight but also write with the same ability in which she fought." Notice Deborah, who, after her victory over the Canaanites, composed a song which is one of the finest specimens of ancient Hebrew poetry found anywhere. Even better than the famous song of Miriam. This song of praise, found in Judges 5, magnifies the Lord as being the One who enabled Israel's leaders to conquer their enemies. Out of this conquest came the moral purification of the nation, and the inspiring influence was a daring and dynamic woman in leadership of her nation. No character in the Old Testament stands out bolder than Deborah." [2]

6. **Deborah describes herself as a "Mother in Israel"** – In Judges 5:7, Deborah describes herself as "a mother in Israel." Notice the wording of the verse. "Village life ceased, it ceased in Israel, until I, Deborah, arose; arose a mother in Israel." Calling herself the "Mother of Israel" is her description of her having watched over her people with maternal care in the same way as job called himself a father to the poor because he supported them (Job 29:16; Isaiah 22:21). She was to God's children the same as a mother would be her children. She was to teach and instruct them in the mind and will of God. She administered judgment and justice to protect and defend them against all enemies. And by doing so for an unspecified number of years, she undoubtedly developed a maternal affection for them. Should not a mother carry these same types of responsibilities for her children, especially Christian mothers? Perhaps that is why God allowed her this honored title, "a mother in Israel" to be recorded in His timeless word.

Through Deborah, God's compassion and love touched people. God can only use someone if his love and compassion flows through them; Is that not the meaning of 1ˢᵗ Corinthians 13:1-2.

> "Though I speak with the tongues of men and angels, but have not love, I have become sounding brass or a clanging cymbal. (2) And though I have the gift of prophecy, and understand all mysteries and all knowledge, and though I have all faith, so that I could remove mountains, but have not love, I am nothing."
>
> 1ˢᵗ Corinthians 13:1-2

No faithful and true love for God, brings no power; no power, produces no mighty works. Perhaps that should be the last lesson in this chapter!

GIDEON — PART ONE: THE BIRTH OF FAITH

Forty years have passed since Deborah and Barak gained the victory over Jabin and the Canaanites. We know nothing regarding those forty years of rest. All we know is it was the same type of rest ("shâqaṭ" idleness, Judges 5:31) mentioned before the start of each "Cycle of Sin." Notice also that the same phrase repeated several times before, appears again in Judges 6:1; "the children of Israel did evil in the sight of the Lord, so the Lord delivered them into the hands of ..." In Judges 6:2 the "cycle of sin" begins again with Israel under servitude for another extended period. A time filled with dreadful conditions (verses 3-6), Then Israel again starts crying out to God (verse 7), God hears and answers their cries and brings deliverance. This time by the hand of Gideon, whose name means "He that bruises, or breaks, he that cuts down; a destroyer or warrior."

Before we get into the finer points of Gideon's story, please keep in mind a valuable lesson seen repeatedly in the Book of Judges. God loves to take people who are willing, available, humble, and sometimes weak and fearful and use them to do great and wonderful works. We have all heard this old but very true Christian axiom "God is not looking for ability, but availability.1

"So, it is in the book of Judges.

In verse 6, we see an overview of the condition of Israel at the time of Gideon. "So Israel was greatly impoverished and devastated because of the Midianites." It is the only time in the Bible that the phrase "greatly impoverished" is used, and it means to be vehemently oppressed, brought low, feeble, dried up, emptied. It was the lowest point in their history. Have you ever felt like you've been there? We all have! However, they remembered God's promises. They possessed a "land flowing with milk and honey." God's abundance and protection was theirs as a result of keeping His covenant. But due to their disobedience and idolatry, they were now destitute, living in caves and in the clefts of the rocks, too scared to face their enemies. Even when they managed to gather enough courage to go out and plant crops, the crops were stolen or destroyed, bringing discouragement, defeat and compromise and capitulation. A detailed account of the extent of their oppression is found in Judges 6:2-5. Their condition could not get any worse. It was at this point that Israel cried out to God for help and deliverance. This set of circumstances begs the question again; why did it take seven years (verse One) under these conditions for Israel to cry out to God? Could it be spiritual blindness? Maybe pride! Perhaps brokenness! Or was it their overwhelming desire to live without acknowledging Jehovah God or His covenant! In this time of Israel's most desperate state, God in His infinite and boundless love and mercy let His people know, through an unnamed prophet, that He was aware of their situation and that He had a plan to deliver them. He explained to them the reason for their distress, in the hope that if they were aware of what got them in this situation, they would not repeat the same actions. This time, God preceded the calling of a deliverer by sending a prophet to Israel with a direct and robust pronouncement of what brought them to this state and a clear message of hope. In the New Testament, God repeats this same event. The prophet God sent before (Jesus) His deliverer, was John the Baptist.

"Jehovah sent a man, a prophet, to the sons of Israel. And he said to them, so says Jehovah, the God of Israel, I have brought you up out of Egypt; and I have brought you out from a house of slaves. (9) And I have delivered you out of the hand of the Egyptians and out of the hand of all your oppressors, and I have driven them out before you, and I have given you their land. (10) And I said to you, I am Jehovah your God. You shall not fear the gods of the Amorite among whom you are dwelling in their land. But you have not listened to My voice."

Judges 6:8-10

Notice what the Lord said through this unnamed prophet.

1. I have brought you up out of Egypt.
2. I have brought you out from a house of slaves.
3. I have delivered you out of the hand of the Egyptians and out of the hands of all your oppressors.
4. I have driven them out before you.
5. I have given you their land.
6. I said to you, I am Jehovah, your God.
7. You shall not fear the gods of the Amorite among whom you are dwelling in their land.

Then God openly and frankly states the root of their entire problem.

8. **But You have not obeyed my voice.** (c.f. Judges 2:2, 6:10, 3:13 Is this not the case with many of God's people today? Is this not the case of our nation? Taking it one step further, is it not the same for the entire world? We have forgotten many of God's graces and have disregarded God's commandments, statutes, and laws due to arrogance, pride, discomfort, inconvenience, or dissatisfaction. As a result, we find ourselves distressed, fearful, and in dire consequences and under severe judgment. God said that if His children choose this course:

"I also will choose their delusions, and will bring their fears upon them; because when I called, none did answer; when I spoke, they did not hear: but they did evil before mine eyes, and chose that in which I delighted not." (Isaiah 66:4)

For many years I have heard the same argumentative excuse from people who do not wish to know God, and frankly, it is becoming tiresome to answer it. The argument goes like this. "How could a God of love allow all the evil in the world? If God was a God of love and He is with us today, why doesn't He do away with all evil and be done playing this malicious game?" Now in all fairness to these questioning individuals, I must admit that Gideon asked almost the same question,

So, let me attempt to address the issue. Notice verse 13. "Gideon said to Him,

"O my lord, if the Lord is with us, why then has all this happened to us? And where are all His miracles which our fathers told us about, saying, 'Did not the Lord bring us up from Egypt?' But now the Lord has forsaken us and delivered us into the hands of the Midianites." (Judges 6:13)

Ask yourself – Who was it that forsook whom? When we read the rest of the chapter, we notice that God did not bother to answer Gideon's question. The exact reason why God did not answer we do not know, but one possible answer is that the unnamed prophet already explained why; notice verse 10b, it says, "But you have not obeyed my voice." Another reason could be that throughout the time of Israel's existence, the answer was obvious. The history of Israel's covenant with God, with all their successes and failures were well known to every Israelite. Parents taught all their children as well as preserving the reasons in written form.

Let me ask all who have ever questioned God's motives. Are you evil, and are you playing a malicious game when you scold or punish your children for doing something you know will hurt them now and more so in the long run? Of course not! You are a good parent. So is God!

Due to fraudulent misrepresentations of who God is, comes a direct and proportional devaluing of God Himself, His Word, His precepts, and His laws. How much one believes in "God" directly determines his relationship and obedience to Him. Devaluing God extends much farther than just our relationship and obedience; however, it reaches into the depth of our soul. Our concept of God directly affects our desire to know Him or His ways. More importantly, it directly affects our need of salvation. Once our idea of God is skewed, how can we believe in the need for redemption or anything God has to offer? A wrong concept of God can become a catastrophic and lethal concept. Therefore, we need to rectify our understanding of who and what God is.

The Puritans believed that the Law was God's holy nature in written form. They considered the moral law as a revelation of God's divine nature, an unchanging expression of the holy majesty of God. Since God's moral Law originates from His character and His immutable and divine management of cause and effect (moral Law), a perfect revelation of God's righteous character appears.

The moral law of God was given to man beginning with the Promulgation. Promulgation is the binding power of the law or legislation which rests entirely on the will of the legislator. The legislator, in this case, was Jehovah. "I am the Lord your God, who brought you out of the land of Egypt, out of the house of bondage. " (Exodus 20:2); therefore, the standard man must use to decide what is right or wrong, good or evil, is fixed in the unwavering and perfect holy character of God. His nature, attributes, character, power, and qualities provide the measuring stick for all ethical decisions. With that said, let this writer explain to you a Biblical principle. All actions, good or bad, bring with them two things; one is a consequence, and the second is judgment. Recently there was a story in the news of a local bus driver who rammed his bus into the back of a marine convoy truck forcing the truck to turn over in a ditch, injuring many in the transport. The impact hospitalized the driver of the bus. The consequences of his actions were obvious; many marines along with the bus driver paid with their lives. The accident traumatized and inconvenienced many others as well Judgment, however, will come when he faces the DUI charge.

It is the same when we disobey or ignore the commandments of God. Mankind is now doing precisely this! We have told God that we are not interested in Him or His laws, thereby breaking His covenant. The result of this decision has immediate consequences and an everlasting judgment. All the evil we see in the world today is directly due to our disobedient actions and God's moral and spiritual law of cause and effect. Perhaps I can make the point in a more obvious way. Remember what Judges 6:1 says; "the children of Israel did evil in the sight of the Lord, *so the Lord delivered them into the hands of Midian for 7 years*" Change the name Israel; "the children of God did evil in the sight of the Lord, *so the Lord delivered them into the hands of ...*" Or perhaps change it, so it reads like this; "America did evil in the sight of the Lord, *so the Lord delivered them into the hands of ...*" Or more accurately, "I have done evil in the sight of the Lord, *so the Lord delivered me into the hands of ...*" Hopefully, any of these rephrases should make you completely comprehend the truth of what was happening to God's chosen people, which includes all believers today.

The consequences upon us are due to our dismally poor decisions regarding God, and His precepts have manifested in fear. Fear for our lives, futures, jobs, our finances, retirement, marriages, our children's future, and safety. Do any of these bring you concern or fear? Don't worry; God has good news! He has the answer that will take away your fears. God encourages us to "Fear Not." God then gives us nine reasons for encouragement if we obey Him.

1. Blessings in the journey of life (Genesis 26:24; Numbers 21:34; Judges 6:23)
2. Supplies in time of famine (1st Kings 17:13)
3. Protection in times of peril (2nd Kings 6:16)
4. Strength in times of weakness (Isaiah 41:10)
5. Companionship in your trials (Isaiah 43:1-3)
6. Overshadowing parental care (Matthew 10:30-31)
7. A future and a hope (Jeremiah 29:11)
8. Life beyond the grave (Revelation 1:17-18)
9. His never-ending companionship (Hebrew 13:5)

Anyone who wishes to escape personal consequences must obey God's moral law without exception; if we fail, we must turn to God with a pure heart of repentance (Ref. 1st John 1:9). Unfortunately, the consequences and judgments against the world's evils will not go away until the world turns to God in obedience. The good news is that we can minimize the effect the evil in our society has on us by living above sin's influences, and obeying God, His laws and precepts. Jesus speaking to his disciples told them, "Woe to the world because of offenses, *For offenses must come!*" (Ref. Matthew 18:7) The fact is that the world will suffer because of offenses, but for the man after God's own heart, God will elevate him above them.

Israel did not obey God's precepts, and as a result, three different nations ruled over them (Ref Judges 3:6). The first was the Midianites. Midian means "strife" or "judgment." Second, the Amalekites from Amalek, Esau's grandson, which means (the people who lick up) and third were the children of the east thought to be the Kedemites or the Arabs. Both the meanings of Midian are appropriate for the conditions experienced by Israel at this time. Midian speaks to us of consequences, strife, judgment, and evil effects that come to Christians while living in this world.

These nations represent the character of "wickedness" (1st Samuel 15:18); "oppression" (Judges 10:12). They were "warlike and cruel" (1st Samuel 15:33), and they were mighty and influential nations (Numbers 24:7). Also mentioned in Judges 6:3 are the people of the East, who were probably the Arabians, as Josephus expressly affirms. The name is perhaps a synonym for the Bene-Kedem — the "children of the East." Orientals, the name of a Canaanitic tribe which inhabited the north-eastern part of Palestine in the time of Abraham (Genesis 15:19). Probably they were identical and identified as the "children of the east," who inhabited Palestine and the Euphrates countryside. These three nations all contributed to the desperate state of Israel at this time.

Consequence, strife, judgment, fear, and evil are the results that stream from any of three causes.

1. from the personal desires for a sinful nature
2. by personal sins
3. they can occur from living in a sinful world.

But no matter the cause, fear, consequences, and judgment are inevitably the result. Brethren realize one thing about fear; God can and does use it to teach us His truth. It stops us from committing sinful, foolish, and dangerous acts. Once we learn to obey His truth, fear vanishes, hope becomes a reality, and the path back to a victorious life in Christ becomes assured; Why? Because God's perfect love casts out all fear (Ref 1st John 4:17-18).

In Judges 6:8-10, God sent a prophet to His people to deliver His message of deliverance and hope. God's unfathomable and boundless mercy continued even though there were no recorded signs of true repentance by Israel. An Angel of the Lord then came to confirm the word of the prophet and to call and commission Gideon. He was to be their mighty warrior and their deliverer. God also gave Gideon the ability to work miracles to infuse him with supernatural courage and the confidence he needed for success. This "Angel of the Lord" was not a mere created messenger of Jehovah but the Son of God Himself (Ref. Judges 6:14, 23); notice verse 14 "Then the "Lord" turned to him and said..." Here the word "Lord" is "yehôvâh" (Jehovah), the national name of God, which means the "self-existing one," and here used in reference to the Angel who was speaking to Gideon. The Hebrew word "yehôvâh" shows us that the Angel was, in fact, the Lord Jesus Christ, who appeared as a visible self-revelation in human form, a "theophany."

There is another attribute of Gideon that needs mentioning at this time, and it is his "steadfastness." Despite the circumstances surrounding Israel's oppression and devastation, we find Gideon threshing wheat in a winepress so that the Midianites would not confiscate or destroy it. Under normal circumstances, they would use threshing carriages, threshing shoes, or oxen, which they drove over the scattered sheaves to tread out the grains with their hoofs. Hitting the wheat with a stick was another common way to thresh wheat, but only the poor did it that way (Ruth 2:17). During this time of distress, Gideon was beating out the grain in a winepress, which was below the ground, to hide the grain from the oppressors (Judges 6:11).

Now let us get back to the Angel of the Lord, who called Gideon a "mighty man of valor" (Judges 6:12). The first thing to notice is the words that the Angel of the Lord spoke just before calling Gideon a "mighty man of valor." They were, "The Lord is with you..." (Ref. Judges 6:12) Think about that for a moment. Gideon, like all the Israelites, were very familiar with their history and heritage. Gideon undoubtedly had fond memories of how God delivered them from Egypt and brought them, by way of many miracles, to this Promised Land filled with milk and honey. But now the reality of this present situation flies in the face of the greeting that the Angel of the Lord gave. Can you imagine how the humiliating circumstances under which he was working must have filled his soul with sadness, discouragement, doubt, and longing? But it was when God's "mighty man of valor" was at his lowest, that the Messenger of the Covenant suddenly appears to encourage and strengthen him.

The first thing the Angel did, was He immediately gained the confidence of Gideon. Perhaps it was the brightness of His face and form or the tone in which He spoke, and even possibly the words He spoke that immediately struck deep in Gideon's heart. "The Lord is with you, you mighty man of valor" (Ref. Judges 6:12)! To this unknown stranger, Gideon pours out his innermost doubts, sorrows, and fears. It is not that he is ignorant of Jehovah's past dealings, nor that he questions His present power, but he believes that if Jehovah had not withdrawn from Israel. Notice who is blamed and whose blame went unignored! We do the same today. Understand that their present calamities would not have fallen upon them if Israel would have remained faithful to God and His covenant.

Notice again what Gideon says; "O my lord, if the Lord is with us, why then has all this happened to us? And where are all His miracles which our fathers told us about, saying, 'Did not the Lord bring us up from Egypt?' But now the Lord has forsaken us and delivered us into the hands of the Midianites." (Ref. Judges6:13) Gideon's concluding statement was right so far as it went. Israel's prosperity or sufferings depended on the presence or the absence of the Lord. Thus, Gideon's announcement was a truthful confession of Israel's condition and Jehovah's justice. It was the beginning of repentance. But Gideon had more truth to learn. First, would Jehovah turn from His anger, if Israel turned to Him in repentance? The second lesson was for Gideon. He had to put personal trust in the promises of God (Ref. verse 14).

We can see Gideon's need for these lessons by his response to the Angel's greeting.

"But how can I rescue Israel? My clan is the weakest one in Manasseh, and everyone else in my family is more important than I am. It's hard to believe that I'm talking to the Lord. Please do something, so I'll know that you are the Lord." Judges 6:15, 17 (CEV)

Can you imagine what Gideon is saying to himself? Who is this guy? What is he nuts, a mighty warrior, who is He talking about, surely not me? Gideon does not exactly think of himself as a mighty man of valor, and as for delivering Israel by himself, he's saying to himself, not going to happen! Notice the excuses given by Gideon in verse 15, and the proof he needs regarding this Angel's identity is in verse 17.

Let me try and interpret this verse in modern vernacular. "Say what?

Lord, you don't understand – my family is at the bottom of the barrel. We are insignificant. Not only that, but I'm the youngest and weakest of all my family members! You must be asleep at the wheel if you think I can deliver Israel. Lord let me make this easy for you, no way – I can't do this – You got the wrong guy!" Lord, is this you, or is this a result of the chili I ate last night? Do any of these excuses sound familiar? Have you ever felt like Gibeon when God asked you to help Him? You are not alone; most Christians feel precisely that way. Welcome to the club! One thing is for sure, if you keep your eyes on yourself or the situation – you will undoubtedly fail, and you would have proven yourself right. Still, if your eyes are placed solely on Christ, victory is assured and the ability to succeed no matter the endeavor, you will find (Ref Matthew 14:25-31).

Gideon might have understood by the statement "The Lord is with you, you mighty man of valor," that being God's mighty man of valor is contingent on what was said just before it, which was "The Lord is with you." or, as the Chaldeans translate it, "the Word of the Lord is thy help." But to eliminate Gideon's doubt and make God's word living and powerful, Gideon needed support and confirmation So;

1. God gives Gideon the promise that He would be with him.
2. God gives Gideon His assignment. When God is with us, He will justify us and bear us up in our undertakings.
3. God furnishes Gideon with all the necessary qualifications and abilities for the completion of his task. "The Lord is with you to guide and strengthen you."
4. God assures Gideon of success; for, He confirms who he was through the fire (Ref. Judges 6:21. For success in whatever we do for God, God's presence is vital. Gideon was a mighty man of valor, yet he could bring nothing to pass without the presence of God. God's presence is enough to make any man mighty in spirit and is enough to give any man courage and victory in any challenge. When God acts powerfully on the heart of His children, the first thing that should happen is that their hearts and minds become focused on God, and no distractions are possible. Gideon occupied his heart and mind only with thoughts of Jehovah. Gideon's heart and mind being steadfast

filled with thoughts of Jehovah caused Gideon to express his deepest feelings and concerns to the Angel of the Lord.

Now notice how God responded to the extreme bitterness that filled the questions of Gideon. God responded with love and understanding, not condemnation. Jehovah answering in this manner put to rest all Gideon's doubts and fears. It gave him a real inner peace. It also immediately turned Gideon's attention to worship. Gideon builds an altar to God and worships (Judges 6:18-19). This action results in a personal relationship and a covenant of peace between God and His servant. When we develop a real relationship with Jesus, He becomes our peace, for He is the God of peace and rest (Ref. Isaiah 53:5; John 14:27, 16:33; Romans 5:1, 15:33, 16:20; Ephesians 2:14, Philippians 4:9; Colossians 1:20: 1st Thessalonians 5:23; Hebrews 4, 13:20).

The Angel of the Lord promised that He would be with Gideon and that Gideon would prove himself a mighty hero through the strength of the Lord. This promise was to be a guarantee of strength and victory in the conflict with the Midianites. This guarantee is for us as well in all our battles. Notice:

> "Let your character or moral disposition be free from love of money [including] greed, avarice, lust, and craving for earthly, possessions and be satisfied with your present [circumstances and with what you have]; for He (God) Himself has said, I will not in any way fail you nor give you up nor leave you without support. [I will] not [I will] not, [I will] not in any degree leave you helpless, nor forsake nor let [you] down, [relax My hold on you.] Assuredly not! (6) So, we take comfort and are encouraged and confident and boldly say, The Lord is my Helper, I will not be seized with alarm, I will not fear or dread' or be terrified. What can man do to me?"
> Hebrews 13:5-6 AMPV

"I will be with you" (Ref. Judges 5:16) God guarantees, is this not all we need to know. Rest assured brethren, "If God is for us, who can be against us" (Romans 8:31b)? With God, you are a majority, no matter the odds.

It is at this point that Gideon asks the Angel of the Lord for a sign that would prove that He was indeed God and it was His will to battle the Midianites. How often as Christian believers have we done the same thing? Now many might consider Gideon a man weak in faith because of this request? But let us not make that mistake. Gideon was not a man of no faith or weak faith. After all, God asked him to fight against and defeat the entire Midianite army estimated at 135,000 men; that takes faith! (Ref. Judges 8:10)! When asked to do something of that magnitude, wouldn't you want to be sure it was God? We need to remember that Gideon was not an extraordinary warrior or leader. He was an ordinary man from a small tribe. Gideon fits God's requirements for a servant perfectly. He was a man weak enough for God to use, and faithful enough to follow God's orders, even in the face of this extreme challenge.

One thing many of us miss when reading this passage is that the sign-in which God used to strengthen Gideon's faith required a great sacrifice on Gideon's part. He was to bring certain things before the Angel of the Lord as a sacrifice (verse 19-20). These objects included a young goat, unleavened bread, and an ephah of flour (about one bushel or 35 liters). During this time of extreme impoverishment and famine, it took a lot of faith to provide that amount for an offering. Gideon demonstration of faith God Honored in that fire came out of a rock and immediately consumed the offering, and the Angel of the Lord disappeared right in front of Gideon (verse 21). Gideon immediately upon seeing the Angel's disappearance realized that the man he had been speaking with was the Lord Jehovah Himself (verse 22). This assurance was all Gideon needed. He stopped focusing on his inadequacies, stopped looking at the odds against him, and obeyed God's command. If there is a downside to any of Gideon's actions, it would be that his faith and assurance needed some confirmation by an outward physical sign.

Gideon received a sign, which proved to him that the person who had appeared to him was God. But seeing God face to face filled his soul with fear, so much so that he cried out, "Alas, Oh Lord God! I have seen the Angel of the Lord face to face." (Ref Judges 6:22). Seeing the Angel of the Lord face to face is an expression of alarm, fear, and death, which would be the consequence of seeing God face to face (Ref. Exodus 20:19, 33:20; Judges 13:22; Isaiah 6:5). The Lord knowing and understanding the fearful heart of Gideon assured him with the words, "Peace be with thee; do not fear: you shall not die" (verse 23). When we face the toughest times in our lives, and we cry out to God in fear, rest assured that He will give us that same assurance. "The Lord is with you, you mighty man of valor... Peace be with you; do not fear: you shall not die." (Ref Judges 6:23

The Lord spoke these words from heaven after the disappearance of the Angel, giving added assurance to Gideon. And in gratitude for this comforting assurance, Gideon built a permanent altar to the Lord, which he called Jehovah-shalom, "the Lord our peace" (Judges 6:24). The intention of this altar was not of sacrifice but as a memorial witness of the revelation of God's ultimate victory over the Midianites. It was a physical monument of the proof Gideon had received that Jehovah was peace and that He would not destroy Israel in wrath, but He only cherished thoughts of peace for Gideon and his people. This altar was also a symbol of God's announcement that Gideon would conquer the Midianites in the strength of God, and deliver Israel from its oppressors.

That very night Gideon got his first set of instructions because "God is not slack in the performance of His promises" (2nd Peter 3:9). Notice what the first order of business was, God calls Gideon to get his own house in order (verse 25)! Does this not remind you of the first step of Othniel when he was to deliver Israel from Cushan-Rishathaim king of Mesopotamia. Gideon was now set apart as the "Deliverer of His People." To be able to carry out the work entrusted to him, it was, therefore, necessary that Gideon first purify his father's house from idolatry, and sanctify his life and labor to the Lord by sacrificing a burnt-offering. That very night God commanded him to destroy his father's Baal altar, with the Asherah-idol with it. Then build an altar to the Lord, and offer two bullocks upon the altar. He was to provide one for himself, the other for the sins of his people. All blessings will come after one, deals with their sins. Notice how vital cleansing one's house first is before a work of God can go forth (Ref. Judges 3). Gideon like Othniel had to judge himself and his house before God would give, them their marching orders.

Today Christians must deal with their battles in the same two-step approach.

"For the time has come for judgment to begin at the house of God; and if it begins with us first, what will be the end of those who do not obey the gospel of God?" 1st Peter 4:17

We, like Gideon, could not even begin a work for God until we first purify our own house. For God is looking for a faithful and wise servant, someone on whom He can pour out His blessings. How can God give authority and power to unfaithful servants? Do you remember the parable of the Talents (Ref. Matthew 25:14-30)? The more faithful a servant is in doing the things of God, the more blessings. Reprimand comes to the servant who does not use his talent, in fact (Ref. Matthew 25:23-25). The unfaithful servant found himself in outer darkness. Often overlooked is the one thing that this parable teaches that is, a "servant of God;" a servant that decided not to be faithful in his assignment loses all blessings. The excuse given by God's servant was that he "was afraid!" Afraid of what, you might ask. Let us look and see what we can glean from the servant's attitude and response. But first, we must understand that all excuses are reasons for disobedience, idleness, sloth, and a worldly outlook. The effects of such explanations are that they bring trouble and sorrow. Such is the case with everyone for not doing their God-given duties. The servant's response was, "Master, I knew that you were a hard man, harvesting where you haven't planted and gathering where you haven't scattered any seed" (Matthew 25:24 ISV). The bottom-line Jesus did not deny what he said but used it to judge the slothful servant's excuse, Jesus told him that if he knew that he was such a man he ought to have acted accordingly, to have escaped punishment.

1. I will have more to answer for; if I improve my talents,
2. If I do not gain enough, or if I should lose the talent itself, the Lord might not have mercy on me. This fearful excuse is a pretense. Notice that all the servant's talents came in accordance with their abilities. When one' uses his abilities, they are rewarded. When one does not use his talents, they get condemned. God is looking for servants, not slackers.

3. "I was afraid," (Ref Matthew 25:25) is this not what the servant said. This ill-conceived fear of God arose from the type of man he mistakenly thought his Lord to be; his false concept of God. Nothing is more unworthy of God, and no more hinders our duty for Him than mindless fear. This type of fear has bondage and torment, associated with it, and is directly opposite to the very nature of God, which is love.

Let us examine this misconception of God for a moment. Question; Can a man understand, devote himself, or be obedient to God and His Word without understanding God's divine nature and wisdom? When we thoroughly and thoughtfully examine this question, it becomes clear that our concept of God is the most important fact upon which our understanding of God and His will exists. A.W. Tozer, in his classic book on the attributes of God, "The Knowledge of the Holy," makes an incredibly profound assertion? "Man's spiritual history will positively demonstrate that no religion has ever been greater than its idea of God." Worship is pure or base as the worshipper entertains high or low thoughts of God."

In our hearts, we know the above statement is true. If we have lost or skewed our concept of God, how can one follow God properly? Today God has become a word meaning anything from an idea of man, to a ritual based on personal needs and likes, or a psychological crutch used by weak, hurting, unintelligent people. The word "god" can represent an all-powerful creature that is indifferent to our problems, a powerless overseer, or a complete myth. God has come to mean so many different things, that a man can freely set his moral standards, likes, and dislikes up as divine truth (cr. Judges 17:6, 21:25) while never having to worry about consequences. In other words, "we have made God **in our** image

Due to these skewed and fraudulent misrepresentations of who and what God is, comes, a direct and proportional devaluing of God Himself, How much one believes in God directly determines his relationship with the almighty and their obedience as well. There is no need for salvation if our concept of God's will, His precepts, grace or love is false. This wrong concept is a catastrophic, lethal, and eternal error if not rectified. I know some individuals that are living together while at the same time being married to others. They explain it by repeatedly telling me and others that they are okay because God understands their situation. Therefore, God is OK with living together and acting like they are married. Furthermore, it will not carry any judgment because God understands the situation and what caused it.

With that said, let us turn our attention back to Gideon. Despite God's assurances and signs, fear was still apart of Gideon. Gideon obeyed God, but only after finding ten men to accompany him and then he waited until he was under cover of night (Judges 6:27). Now the fact that he feared, one might say, was because he would suffer for destroying the Baal altar, if he was discovered. Be that as it may, Gideon still feared, but notice God did not scold him for his fear. Not at all! God knows Gideon's heart and ours, as well. He knows we are weak and fearful creatures. The real lesson and challenge for us is not to allow fear to prevent us from being obedient. Total obedience to God admittedly is easier said than done, but it must be done nevertheless. God will teach us how to achieve fearless faith if we trust Him. Gideon, being weak and fearful just like you and I, still obeyed God's command. We would do well to do the same!

Gideon's fear became a reality the next morning when; the town came looking for him. They wanted to put him to death. But to Gideon's surprise, Joash, Gideon's father, yes, the same one who worshiped Baal so intently that he built the altar for himself and the entire town, came and stood as Gideon's savior. Notice how Joash defended not only his son but Jehovah as well.

> "But Joash said to all who stood against him, "Would you plead for Baal? Would you save him? Put to death by morning, the one who would plead for him! If he is a god, let him plead for himself, because his altar has been torn down!"
>
> Judges 6:31

These words of Joash in the Hebrew are very emphatic: "Will you plead in earnest for Baal? Will you save him? If he is God (Elohim,) let him contend for himself, seeing his altar is thrown down." In these words, Joash brings out two truths.

1. **It is absurd and senseless to plead for Baal for as Israelites you know that Jehovah is the only living and true God, so why plead for Baal, a false god?** Will you be so stupid, so senseless? Are you who worship and plead for Baal more excusable than you who knew Jehovah? Tell me what has the worship of Baal brought you, look around, why would you plead for him? Note, it is wrong to sin, but it is a greater wickedness to plead in defense of it.

2. **It was needless to plead for Baal. If he is God, let him fight for himself; for they have destroyed his altar,** if he is not a god, why say anything for him; if on the other hand, he is a god, is he not able to plead for and avenge himself. Why do you take it upon yourselves to save your god! Can he not save himself? In truth, he ought to save both himself and you. If he is a god, then there is no need for you to save him. Is this not a fair challenge for Baal to stand up for himself?

It was evident that Gideon's daring act of faith had inspired his father Joash and filled him with faith and courage, for he is now standing with his son against the multitude of Baal worshipers. Joash's change of heart is the inevitable result of actions believers take in obedience to God. Although it is true that God's word; shall not return void, and it will accomplish what God pleases (Isaiah 55:11). It is also necessary for those words to manifest in physical actions. Even Jesus said if you do not believe Him for what He said, believe Him for the works that He did (Ref. Matthew 11:4; John 2:11, 3:2, 7:31, 10:25, 10:38, 20:30; Acts 8:6).

All too often, our witness goes unnoticed and unaccepted because our words do not reflect our actions. Imagine what great results would appear if we testified of God's love and power and backed it up with the mighty works of God. If we believe God's word as truth and believe in His power, should this not be our hearts cry, "Lord, let my testimony of your wondrous love and power, be supported and confirmed as truth by your miraculous works. For you promised that signs and wonders would follow them that believe, and you would confirm your words with signs following (Mark 16:20) Amen!

After this (no specific period given), Israel's enemies gathered together to destroy Israel. All is now ready for the Lord's intervention. The Spirit of the Lord comes upon Gideon (verse 34a). This phrase "the Spirit of the Lord comes upon" appears only one other time in Biblical history (Judges 3:10) when the Spirit of the Lord came upon Othniel, who delivered Israel from Cushan-Rishathaim king of Mesopotamia. The last time this happened, God's Spirit brought faithfulness, power, and victory. Gideon blows the trumpet, and those who shortly before would have slain him, now follow him to accomplish his God-given assignment. He sends messengers to all Israel's tribes, and many came up to meet him. This action and response can only come by the power of the Spirit, which sways the minds of men. This power of the Spirit can only come through a man who, by faith, acknowledges his relationship with God, and his people, and faithfully puts away the evil which is incompatible with those relationships.

But as we can see by Gideon's request for signs, Gideon's faith was not constant; it knew the depth of uncertainty as well as heights of confidence as it is with all Christians. The Lord shows his remarkable patience when Gideon, who twice sought confirmation of the assignment God had presented to him by the use of a fleece. The Lord very graciously accommodated Gideon's requests. God completely understands the frailty of human nature (cf. Psalm. 103:14). The reason why Gideon asked for two signs and requested a reversal in the details of the first sign might be that Gideon realized that when the sun came up, the rocks on the threshing floor would dry much quicker than the wool fleece, making void the first sign due to natural occurrences. Gideon's second request in which he reversed his conditions would be a more miraculous sign. This time he asked for the fleece to be dry and the surrounding rocks wet. Gideon knew that if this happened, it could not be natural, and therefore it had to be a sign from God. Now despite Gideon's other desperate search for confirmation, we see that the Lord deals more tenderly and graciously with His child than any earthly father could. Notice how gently the Lord condescends to the weakness of his servant's faith, and once again empowers Gideon's confidence. The Lord, with the same love and tenderness, gives us similar signs to confirm our faith. He will respond in love. His nature is one of love (Ref. 1st John 4:7-8).

Brethren, if we were to take this one event and pull it out of the entire story, one might understand Gideon's wavering faith and the need for confirmation. I dare say that if we were in the same situation, we might do the same as Gideon. When we consider the whole story, however, it leads us to an entirely different conclusion. When we consider all the things that Gideon had seen and heard, like the Angel of Jehovah, the fire coming out of the rock, the disappearance of the Angel, the words addressed to him that night, his fathers' conversion and stance in defense of Gideon, and the peoples change of attitude and heart toward Gideon's call, Gideon did indeed have faith enough to believe that God could and would deliver Israel through him.

But there is a battle much more intense than just believing if God can do a thing, or if God will do a thing. There is a battle that takes much stronger faith, and it's the battle against the flesh. When the time came for the physical battle and Gideon seeing the overwhelming odds he faced, it becomes easy to understand why his faith wavered. And why it needed a confirmation, a confirmation that would once and for all assure him that he would prevail against his flesh, the natural man.

Too often, Christians know that God can and will do a thing. Wavering faith occurs when they have nowhere else to turn, no way of escape, and they are facing impossible circumstances. It is in these circumstances that our enemy presents us with a question like: "Is God willing and able to do this for you?" It is easy to believe God can and will provide when our bank accounts, our pantries, and our stomachs are full. It is not so easy to believe the same thing when they are not! I dare say that Gideon is not better or worse than any of us. Our situations determine our actions. Will we follow God faithfully, or will we wane before them?

GIDEON — PART TWO: THE MATURING OF HIS FAITH

All things are possible to them that believe

The battle now begins. But wait, God is not ready. Gideon had too many followers. Thirty-two thousand men followed Gideon after his emotional appeal. But Jehovah will not have that many even though these 32,000 men of Israel were, for the most part, farmers without military hardware, and they were not battle-hardened soldiers like the 135,000-armed Midianites soldiers who were prepared and trained in war. Gideon's aware of his men being way outnumbered and overmatched, would have every reason to be fearful and anxious; Right? Absolutely! You can probably imagine his utter astonishment when the Lord spoke to him, saying, 'Gideon, you have got too many men for this battle (Ref. Judges 7:2)!' In the natural, this statement seems absurd and impossible! In the spiritual, the impossible and absurd is the very thing God is easily capable of handling and desires in order to teach us that placing our faith in him is well entrusted!

Israel's faith was indeed weak, even while the Spirit of God was at work. Twenty-two thousand men who knew the horrific consequences of life under the Midianites still took a selfish action and disregarding their brethren and country. They were content to leave the battle and return home after they heard Gideon's offer. The offer was, "Whoever is fearful and afraid, let him turn and depart at once from Mount Gilead" (Judges 7:3). These men left their brethren to incur whatever fate awaited, while in heart, they accepted whatever repercussion awaited them. These men were weak in faith, comfortable with any outcome, fear-filled and cowardly! They lacked the experience of personalized faith in God. The truth is that the faith produced by others is of quite a different quality than the faith produced by personal experience. When one's experience brings about personal faith, one can withstand anything. God only wants to use men who have personal faith in Him and who are faithful and committed to His will. Drawing faith from another is what I call "second-hand faith," it is weak, and it is almost useless and undependable. Second-hand faith was the type of faith that these twenty-two thousand men had. They were somewhat Committed to the cause, but not grounded in faith or trust in the Lord.

Let me give you a Biblical example of the weakness of second-hand faith. In Genesis 2:16-17 Adam, heard God tell him not to eat of the tree of the knowledge of good and evil, Eve, got her instructions through Adam, which produced "second-hand faith." Now let me ask you, who was the one the serpent (Satan) approached? Eve! Why? Because she, due to her "second-hand faith" was weaker in faith. Remember, Adam told her what "God said," she did not hear from God directly! After all, man makes mistakes.

On the other hand, Adam was stronger in faith because he heard the instruction directly from God, and God does not make mistakes. When you wish to do God's will, you must hear directly from God. Or else there is a good chance you will fail, and injury will result. Remember doing any work for God is still sin if you do not have His blessing!

Twenty-two thousand men got up immediately upon hearing God's offer and went home (verse 3). That must have been an enormous shock to Gideon. The ten thousand men that remained must have stood there watching in absolute astonishment as they watched any chance of survival and victory walk away. I would say that this circumstance gives us a perfect definition of "shock and awe." If that was not enough, imagine how far down emotionally, the remaining men's outlook fell when they saw 22,000 men turn tail and run away in fear? But there was more weeding out yet to come. God was not through weeding out the chaff. God now orders the second reduction in the number of His troops. Why? What could be the possible reason for this? Perhaps it is that you must give God all the glory and hold nothing back from Him (Ref. Judges 7:2). If the men that remained were men of valor, Israel would have thought it was their heroic actions and battle skills that won the victory, and God would not get the glory in the victory. God, therefore, said to Gideon that their number was still too high.

Could there be another reason why God allows or even creates times of weakness, and times when we face overwhelming odds? Could it be that when we face times of weakness, overwhelming odds, and impossible situations that it forces us to be more reliant upon God and through that situation, God can teach us more about Himself, His work, His power, and His care for us? God teaching us more about Him develops a stronger faith. Oh, how the human heart loves to claim credit for any achievement. If God had allowed Israel to defeat Midian with 10,000 men, guess who would have taken the credit? Israel, of course! (Ref. Judges 7:2) And they would not have learned the lesson God wanted them to learn. "Amid all these things, we are more than conquerors and gain a surpassing victory through Him Who loved us (Romans 8:37 AMP).

Gideon was now to divide the people into two groups. One was those who would lick the water with their tongue like a dog, and the other were those who knelt and lifted the water to their mouth with their hand. The number of those who raised the water to their mouth by their hand was 300. God sent all but that 300 home. It is important to make note of another point here. The 10,000 brave and faithful men who remained to fight with Gideon didn't know that Gideon was testing them when he suggested they go and drink some water. In like manner, God tests us, looking for hearts that are indeed His, and these tests come in the ordinary events of our daily lives often without our knowledge. After the test, God sent all but 300 home. That's 300 Israelites against 135,000 Midianites. Israel being outnumbered 450 to 1! Question! Would you want to be one of the 300 Israelites facing odds like that? I wouldn't! But that is what God requires of us; complete obedience and total faith in Him despite all odds. We are told in Psalm 91:7-9, that "A thousand shall fall at thy side, and ten thousand at thy right hand; but it shall not come nigh thee. (8) Only with thine eyes shalt thou behold and see the reward of the wicked. (9) Because thou hast made the LORD, which is my refuge, even the Most-High, thy habitation."

It is barely possible to conceive a more severe trial than to attack the overwhelming forces of the enemy with such a handful of followers. Previously, Gideon hesitated, questioned, and needed proof. The weakness of Gideon's faith had strengthened he no longer looked to himself, instead of looking to God. Now, having the assurance that Jehovah would deliver Israel by his hand, he trusts entirely in God (Ref. Proverbs 3:5-8; 2nd Corinthians 12:9) and displays absolute confidence. He, without hesitancy and doubt, obeys God and prepares to go to war with only 300 men. I suppose this is an excellent time to remember the verse that says: "for we walk by faith, not by sight" (2nd Corinthians 5:7). In other words, walk in such a way as to develop your faith in God, where it is stronger than earthly reality itself. God's testing brings stronger faith!

Gideon's faith during the day waned; however, due to obvious natural circumstances. As he continued to see the overwhelming odds he was facing, Gideon started to fear in the same way as Peter's faith did after he started to walk on water and as he noticed the wind and waves. But God is so incredibly gracious. He shows His loving-kindness by bringing encouragement and strength when His people are in a place of utter weakness. It is then that God calls upon a believer to believe beyond their level of faith. When we need faith the most, God strengthens our faith through a dream, a verse, or a prophetic word of encouragement or directly from Himself. For Gideon, it came through a dream with a clear interpretation, "Into Gideon's hand, God has already delivered Midian and the whole camp."

When one needs a great mountain of faith, a mountain of faith so immense that we do not believe we have, do not be surprised if God asks you for only a small, faithful action to bring about the faith you need. Remember what Matthew 17:20 says? In order to remove a mountain of doubt, all that is necessary is a mustard seed of faith! God tells Gideon to "Go down to the Midianite camp with Purah, his servant, and you shall hear what they say, and afterward, your hands shall be strengthened to go down against the camp" (Ref. Judges 7:10-11). What I believe is happening is God giving Gideon a conformation to reassure Gideon of His promised victory, you and Purah sneak down into the camp, and I will provide all the proof you will need to believe for the victory. (Ref. (Ref. Judges 7:10~Have, you ever heard this old saying? "A journey of a thousand miles begins with a single step."[1] That is all God is asking from us. Even though the journey looks long and impossible, take the first step, God will get you to where you need to go. Gideon obeyed God's request for that small first step of faith, and God provided all the proof Gideon required for finding the mountain of faith he needed for victory. Notice from whom, the proof came. It came from the enemy's mouths!

The fact is all interpretations belong to God? God put it into the head of a philistine soldier and the interpretation into the mouth of another. Gideon hearing the interpretation from the mouth of the enemy would not only confirm that it came from God but also, it was undeniable evidence that the enemy had become so frightened and disheartened at the name of Gideon that Gideon could believe in victory. Gideon, now hearing the interpretation of the dream realized that Israel's victory being assured and that God was with them, it was from that point Gideon had no more problem with his faith or his duty.

Look at Gideon's reaction once he heard the interpretation of the dream – He worshipped God, praising the Lord with joy! Gideon now walked forward in faith, even though in the natural, the circumstances had not changed. We, like Gideon, must hold on to the promises and encouragements God gives us in whatever form it comes, even despite what we see in the natural. Because if it is from God, it is as real as it gets!

Gideon did not only worship God when he heard the dream and its interpretation, but he returned to the camp, shared the encouragements he had received from God, and then immediately called for the attacked on the enemy. This action of testifying is a natural outpouring of the Spirit of faith (Ref: 2nd Corinthians 4:13; 1st Peter 5:12). It produces faith, and it enriches the lives of those who hear it (Ref. 1st Corinthians 1:5-6). It also, as it did in this particular case, overcame the evil one and the fear which he brings (Ref. Revelation 12:11).

Gideon then divides the 300 men into three companies, i.e., three attacking columns, and he put a trumpet into every man's hand, with empty clay pitchers, and torches inside the pitchers. The pitchers were so they would hide the light of the torches during their attempt to surround the enemy's camp. At Gideon's command, he placed his men in strategic places, and at his command, the trumpets sounded, and the soldiers shattered the pitchers revealing the light inside the torches. Gideon commanded them to shout "The sword of the Lord and Gideon" (Judges 7:18). How astonishing and overwhelming this was to the half-awakened eyes of the Midianites. Consequently, the earsplitting noise of the trumpets and the shouts of the 300, and the sudden lighting up of the burning torches, un-nerved, overwhelmed and completely deceived the enemy as to the strength and number of Gideon's army, the Midianites then fled for their lives turning their swords against each other.

Then God inflicted terror and dread on his enemies. As we have already seen, the name of Gideon brought dread to the numerous armies of the Midianites. Adding the name of Jehovah to that of Gideon's, it became too much for the Midianites to bear. The confidence and strength of the Midianites melted away before the power of faith; When you feel the enemies fear tactics remember what God assures us "Fear not, for I *am* with you; I am your God. Be not dismayed, for I will strengthen you, Yes, I will help you, I will uphold you with My righteous right hand.' (11) "Behold, all those who were incensed against you Shall be ashamed and disgraced; They shall be as nothing, and those who strive with you shall perish. (12) You shall seek them and not find them - Those who contended with you. Those who war against you Shall be as nothing, As a nonexistent thing. (13) For I, the Lord, your God, will hold your right hand, saying to you, 'Fear not, I will help you'" (Isaiah 41:10-13).

It was the Midianite's weapon (fear) that God used to defeat them. It is Jehovah who is omnipotent; fear melts before Him and before them who stand in His name, by faith. The trumpets and the lamps alone announce His presence and that of His servant Gideon. God's enemies flee before His children and the 300 faithfuls. The brave men of Israel pursued their enemy, utterly destroying them. As a result of their faith, they gained a miraculous victory.

Now let me bring this home a bit. You may remember from the last chapter that Midian means "strife." The Midianites represent trouble, trials, and the strife that occurs while we live in this world of sin. We all run into our Midianites and the Amalekites from time to time, more times than not I'm afraid, so what are the clay jars, torches, and trumpets that we can use to gain the victory over our enemies today?

The answer to this question is found in 2nd Corinthians 4:1-11.

"Therefore, since we have this ministry, as we have received mercy, we do not lose heart. (2) But we have renounced the hidden things of shame, not walking in craftiness nor handling the word of God deceitfully, but by manifestation of the truth commending ourselves to every man's conscience in the sight of God. For we do not preach ourselves, but Christ Jesus the Lord, and ourselves, your bondservants for Jesus' sake. (6) For it is the God who commanded light to shine out of darkness, who has shone in our hearts to give the light of the knowledge of the glory of God in the face of Jesus Christ. (7) But we have this treasure in earthen vessels that the excellence of the power may be of God and not of us. (8) We are hard-pressed on every side, yet not crushed; we are perplexed, but not in despair; (9) persecuted, but not forsaken; struck down, but not destroyed – (10) always carrying about in the body the dying of the Lord Jesus, that the life of Jesus also may be manifested in our body. (11) For we who live are always delivered to death for Jesus' sake, that the life of Jesus also may be manifested in our mortal flesh."

2nd Corinthians 4:1-11

Notice verse 7; we are the fragile earthen vessel made from the clay of the earth (Ref. Genesis 2:7); Jesus is the light within the earthen vessel (verse 6); and our testimony of His greatness is the trumpet blast (verse 5, 10)! God has made His light to shine in our hearts (Matthew 5:14-16). We are the epistle written upon our hearts for all men to see (2nd Corinthians 3:2). His presence is the light within our lives. Jesus is the great life-giving light God has placed within our bodies of clay. Fragile human beings – an earthenware vessel which contains the life and light of God! But how does this light shine forth? When cracks appear in the clay vessels, God's light and power reveals itself. Just as Gideon and his army broke their jars to expose the light, so there must be times of weakness that demand us to die to self and reveal God's light (2nd Corinthians 4:11). In other words, we must crack our earthen vessel (break our wills) and allow Jesus' light and power to shine forth.

We have spoken of the jar and the lamp, but there is one last ingredient we should discuss if we are ever to achieve true victory over our enemies. After smashing the pitchers, the light from the torches inside reveals themselves, it was when the trumpet sounded that the Lord brought victory over the Midianite army. Blow the trumpet. Sound the alarm, let God arise, and His enemies will scatter. Not our own horn, however. Blow the trumpet of God. Look at how the Apostle Paul put it in 2nd Corinthians 4 – "For we do not preach ourselves, but Christ Jesus as Lord" (verse 5).

The trumpet call that we must sound is all about Him. It should never be about us. In the midst of difficulty, the only testimony that should sound is God's and His Son Jesus. For as "Moses lifted the serpent in the wilderness, even so, must the Son of Man be lifted, that whoever believes in Him should not perish but have eternal life" (John 3:13-15). God will speak through it and draw Christians and non-Christians alike unto Him. Despite the overwhelming odds, our death to self brings forth the light of Christ, and the trumpet blast of His testimony, along with the declaration of His name, brought God's children ultimate victory in the face of the overwhelming odds. (Revelation 12:11).

Paul says, in 2nd Corinthians 4:8, that there were times when he was 'hard-pressed', 'perplexed,' and 'persecuted,' when he was in a battered and weakened state that the power, light, and life of Jesus was the only thing manifested in his body. So, like Paul, Gideon, with his limited followers, as with us, are only armed and dependent on our jars (our flesh), a torch (the light and strength of Christ in us), and a trumpet (Our shouts of praise.) Like Gideon, it is daunting and scary when you are facing overwhelming odds and facing an impossible task; but by faith in Christ, we will prevail. Remember, Psalm 23: 4 says, "Yea, though I walk through the valley of the shadow of death, I will fear no evil; For You are with me; Your rod and Your staff, they comfort me." The most critical words in this verse are the words **"through"** and **"shadow"** I will walk **through** any trial. And that the trial is only a **shadow** and shadows cannot hurt me no matter how large and scary. "Trials are never pleasant. But I will, with God's help, walkthrough all trials out the other side! In this, we can take heart that God has a purpose for us. It is for the strengthening of your faith and the displaying of His life through you that offenses must come (Matthew 18:7)! Each crack in the clay vessel brings forth more of the light of Christ and more destruction of our flesh and its desires.

> "And He said unto me (Paul), 'My grace is sufficient for you, for My strength is made perfect in weakness.' Therefore, most gladly, I will rather boast in my infirmities, that the power of Christ may rest upon me. (10) Consequently, I take pleasure in infirmities, in reproaches, in needs, in persecutions, in distresses, for Christ's sake. For when I am weak, then I am strong.
> 2nd Corinthians 12:9-10

Brethren hold fast to the promises of God "For the gifts and the calling of God are irrevocable" (Romans 11:29). When God instructs you in any action, obey it without question or hesitancy. Faith in God will make you more than a conqueror, and "Faith comes by hearing and hearing by the Word of God" (Romans 10:17). Remember "The fear of man brings a snare: but whosoever puts his trust in the Lord shall be safe" (Proverbs 29:25), "You shall not be afraid of the face of man; for the judgment is God's: and the cause that is too hard for you, bring it unto Me, and I will hear it" (Deuteronomy 1:17b). "There is no fear in love, but perfect love casts out fear because fear involves torment. But he who fears has not been made perfect in love" (1st John 4:18). For the eyes of the Lord run to and fro throughout the whole earth, to show Himself strong on behalf of those whose heart is loyal to Him (2nd Chronicles 16:9).

God brought victory. The only thing left to do was to destroy those that remained. Israel was now to embark on a period of peace. It was a time to enjoy the accomplishments and spoils brought about by their achievements. But have you ever noticed that when you have accomplished your God-given task, there is always somebody unhappy about it or disgruntled because you did not involve them? Or they complain because they did not have a more significant role in the accomplishment? The devil always attacks when we least expect it. That is what is about to happen to Gideon in Judges chapter 8. Remember, Gideon did call all the tribes to gather for battle. He sent messengers throughout all the mountains of Ephraim, asking for assistance (Judges 7:24). How true it is when there is success, everybody thinks that they ought to have taken part in it, and then they blame someone else for their lack of participation. We do not know whether the Ephraimites got the call or not, despite Gideon's efforts, but it is also not known that had the Ephraimites heard the call, they would have welcomed the invitation. What is known is that more often than not those who grow angry because they cannot claim a share in the honor are usually the very people who would have given the least effort

The Ephraimites, by the overthrow of Israel's national enemy, benefited as much as any of the other neighboring tribes. Being upset at not having partaken in the glory of the victory, their leading men could not suppress their wounded pride at Gideon's accomplishment. Their injured pride only served to bring out the old and deep-seated feeling of jealousy and rivalry that existed between the tribes (cs. Ref Isaiah 9:21). Their discontent was groundless, for Gideon acted according to divine directions, all Israel now knew that. The Ephraimites' territory bordered that of Gideon's; they could have readily volunteered, once they were requested, had they wanted to.

Notice how Gideon responds to the unreasonable criticism of his countrymen, he responded with godly wisdom and tact. A soft answer turns away wrath, does it not (Ref. Proverbs 15:1)? Gideon's response shows his noble Spirit. Though Israel knew he was the sole reason for their victory, he does not covet the praise. He magnifies the exploits of the others beyond his own (Ref. Philippians 2:3). Notice how Gideon soothes their wounded pride by telling them that Ephraim had done more, even though they had joined the battle late, in fact more than he had been able to do in the whole campaign. Notice the metaphor given "The grape-gleaning of Ephraim was better than the whole vintage of Abiezer." Gideon is presenting the fact that even though he began the fight, the Edomites had finished it. Their actions were much preferable to what he had done. He stresses the point that the taking of the two Midianite generals at the Jordan River was of greater value than sending the Midianites running, which is all he accomplished. The victory gained by the Ephraimites must indeed have been a significant one, (c.f. Isaiah 10:26) as a great blow of the Lord upon

Midian. The Ephraimites being told of their significant aide satisfied them; notice, "Then their anger toward him subsided when he said that" (Judges 8:3). Gideon played to their pride.

In spite of this distraction, Gideon never lost sight of his God-given calling. Once he solved this confrontation with the Ephraimites, he started once again after the fleeing enemy over the Jordon River. Gideon was a good commander and chief. His men were exhausted, thirsty, and hungry, so he stopped and asks his Israelite brethren from Succoth and Penuel for provision so that his men could continue the pursuit of their common enemy. His request met with an insolent and time-serving reply. It was insolent because it implied Gideon was confident of a victory which they believed he would not gain. It was time-serving because living in the near neighborhood of the Midianites, they dreaded future vengeance, so they delayed Gideon, and by not giving them provisions, they reduced the effectiveness of Gideon's army, or so they thought. This manner of action was heartless and disgraceful.

Edmund Burke, an 18th-century Irish statesman, political theorist, and philosopher, said, "All that is necessary for the triumph of evil is for good men to do nothing." Gideon's brethren at Succoth and Penuel did precisely that, "nothing," and by doing so aided the Midianites in their fight against Gideon. Have you ever been in a situation like that? Where God tells you to do something that your family and friends do not agree with because if you fail, it will adversely affect them. So, you get ridiculed, and they do nothing to help you achieve your God-given assignment. If the answer is – yes, remember, "If you are reproached for the name of Christ, blessed are you, for the Spirit of glory and God rests upon you. On their part, He is blasphemed, but on your part, He is glorified. (Ref. 1st Peter 4:14).

Gideon and his men remained undaunted by the inappropriate actions of his brethren; they continued the pursuit and defeated Midian's entire army capturing the two Kings of Midian, Zebah, and Zalmunna as proof of victory. It is at this point that Gideon turns his anger back upon those who had ridiculed him, and who by not helping aided the cause of their common enemy and the death of additional Israelites. He tore the flesh off the seventy-seven leaders of Succoth, and then killed the men of Penuel and tore down the city tower in retribution for their treachery and faithlessness.

The punishment inflicted by Gideon, both cities deserved. The inhabitants of these cities had not only acted treacherously against Israel as an action founded on their selfish interests. They did so against a holy conflict, the glory of the Lord, and the freedom of God's people. Their contemptuous treatment of Gideon and his men poured contempt upon the Lord because God had shown his support for these men to the whole nation by their miraculous victory. Gideon called by the Lord to be the deliverer and judge of Israel had a duty to defend the honor of His creator and to punish God's faithless children. The judgment of God begins in His own house (1st Peter 4:17). Christians that do nothing, aid in the advancement of evil, and judgment came upon them as it will against all who do nothing in accomplishing God's will. They lost their position, calling, wealth, and ultimately, they will suffer in outer darkness (Matthew 25:14-30). Christians cannot afford to stand idly by and do nothing. Remember A battle not fought is a battle lost!

Gideon had one more job to do, to make the victory complete. By the ancient laws of war, Prisoners were either slain, sold, or kept for slaves. Putting a captive enemy to death needed no executioner. The nearest of kin was the blood-avenger (Numbers 35:12; Deuteronomy 19:6), but a magistrate might order anyone to do the work of the executioner. The person selected was always of a rank equal to that of the party doomed to suffer (1st Kings 2:29). Gideon intended to give his son this honor by commissioning him to slay the two enemies of his country, who were the slayers of his two uncles, and adding to them the disgrace of falling by the hand of a boy. The youth due to fear refused and Gideon not slack in his duty or his dedication to the Lord and His people, immediately killed the two Kings of Midian Zebah and Zalmunna (Numbers 35:30-31). Gideon ordered it with the same authority that Samuel cut Agag in pieces (1st Samuel 15:33), Benaiah slew Joab (1st Kings 2:25), Saul ordered his guards to slay the priests who had contributed to the escape of David (1st Samuel 22:17); and David ordered one of his attendants to slay the Amalekite who lied about having killed Saul (2nd Samuel 1:15). Do we possess this type of dedication to God and His commands especially in the face of overwhelming trials?

[1] Chinese Proverb - Chapter 64 of the Tao Te Ching

GIDEON — PART THREE: MISPLACING ONE'S FAITH

Sin lies at the door. And its desire is for you.

Judges 8:22 to the end of the chapter gives us the history of the third part of Gideon's life. In the first part, we saw a frightened farmer called anointed and made into a mighty warrior by God. Gideon's faith came alive. The second part was the exploits of this anointed mighty warrior and the faithful obedience he demonstrated. Gideon faith growing and active. Gideon received a place of honor and respect, and he became a national hero by his faithful obedience. The third part of Gideon's life was his fall from a national hero to a ridiculed, disrespected, and despised Israelite. Gideon's actions as a deceiver caused him to lead his people into apostasy?

The third part of Gideon's life begins after the killing of the two Midianite Kings. When the awestruck, and extremely grateful Israelites offered Gideon an unlimited hereditary monarchy in gratitude for his miraculous victory. "Rule thou over us, both thou, and thy son, and thy son's son also: for thou hast delivered us from the hand of Midian" (Judges 8:22). This offer is the first recorded attempt to establish a hereditary monarchy in Israel. A form of government Moses had already foreseen and had given them guidelines and warnings of what would happen once they chose their earthly king (Ref. Deuteronomy 17:14~).

What a weak, foolish, and hypocritical people! Up to now, Israel's government was a theocracy. The people now dazzled by the success of a man whom they believed to be an instrument in the hands of God. Wanted him to rule and by doing so, threw away God's divine rule and shackle themselves with an earthly monarch! Have we not learned through our study of the scriptures that those who cast off their allegiance to God are guilty of foolishness and extravagance and are destine to failure? Jehovah's relationship to His people needed restoration. God alone accomplished the deliverance of His people; Gideon was the vessel God used. The people must not take credit for it, or give credit to the vessel God chose. The farther off one is from God; the readier one is to ascribe to themselves that which is due only to God. Gideon demonstrated his praiseworthy modesty; by refusing to accept their offer of a monarchy. Notice his commendable refusal, and the rebuke and instruction contained in it. "I will not rule over you; neither shall my son rule over you: The Lord shall rule over you" (Judges 8:23).

Gideon's refusal of lordship shows His modesty and His Piety. Gideon knew God's desired government. He had no ambition for a dynasty; he knew that Jehovah wanted a theocracy, not a monarchy; and neither he nor any man had a right as a monarch. If the Lord Jesus has indeed set us free from sin and Satan, it is but necessary and right that He should rule over us. Notice what Gideon said; 'the Lord shall rule over you;" God was to be their chief magistrate, and Gideon would not be the instrument in changing to a monarchy. Gideon, therefore, would willingly act as judge, but he acknowledged the Lord alone as King in Israel. A wise man of God will not covet an increase of power, position, and responsibility unless it is the manifest will of God for him to accept it.

The apostle Paul shared this exact sentiment in the New Testament book of Philippians.

> "Let nothing be done through selfish ambition or conceit, but in lowliness of mind, let each esteem others better than himself. (4) Let each of you look out not only for his interests but also for the interests of others. (5) Let this mind be in you which was also in Christ Jesus, (6) who, being in the form of God, did not consider it robbery to be equal with God, (7) but made Himself of no reputation, taking the form of a bondservant, and coming in the likeness of men. (8) And being found in appearance as a man, He humbled Himself and became obedient to the point of death, even the death of the

cross. (9) Therefore, God also has highly exalted Him and given Him the name which is above every name, (10) that at the name of Jesus every knee should bow, of those in heaven, and of those on earth, and of those under the earth, (11) and that every tongue should confess that Jesus Christ is Lord, to the glory of God the Father."

Philippians 2:3-11

In this passage, our apostle discourages God's people from a double vice, which is destructive to unity; ambition and conceit are the very enemies of unity (Ref. Philippians 2:3). A selfish or conceited individual overrates himself, undervalues others, disrupts unity, and strife accompanies him with jealousy and contention. Paul is calling for humility to be the author of peace and unity, which he calls lowliness of mind, whereby a man thinks little of himself, and highly of others.; even though that might be the case.

"Let nothing be done through selfish ambition or conceit, but in lowliness of mind, let each esteem others better than himself" (Philippians 2:3). Gideon's response to his people's offer of a hereditary monarchy is a true example of a humble heart and mind. Paul, in this passage, also sets before us a Gospel pattern one we should try to emulate. It is the example of our Lord Jesus Christ: "Let this mind be in you, which was also in Christ

> **IT IS NO CRIME TO JUDGE ANOTHER BETTER OR WISER THAN YOURSELF; THOUGH THAT MIGHT NOT BE THE CASE; BUT IT IS PRIDE TO JUDGE ANOTHER WORSE THAN YOURSELF.**

Jesus" (Philippians 2:5). Christians must be of the same mind as Christ. We must bear a resemblance to His life if we would have the benefit of His death. If we have not the Spirit of Christ, we are none of His, according to Romans 8:9. Now, what is the mind of Christ? He is eminently humble. If we were like Christ and had a like mind, we would be lowly-minded as well. We must walk in the same Spirit and the same steps as the Lord

Jesus, who humbled Himself, came to earth as a servant, and suffered and died for us. This action was to satisfy God's justice, and pay the price of our redemption, but to set us an example, that we might follow.

Gideon, like so many Christians throughout history, made an immediate and devastating error after the highest point in his life. Like, Elijah, after his battle with the 450 prophets of Baal on Mount Carmel (1st Kings 18), he ran and hid in a cave for fear of a woman (1st Kings 19). Moses? After seeing God in the burning bush and instructed to set God's people free. Moses goes to Egypt to face Pharaoh, he performs a miracle, and when Pharaoh ridicules him and refuses to comply, what does Moses do? He doubts God and accuses God of not fulfilling His promise and bringing evil on His people (Exodus 5). What about the un-named prophet of 1st Kings 4, who God sent to cry against the altar of Baal at Bethel. Jeroboam was so upset by the prophecy that he reached out to touch the prophet, and Jeroboam's arm withered. Immediately upon healing Jeroboam's arm, the un-named prophet left only to disobey God, and a lion killed him along the way home. Brethren let us remember the words of the apostle Paul to the Corinthians.

> "Now all these things happened to them as examples, and they were written for our admonition, upon whom the ends of the ages have come. (12) Therefore, let him who thinks he stands take heed lest he fall."
>
> 1st Corinthians 10:11-12

However, brethren, we do not have to fall into this sin. Notice that in the very next verse, after this warning, Paul gives a guarantee of God's strength to assist us in these times of potential weakness.

> "No temptation has overtaken you except such as is common to man; but God is faithful, who will not allow you to be tempted beyond what you are able, but with the temptation will also make the way of escape, that you may be able to bear it."
>
> 1ST Corinthians 10:13

In the case of Gideon, he allowed avarice to take control, and it caused his downfall. First, he took the crescent ornaments, which the Septuagint translates as half-moons off the two slain kings and their camels. These "half-moons" were crescent-shaped ornaments of silver or gold, which men and women wore upon their necks (see Judges 8:26, and Isaiah 3:18) and hung upon the necks of their camels. These emblems are a custom still prevalent in the Arab countries today. Then he asked for the 135,000 enemy soldier's gold earrings as a reward for his efforts. Taking the spoils of war is in itself, not evil. So, what did Gideon do wrong? He was not mindful of what he took and the reason he wanted to take so much. We must be sober and vigilant; because our adversary, the devil, walks about like a roaring lion, seeking whom he may devour (1ST Peter 5:8). The devil is the most cunning of all God's creations, and far too often, we unsuspectingly fall into his evil traps.

The worship of the moon and the sun was very ancient; it constituted the earliest form of idolatry. Gideon would have known that these ornaments were badges of the Ishmaelites loyalty and idolatry toward Ashtaroth, symbolized by the moon and Baal by the sun. Gideon, as an Israelite, knew very well that God demanded that His people put away all foreign idols (Ref. Genesis 35:2; Exodus 20:3; Joshua 24:14). The Ishmaelites, who were known as the Arabs, used golden earrings, which contain a crescent moon; and the Arabs were addicted very early in their history to the worship of the moon, so we learn from the Targum, Syriac, and Arabic translations. They used these as symbols of false religion up until the time of Mohammed (570-632 AD), who destroyed the idolatrous use of the crescent, as ornaments. However, today, their flags, coins, military banners, and their mosques still use them as a symbol of their worship of false gods. "Among the symbols are the night and day, the sun and the moon. It is said in the Qur'an to "Prostrate not to the sun or moon but prostrate to Allah Who created them, and it is Him ye wish to serve" (Ref. Qur'an 41:37). This idolatrous worship still exists in Arab countries today! Examples seen today below.

Gideon being well aware of their significance, took them and did not stop at just accepting the crescent ornaments that were on their camels' necks; Gideon took all their ornaments off the slain as well (Judges 8:24-26). Gideon's monstrous error was that he did not destroy them, nor did he put them to good use.

It could be that Gideon intended to build something to signify this great victory though it is very unlikely because the ephod he made with these ornaments was a vestment worn only by the High Priest when the priest inquired of God. It was evident that Gideon intended to consult this false ephod he made. Setting it up in Ophrah, his home town had a lot to do with his tenuous relations with the tribe of Ephraim, which made him unwilling to consult with the real ephod which God had placed in Shiloh (c.f. the act of Jeroboam 1st Kings 12:28). Now notice the result of this unwise decision. "And all Israel played the harlot with it there. It became a snare to Gideon, to his house, "and his people (Judges 8:27b).

This unwise act of Gideon is not a onetime historical mistake. Many have fallen into false ways by a false step of a good man. That is why God commands us to "Study to shew thyself approved unto God, a workman that needs not to be ashamed, rightly dividing the word of truth" (2nd Timothy 2:15). God's word is the lamp to my feet and the light to my path" (Psalm 119:105). Look, men are fallible, and because of that, we should not completely and wholeheartedly trust men with the most precious gift you possess; your eternal soul! Refer again 2nd Timothy 2;15 We must study and know His word; we must use God's word as the anchor for our soul. We are responsible for our soul's wellbeing. How unwise is it to hand your eternal soul over to another man's care? Do you not realize that the consequence of this action, good or bad, is on us and the accountability for it is ours? Therefore, work out your salvation with fear and trembling" (Philippians 2:12b). And because it is God who works in you, we should do our utmost, because our labor shall not be in vain.

Understand; there is no excuse for not going to church, or trusting in your church leaders. The point being made here is "Trust but Verify[1]. Double or triple check everything heard from the pulpit no matter who it is that you have decided to follow or from whoever one claims to have heard it from. Again "Trust but Verify."

A few years ago, at a meeting with a pastor friend who had a very large church in Beaumont, Texas, he related an alarming experience that he and all his elders experienced during a twenty-four-hour prayer meeting at his church. This prayer meeting came directly after the conclusion of the churches twenty-one day fast. The pastor and each leader received the same vision from the Lord at the same time. The vision was so troubling that they immediately started to discuss it with each other. None of the men knew what the vision meant, so they decided to continue to pray, believing for God's revelation. About an hour later, God answered their diligent heartfelt cries. What these men had seen was a man running through the flames of hell, reaching down into the fire and pulling up, by the hair, another individual. Each time the man would look intently at the individual and then threw him back into the flames then ran to another to do the same thing. This wild search happened over and over again. The Lord's revelation of what was happening was that the man running through the flames was a church member looking for the pastor that steered him wrong. "Trust but Verify" your soul's place in eternity depends upon it.

Gideon's later life became a distinct anticlimax to the heroic actions of his earlier life. This man who had given such a magnificent testimony to his fellow countrymen is now setting a deplorable example of self-indulgence. By which he, his family, and the whole nation was led into cultic idolatry as evidenced by Gideon making an Ephod out of the spoils and setting it up as an altar in his city (Judges 8:27). An Ephod is an object of worship and a sacred vestment designed initially for Jehovah's high priest (Exodus 28:4; 39:2). No doubt, it is easier to honor God in some courageous action than to honor Him consistently in the ordinary activities of everyday life. Giving this type of day-to-day commitment requires a different kind of courage. A much more refined, and purer form of courage, one, the Apostle Paul described in Romans 12:1-2 "I beseech you therefore, brethren, by the mercies of God, that ye present your bodies a living sacrifice, holy, acceptable unto God, which is your reasonable service. (2) And be not conformed to this world: but be ye transformed by the renewing of your mind, that ye may prove what is that good, and acceptable, and perfect, will of God." In other words, dying once, is much easier than to die every day, all day long, and it is up to us to protect our eternal soul and not leave it to another person.

Gideon, who came through the test of adversity with flying colors, was not the first nor will he be the last to be unsuccessful in the test of prosperity. The amount of gold he asked for was incredible. It was approximately 1,007 to 1700 shekels or 50 to 75 lbs. of gold, depending on whether you use the lighter or heavier weight of a shekel., the value using today's prices, could be anywhere between $726,400.00 and $1,362,000.00. The granting of Gideon's outlandish request illustrates two things; one – the extent of the victory gained by Gideon and two – the high esteem in which Gideon obtained in the eyes of people as a result of this victory. Gideon's success and standing were but for a fleeting moment, however, which is often the case when a man who accepts honor based on God's blessing and then dishonors God in the duties associated with it.

The last days of Gideon and the time shortly after his death were times of national decay, according to verse 33. The decay and apostasy that characterized Israel's history under the last days' judgeship of Gideon was also characteristic of Gideon's family. We see this in Judges Chapter 9 with the rebellion of his son Abimelech, who was the only judge to win leadership through treachery.

The story of Gideon is a study in contrast. It is an excellent example of what God can do with a weak man who is open and available. One who, when called, acts in faith in spite of the impressive numbers and military strength. Gideon, the youngest member of the smallest tribe of Israel, a man found working underground due to fear, a man angry with God, and one who questioned God's trustworthiness, yet God used him and gave him a mighty victory, along with great honor, and prestige. This simple man of faith who was available to God, God made a national hero and gave a place in His honor role of faith (Ref. Hebrews 11:32). But he miserably fell after God gave him victory, honor, prestige, and abundance. Remember what 1st Timothy 6:10 warns us about.

The danger of failure in spite of initial victories is a danger all Christians should be aware of, be on the lookout for, and pray against for offenses that must come (cf. Matthew 18:7, 24:6; Luke 21:9).

> "Because there were also false prophets among the people, even as there are false teachers among us, who will secretly bring in destructive heresies, even denying the Lord who bought them, and bring on themselves swift destruction. (2) And many will follow their destructive ways, because of whom the way of truth will be blasphemed. (3) By covetousness, they will exploit you with deceptive words; for a long time, their judgment has not been idle, and their destruction does not slumber."
>
> (2nd Peter 2:1-3).

Gideon enjoyed unparalleled success in military matters, but the victory brought him access to tremendous wealth, and this, in turn, led him away from God. He turned to cultic practices, which resulted in his downfall and the downfall of the very people he set out to free. He fell from a respected national hero to a disrespected national fool. The implications of this story should be evident to all readers. Even though one might enjoy significant success in spiritual matters, one should be aware of the fact that in being human, one is open to the subtle whiles of Satan. If a great man such as Gideon could fall, how much more should we be aware of the same and take care that we stand in full obedience to the Word of God?

> "You, therefore, beloved, since you know this beforehand, beware lest you also fall from your steadfastness, being led away with the error of the wicked; (18) but grow in the grace and knowledge of our Lord and Savior Jesus Christ. To Him be the glory both now and forever. men."
> Amen.
>
> 2nd Peter 3:17-18

Could Gideon's fall from faithfulness be from his love of money? Why would he ask for such an abundance of silver and gold all dedicated to false deities; If not for their economic value! He had already repeatedly demonstrated his loyalty, faith, and dedication to Jehovah God through this ordeal?

For the love of money is a root of all *kinds of* evil, for which some have strayed from the faith in their greediness, and pierced themselves through with many sorrows. (1st Timothy 6:10) Does this verse not describe what Gideon later life confirmed.

[1] Ronald Reagan – 12/87

ABIMELECH — AMBITION AND PRIDE BRINGS DESTRUCTION NICKNAMED "THE BRAMBLE KING"

Gideon's idolatrous practices, which had been quietly creeping into Israel during his later years, were now openly professed and brought great sorrow to Gideon's family and great sin to Israel after his death.

> "So, it was, as soon as Gideon was dead, that the children of Israel again played the harlot with the Baals, and made Baal-Berith their god. (34) Thus, the children of Israel did not remember the Lord their God, who had delivered them from the hands of all their enemies on every side; (35) nor did they show kindness to the house of Jerubbaal (Gideon) in accordance with the good he had done for Israel."
>
> Judges 8:33-35

These verses have shown us the internal struggles of the children of Israel. No sooner were the children of Israel freed from their bondage; they showed their wickedness by voluntarily engaging in awful ingratitude towards God and Gideon both. They went from worshipping God to the worship of Baal-Berith which means their covenant God the False God they made a covenant with. This wrong choice is not a hard thing to do; once we establish compromise in worship. False worship is but an easy step-down.

Gideon's son Abimelech, born to him by a concubine (Judges 8:31), decided unlike his father and his brothers, that being Israel's king was a legitimate office and that he was the best candidate for the job.

Abimelech's mother was from Shechem; that is why he returned to that city to gain popular support for his proposed reign over Israel (Judges 9:2-3). He won the support from both the inhabitants of Shechem and from the priest of the local shrine (verse 4).

Judges 9, which contains the rise, rule, and fall of Abimelech, whose name means "the father of the King," is of outstanding interest. It offers clear evidence of what can happen when the children of God disobey God's commandments and leave evil influences of an ungodly nature (Canaanites) living within their midst.

The city of Shechem, a city in Ephraim's territory, played an essential role in the history of its day. Many of the trade-routes came together in Shechem, Shechem, a city, hollowed in Israelite tradition as the place where Yahweh first revealed Himself to Abraham after his arrival from Haran (Genesis 12:6, 7). It is also the place where Jacob had lived on friendly terms with the children of Hamor until the evil actions of Simeon and Levi destroyed their friendly coexistence (Genesis 33:18 – 34:31).

The fact that the Shechemites were 'the men of Hamor' (Judges 9:28; cf. Genesis 33:19), and their allegiance to the Canaanite deity Baal-Berith (verse 4) made it clear that the population of Shechem was predominantly Canaanite. Abimelech, by the use of very subtle and cunning words, shows that there was an active and robust friction between the men of Hamor and the household of Gideon. Judges 9:1-2 indicates that Abimelech, the son of Jerubbaal (Gideon), returns to Shechem after his father died. Shechem was the home of his mother and her entire family. Notice how he addresses them: He refers to them as the "Baals of Shechem." "Speak, I pray you, in the ears of all the "men of Shechem" (verse 2). The word "men" in the original Hebrew is the word "Baal," meaning 'lord,' 'ruler' or 'owner' (cf. Joshua 24:11; Judges 20:5; 1st Samuel 23:11, 12; 2nd Samuel 21:12). Abimelech did not use "Adam" or "Enosh," the two most common Hebrew words used for men. Also, notice how Abimelech purposely and continuously refers to his father by the name of "Jerubbaal," which means "contender with Baal." A name which he acquired in consequence for destroying the altar of Baal (Judges 6:32). Using that name was an evil plot directed at bringing controversy and conflict between the "Baals (men) of Shechem," and

Gibeon and his children, and at the same time distancing him from this conflict of ideology.

There are a few essential facts Christians should know about Abimelech and his actions. First, Abimelech's background was an environment of false worship. So, let us guard against this by obeying the words of Titus. (Titus 2:1-8.)

"Wherefore rebuke them sharply, that they may be sound in the faith; (14) not giving heed to Jewish fables, and commandments of men, that turn from the truth. (15) Unto the pure, all things are pure: but unto them that are defiled and unbelieving is nothing pure, but even their mind and conscience is defiled. (16) They profess that they know God; but in works they deny him, being abominable, and disobedient, and unto every good work reprobate."

> Second, Abimelech, unlike his brothers who were Gideon's "direct descendants" (Judges 8:30)," was Gideon's son through a Shechemite concubine (Judges 8:31), Was not of the tribe of Judah like his father. Gideon's legitimate heirs lived in Ophrah, whereas Abimelech's hometown was apart from them in Shechem. Abimelech can easily represent someone who, on the surface, appears to have a legitimate pedigree and qualifications, but in reality, does not. He is a representation of a false believer who establishes himself as a ruler wanting to rule over the sons of God. Remind you of anyone? The "false Christ" or "Anti-Christ" perhaps!
>
> Titus 1:13-16

> "For there are certain men crept in unawares, who were before of old ordained to this condemnation, ungodly men, turning the grace of our God into lasciviousness, and denying the only Lord God, and our Lord Jesus Christ."
>
> Jude 1:4

Abimelech is an example, not of the world attacking the church from without, but attacking the church from within. These deceptive wolves in sheep's clothing do not hold to the truth of God's Word but twist it for their gain. Brethren remember Genesis 3:1, Satan "the serpent was more cunning than any beast of the field which the Lord had made." (Ref Genesis 3:1) He loves to attack the weak, unsuspecting, naive, and unknowledgeable. He will always exploit any weakness he can find in us and use it for our destruction.

The church, because of their own goals and desires, brings in people who look legitimate, use the methods that God uses to provide the appearance of legitimacy, but in reality, they are committed to worship practices and doctrine not adhering to what God proclaims as right and true. We see this too often in churches looking for leaders today. They look sound and legitimate, but in reality, they are people who bring into the church practices from other religions. Such as the practice of claiming and declaring things that on the surface seem like legitimate Godly doctrines, but in reality, they are not. They forsake the holiness and power of God and embrace worldly practices and gimmicks designed to stimulate the senses of the unsuspecting, unlearned and unaware, to achieve greatness in their own eyes and the eyes of the world. They tell the saints what they want to hear and what makes their ears tickle to enlarge their audience (Ref. 2nd Timothy 4:3-4). Of these be aware. Brethren, there is only one sure way of avoiding this tragic and deadly attack of the enemy. We must do what Samuel did when he chose David over all his other brothers. He looked to God for the right man to anoint; Why? Because as the Lord explained to Samuel;

> "Do not look at his appearance or his physical stature, because I have refused him. For the Lord does not see as man sees; for man looks at the outward appearance, but the Lord looks at the heart."
>
> 1st Samuel 16:7

> "The heart is deceitful above all things and desperately wicked; who can know it? I, the Lord, search the heart, I test the mind, even to give every man according to his ways, according to the fruit of his doings. "As a partridge

that broods but does not hatch, so is he who gets riches, but not by right; it will leave him in the midst of his days, and at his end, he will be a fool."

Jeremiah 17:9-11

Do not delude yourselves brethren, for the Bible warns us of this; "for the time will come when they (Christians) will not endure sound doctrine; but after their lusts shall they heap to themselves teachers, having itching ears" (Ref. 2nd Timothy 4:3). These men are the ones of whom Paul informs Timothy, "they have a form of godliness, but deny the power thereof (2nd Timothy 3:5a). Paul goes on to warn Timothy, saying, "from such turn away (2nd imothy 3:5b). Their goal is to replace the legitimate with the illegitimate, the real with unreal for control, success, to gain fame and fortune.

Third, as mentioned earlier, Gideon was called Jerubbaal throughout this entire story. Never once is the name Gideon, used in this story. Gideon's contention with Baal was the origin of his power Gideon's action of making an Ephod, a holy symbol of the Jewish God, from items dedicated to false Gods, was detestable and unacceptable. And to have Gideon's descendants ruling them was therefore also impossible, and there was no way they could accept it. There is no doubt that Abimelech's strategic use of the name "Jerubbaal" stirred the hearts of the Shechemites against Gideon and away from the evil deed now proposed by Abimelech. Abimelech offered an uprising, which in turn would be the main point of contention between Baal and the house of Gideon. This entire plan hinged on one thing, having a leader who was close to and passionate about the situation. So, who better than the son of Jerubbaal, though illegitimate, one of their countrymen?

After Abimelech's voiced his ambitions, notice how the men of Shechem responded. It was not because the cause was right, but because "He is our brother" (Judges 9:3). It is so true that people's judgment, feelings, and conduct are often towards those who are related to them in some way. Men who earnestly desire power, and flatter their fellow man to obtain it are not worthy of any trust. The only type of men that would choose a leader of this sort are men who are of base character, who have an ulterior motive such as, "what is in it for me,"

The ambitions of Abimelech involved first, the death of his 70 brothers. Notice what Abimelech proposes; "which is better for you that all seventy of the sons of Jerubbaal reign over you, or that one (Abimelech) reign over you? Remember that I am your flesh and bone." Abimelech uses this term when referring to himself in contrast to that of his brethren, where he cunningly uses the term "sons of Jerubbaal. (Ref. Judges (9:2)," i.e., sons of the man who had destroyed the altar of Baal. What a cunning, deceptive, but brilliantly evil tactic employed by Abimelech. He presents his brothers as the sons of the man (Jerubbaal) who fought against their God, their way of worship, and their way of life, and as the only other choice, He, on the other hand, was one of their own; he believes in the same way as they do. He would rule them accordingly, giving them exactly what they want. How often do men do the same; they choose a ruler according to selfish desires rather than the desires of the people, or that of God.

Abimelech, by inferring that his brothers were the "sons of Jerubbaal" (the contender of Baal), turned the people of Shechem's eyes off the fact that no such earthly rule ever existed, nor was it ever sought by Gideon or his seventy sons. They were of their father's mind that the Lord should reign over them, and God did not call them to rule. Gideon's sons did not lust for earthly rule, but that is what Abimelech insinuates to pave the way of obtaining his goal of becoming Israel's earthly ruler. How true it is that those who have evil intentions are the ones most likely to suspect others. And have evil intentions, and how often these evil intentions, unfounded or not, cause one to do monstrous evils in the name of success.

The Shechemites supported Abimelech's quest for kingship by giving him seventy shekels of silver (approximately $489.00) from the treasury of Baal's temple (verse 4). This offering was not strange; for frequently, temple treasuries supported political purposes (Ref. 1st Kings 15:18). This money given to Abimelech was out of respect to their god (Baal) and for Abimelech's protection. This offering they hoped would better prosper Abimelech's plan and free them from the rule of the God of Gideon and his sons.

With the funds from Baal-Berith in his hands, Abimelech now hires vain and heartless men who would follow him to carry out the murderous plot against his brothers. The Hebrew words for "vain and light" translate as "worthless and reckless, empty and unimportant, or worthless and wanton." These men were of such sort that they lived on the public's dime and had nothing to lose themselves. They were men of useless heads and empty brains; whose pockets were as useless and empty as their heads. These were men willing to engage in any enterprise, no matter how wicked and brutal, for the sake of fame and fortune. As the leader is – so are his followers!

Now that Abimelech secured his army, he headed to Ophrah to murder his brothers. He did this publicly and in cold blood, all on one stone that was most likely in the center of the town. Ambitious men, who have given up on God for the gratification of their lusts, will commit any crime to satisfy it. The detail given that all the murders took place "on one stone" (Ref Judges (9;5, 18) suggests a parallel to that of animals offered in sacrifice on a stone altar. There are several supposed reasons why the execution took place on one stone. One may be for revenge. God told Gideon to demolish the altar of Baal, leaving nothing but a heap of rocks, then build an altar to the Lord on top of those stones and sacrifice two bullocks to Jehovah (Judges 6:25-26). Abimelech's decision to use the stone altar could have been one of payback for his father's actions, as well as one of defiance to God.

The second reason could be that it served well as an altar on which they could sacrifice them to Baal, in thanks for their victory. Brethren, did you notice just how far blind ambition can drive a man? Blind ambition will turn men into beasts and will utterly destroy good, wisdom, affection, and conscience. It will cause us to sacrifice that which is most sacred and valuable, to accomplish one's designs. We read this passage, and it cannot help but raise a question. When evil runs its course unrestrained, how far will it go, is there anyone it will not affect?

No matter what the reason was for sacrificing all the brothers on one stone, it gave the youngest brother time to escape. Abimelech vehemently went after the eldest brother first, for, in any monarchy, the eldest son is always the heir apparent to the throne, followed by the next oldest and so on down the line. Killing the brothers, according to their age, was probably the way Abimelech carried out the executions. By murdering the seventy from eldest to the youngest, it gave Jotham the youngest son, time to notice Abimelech's design, but also allowed him to escape. The Bible declares, "he hid himself" (Judges 9:5).

In the salvation of Jothan, we see God's grace and mercy demonstrated (verse 5). Ophrah was in turmoil, the people were running in fear for their lives, so it would not be farfetched to believe that the people would have given up Jothan if they could have. Despite these circumstances and conditions, Jothan escaped by hiding himself. Notice what verse 5 says, no one hid him, "he hid himself." He found no help, no safety or refuge with any of his friends or countrymen; he only found refuge in the grace of God. God put a veil around Jothan so that no-one would find him. God protected him. God always leaves His people a way of escape (Ref. Psalm 91:10, 112:8, 121:3; Proverbs 1:33, 3:23, 12:21, 21:31; Isaiah 32:18; Jeremiah 23:6; 1st Corinthians 10:13). Our trust must be in God alone if we are to survive to fight another day. There is a time coming that this exact situation will come to pass in the earth, be ready for it (Ref. Matthew 10:34-37, 24:7-10; Luke 12:51-53).

Once again, let me refer to the famous quote by Edmund Burke, an 18th-century Irish statesman, political theorist, and philosopher who said, "All that is necessary for the triumph of evil is for good men to do nothing?" That's what happened here. The Israelites were so dull and senseless to what was truly righteous and just that they sat by unconcerned except for their own needs. The men of Schechem took no action to protect the sons of Gideon, or to avenge their deaths; they were complacent toward Abimelech's bloody tirade, these men who had lost their reason, and all sense of honor, and integrity. It was not so many years ago that their fathers took revenge on Achan so vigorously for his evil sin, which caused Israel's defeat at Ai and the death of 36 of their brethren (Joshua 7). Yet, now, they had so completely deteriorated into a state of complacency and blindness that they did not even attempt preventing or avenging the death of Gideon's 70 sons. Proving God's word found in Judges 8:35, "nor did they show kindness to the house of Jerubbaal (Gideon) in accordance with the good he had done for Israel."

The inhabitants of Shechem were no better. Their own twisted beliefs had them so deceived that, they had no thought to prosecute and punish Abimelech for this open and brutal act of mass murder, but to crown him king. In other words, for his crime, he received a crown.

What could they possibly hope for themselves from a king that laid the foundation of his kingdom in deceit, and blood? Could they not understand that his rule would be the same as its foundation?

The inhabitants of Shechem, who worshiped Baal-Berith, carried out the election of Abimelech as king over all Israel (Judges 9:22) in the very same place in which Joshua held the last national assembly, and had renewed the covenant of Israel with Jehovah (Joshua 24:1; 25-26). Could it be that this place signified that they still respected God and His covenant with him; and that they did not worship Baal? Was it to show their disdain for Him? We cannot be sure, for the Bible is silent on the reason. One thing is for sure, worshiping God in conjunction with someone else is not strange for the children of God?

Israel, for many years, had been eager to establish a monarchal government (Judges 8:22); and with Abimelech supposedly being the son of Gideon, He seemed to be a great fit. Although Gideon and his sons refused leadership, Israel might have believed that Gideon had no right to give away his sons' right to rule Israel. Now with Abimelech being the Shechemites great champion, along with Israel's universal desire for a monarchy, the Israelites widespread defection from God to Baal was complete. Oh, but how often does what we want, at the cost of God's will, lead us to sin, hurt, or destruction!

When Jotham, the youngest son of Jerubbaal (Gideon), learned of the election that made his brother's mass murderer King, he went to the top of Mount Gerizim. Mount Gerizim rises like a steep wall of rock to the height of about 800 feet above the valley of Shechem on the south side of the city; and cried out with a load voice addressing the Shechemites with a parable about the trees and the bramble (Judges 9:8-15). Shechem was an appropriate spot for such a parable for it was the place employed for the solemn reading of the law, (Ref. Deuteronomy 11:29, 27:12; Joshua 8:33-34; John 4:20). Despite the warning given by Jotham, which foretold a feud between Abimelech and the Shechemites which would eventually consume both of them, the Shechemites made Abimelech king, and for three years he reigned (verse 22). As we will see everything, Jotham prophesied eventually came to pass. God, as He so often does, uses the instruments of man's sin, as the instrument of their punishment.

When we take a closer look at this parable, we find that the interpretation, as well as the application, is quite apparent, but there are some essential truths to discover in it. Let us look at those truths.

> "The trees once went forth to anoint a king over them. And they said to the olive tree, 'Reign over us!' (9) But the olive tree said to them, 'should I cease giving my oil, with which they honor God and men, and go to sway over trees?' (10) "Then the trees said to the fig tree, 'You come and reign over us!' (11) But the fig tree said to them, 'Should I cease my sweetness and my good fruit, and go to sway over trees?' (12) "Then the trees said to the vine, 'You come and reign over us!' (13) But the vine said to them, 'should I cease my new wine, which cheers both God and men, and go to sway over trees?' (14) "Then all the trees said to the bramble, 'You come and reign over us!' (15) And the bramble said to the trees, 'If in truth you anoint me as king over you, then come and take shelter in my shade; But if not, let fire come out of the bramble and devour the cedars of Lebanon!'
>
> Judges 9:8-15

In this parable, various types of trees are seeking a king. First, notice the expression, "the trees" (Judges 9:8); "the trees" ask the bramble, be king over us," whereas in Judges 8:14 "all the trees" are mentioned. Implying that there were some trees, in the beginning, that did not go along with Abimelech, but due to peer pressure, they finally consented. Oh, how often does peer pressure force, people who are weak, uncommitted, and lack confidence to fall into diverse temptations and failure! They just went along with the crowd for fear of standing out or in some way, humiliated. However, what these people do not understand is that their decision to follow for fear of humiliation is a "lose/lose" scenario; no good can come of it. Ask yourself what sense does it make for a majestic tree to ask a worthless bramble bush to be king over them. The fact that all the trees were seeking a king also shows that not one of the trees wanted to be the king. They were unanimous in transferring the honor to the bramble. The trees asked to be king were the olive tree, the fig tree, the vine, and the bramble, with only the bramble considering it, but that decision came with a catch and a threat; "trust in my shadow: and if not..." (Ref. Judges 9:15)

The briar is nothing more than a thorn-bush; it does not cast a sufficient shadow for anyone to rest under, nor does it protect from the burning heat of the sun. The briar is a perfect symbol of a worthless man who can do nothing but cause harm. Notice the words of the briar "Trust in my shadow," or in other words, "seek refuge under my wings," does this not contain a profound irony, the truth of which the Shechemites were very soon to discover. Now comes the threat. "But if not," or if you do not trust in my protection, the fire will go out from the briar and consume the cedars of Lebanon (Ref. Judges 9:15), the largest and noblest of trees. How easy is it for thorns to catch fire (see Exodus 22:5)? Does this not show us how the most insignificant and most worthless of men can cause harm or even death to the mightiest and most distinguished of men. Have we not seen this throughout history?

Now let us look at perhaps a deeper meaning to this parable then what is first apparent. The trees represent the national life of Israel, each tree representing a distinct aspect of the culture and life of the Israelites. All trees derive their sustenance from the same soil, each tree taking from the soil that which is useful and necessary for its purpose. Each tree is different in respect to their size, form, and worth. Each tree has its glory. For example, strong trees shelter and protect weaker ones from the elements (Ref. Daniel 4:20, 22; Isaiah 32:1). In this parable, all the trees (the people of Israel) were unhappy with a Theocratic government and yearned for a Monarchy instead. They desired a government of fleshly rule, in contrast to one of the Spirit, which was unseen and one of faith. They wanted the same type of government as the heathen nations around them. Is this not representative of humanity today? Even people who profess faith in God live by the flesh in contrast to the living in the Spirit.

Each of the plants approached for kingship in this parable had a special significance. Let us dig a little deeper to discover those special significances.

First, the Olive Tree – The olive tree is one of the most valuable of all the trees. Olive yards were numerous in Palestine. Winifred Walker, in her book, All the Plants of the Bible, says that "a full-sized Olive tree yields a half-ton of oil yearly." This oil supplied light (Exodus 27:20), food, as well as an ingredient in the Meat Offering. Israel ate its fruit, and its wood used for building purposes (1st Kings 7:23, 31, 32). Olive branches were and still are, used as a symbol of peace.

The Olive Tree speaks of Israel's covenant privileges and blessings from God (Romans 11:17-25). The Olive tree named the first king of the trees because being ever-green it speaks of God's enduring covenant made with Abraham. In Jotham's parable, the olive tree characterized fatness, and by its use, both God and man received honor (Exodus 27:20-21; Leviticus 2: 1).

In the passage in Romans 11:11-21, broken and wild branches are grafted in, showing Israel's failure. The Gentiles are now enjoying some of the privileges and blessings of the olive tree. Chief among the blessings granted to Israel was the gift of the Word of God and the Son of God. Today believing Gentiles are proclaiming the Son of God and preaching the Word of God to Israel. Israel's fatness (Olive Tree) will manifest in their final restoration when "all Israel will come to Christ if the fall of them be the riches of the World, how much more their fullness" (Romans 11:12).

Second is the Fig Tree, which represents sweetness and tasty fruit. Its sweetness was highly prized. Its fruit widely consumed, and its wide-spreading branches provided abundant shelter (1st Samuel 25: 18). God used fig-leaves to cover Adam and Eve's nakedness (Genesis 3:6, 7). Figs are the first fruits recorded in the Bible, and they represent God's protection and safety. The fig tree speaks of Israel's national privileges and prosperity (Matthew 21:18-20; 24:32- 33; Mark 11:12-14; Luke 13:6-8).

God planted Israel, His fig tree; (Ref. Joel 1:1-7), but it had corrupted fruit. Instead of sweetness, there was bitterness. So, when our Lord came to Israel, they received Him not (Ref. John 1:11). In bitterness, they branded Him "demon-possessed" and "held a council against Him, on how they might destroy Him." It is the same today; Israel still rejects her Messiah and is bitter against Him. The withering away of the fig tree shows Israel's failure in not receiving Jesus as the messiah (Matthew 21:19- 20). Our Lord came seeking fruit, and when He found none, He cursed the fruitless fig tree, and it withered away. This parable of Jesus represented Israel's condition nationally for centuries. She had no king, no flag, and no home. She was the tail instead of the promised head of the nations. This condition was not to be a permanent one. However, because Christ announced Israel's restoration Notice, the new buds coming out of the fig tree (Ref. Matthew 24:32 and Luke 21:29b-31), notice; "Look at the fig tree, and all the trees. (30) When they are already budding, you see and know for yourselves that summer is now near." (31) "So, you also, when you see these things happening, know that the kingdom of God is near." Many believe that this restoration began on May 14, 1948, when Israel became an independent state.

Third is the Vine. Because of its large cluster of grapes producing wine, it held a great source of wealth in Palestine (Numbers 13:23). To sit under one's fig-tree and vine was a proverbial expression, denoting peace and prosperity (Micah 4:4).

The Vine symbolizes Israel's spiritual privileges (Isaiah 5: 1-7; Psalm 80:9-19; Ezekiel 15; John 15).

What characterized the vine was wine, which cheered both God and man. Wine is God's chosen symbol of joy. When Israel found their wine vats full to overflowing, it was proof positive that the blessings of God were upon them. Of course, joy came with His approval, and conversely, God had joy in the drink offering of His people.

Forth was the Cedar. The Cedar Tree is the greatest of all Bible trees, considered to be the first of trees (1st Kings 4:33), planted by God and created to glorify God (Psalm 104:16; Isaiah 41:19; 148:9). It is a durable and robust tree (Isaiah 9:10); it is fragrant (Song of Solomon 4:11); and referred to as graceful and beautiful (Psalm 80:10; Ezekiel 17:23). Cedars often represented the majesty, strength, and glory of God (Song of Solomon 5:15; Ezekiel 17:22-23); the beauty and glory of Israel (Numbers 24:6); a mighty nation (Ezekiel 31:3; Amos 2:9), and as a result of its power it also represents arrogant rulers (Isaiah 2:13; 10:33-34). Cedars were renowned for their remarkable height, often 120 feet tall and 40 feet in diameter. Because of the quality of its wood, Solomon's Temple and Palace used it in their construction. Cedar is a substance for ritual cleansing. In Leviticus 14:4 the cleansed leper was sprinkled with the blood of a "clean bird." with "cedar-wood, which also contained scarlet, and hyssop," and in Numbers 19:6 "cedar-wood, and hyssop, and scarlet" were to be cast into the fire with the red heifer for the purification of the nation's sin.

In the parable, before us, the Cedars represent all the nobles of Israel, such as the house of Millo, who were at the forefront in carrying out their horrible massacre of Gideon's sons. They felt they did not need God's government, blessings, strength, protection, and glory. Perhaps the men of Shechem specifically and the men of Israel, in general, saw themselves as lofty and robust, and as a result, they felt no need for God. Does this not sound like the world's leaders today? Man feels no need for God, for he is self-confident in his abilities and recourses. Ask yourself, when those alternatives no longer are viable and sure, and there is nowhere to turn where do these self-confident arrogant and atheistic, flesh dependent individuals turn? God, that's right!!!

Finally, we have the Bramble. The Bramble is a generic name in which there are several species. They contain many needles; hence, they are, in common language, any rough, prickly shrub. It is a hurtful and grating bush-like plant flourishing in any soil. It produces no fruit of any value; it is also useless as a means of any shelter. The wood is only suitable for fuel. Fire coming out of the bramble refers to how easy it can be set ablaze and how rapid it burns.

The application of this parable is obvious. The noble Gideon and his worthy sons declined the offered kingdom, but this bramble bush (Abimelech) desired it, and he proved to be like an irritating thorn bush. The course he would take would, for him and his subjects, end up in flames (Judges 9:16-20). Notice how the fire goes forth and then returns. First, "...let fire come out from Abimelech and consume the men of Shechem and Beth-Millo; then let fire come out from the men of Shechem and Beth-Millo, and consume Abimelech" (Judges 9:20). As a burning bramble sets on fire a forest of cedars, so will a burning cedar destroy all bramble bushes, as it was with Abimelech and the men of Shechem. Both proved destructive to each other. They received the due reward for their violence.

Notice how the bramble, the most worthless of shrubs, one good only for burning, was willing to reign over "all the trees" (verse 14), for all the trees were willing to have it that way. This prophecy in Judges 9, could be a foreshadowing of that day when the Anti-Christ will rule the world. As stated earlier, the bramble is a thorny bush, and the thorns symbolize the curse of sin (Genesis 3:18; Jonah 2:5; Matthew 27:29; Mark 15:17; and John 19:2, 5). When the bramble comes, he will say, "Come and put your trust in my shadow." When our blessed Lord was here, He said to them, "Come unto Me,"; and they cried, "We will not have this man to reign over us. Away with Him. Crucify Him!" However, when the bramble comes, they will receive him and enter into a covenant with him for seven years, and put their trust in his shadow (Daniel 9:27). Then a fire shall come out of the bramble and devour them all. That is symbolic of the great tribulation, the time of Jacob's trouble (Jeremiah 30:17), and the bramble destroyed and burnt (Judges 9:20). So, it will be at the coming of our Lord (2nd Thessalonians 2:8). And then shall the fatness, sweetness, and the joy, of the trees, bless Israel and make her a blessing, through the One who died on the cursed tree.

In this parable, we see an image established of a false anointed one. The words "rule over" imply, to float about, and include the idea of restlessness and insecurity. Keil and Delitzsch studies of the Old comment that "Wherever the Lord does not find a monarchy, or the king himself does not lay the foundations of his government in God and the grace of God, he is never anything but a tree, moving about above other trees without a firm root in a fruitful soil, utterly unable to bear fruit to the glory of God and the good of men." Now notice the ironic words of the bramble. "Trust in my shadow." (Ref. Judges 9:15)

The shadow or shade referred to in this parable represents protection, protection from themselves, their actions, and their enemies. It also represents guidance, direction, and representation. How can something so foreign and different provide shade to anything, especially the mighty Cedars of Lebanon?

Trust in my shadow represents the vain boast of the would-be sovereign; and one seeking power by the vote of the people. The bramble was too low in stature and too dangerous to give shelter and protection to any tree. Abimelech was the bramble, and the cedars of Lebanon were all the nobles and people of Israel. Could they, therefore, suppose that such a low-born, uneducated, cruel, and murderous man, be a proper protector, or a humane governor? He who could soak his hands in the blood of his brethren to get power, would not stop at any means to retain that power when possessed. If, therefore, they took him for their king, they might rest assured that desolation and blood would mark the whole of his reign. The moral meaning of this fable is: Weak, worthless, and wicked men will always try to put themselves into power. Once obtained, they will eventually bring ruin upon themselves and on the people over whom they preside. The Shechemites soon discovered this truth.

When man disregards the wisdom of God and all His blessings, all that remains is the foolishness of one's sinful heart and the destruction it inevitably brings. Despite Jotham's skillful use of imagery, which captured the attention of the men of Shechem, it went unnoticed. So often throughout the scriptures and life, we see the same arrogance and pride, resulting in deafness occur. Destruction follows every time. When will we ever learn that "Pride goes before destruction, and a haughty spirit before a fall"? (Ref. Proverbs 16:18).

For three years, Abimelech reigned, without any disturbances; however, it is essential to note that He did no service to his country. All that can be supposed is that he enjoyed the title, dignity, respect, and riches of a king. His kingship was short-lived, however. After three years, God sent an evil spirit of arrogance and suspicion upon them, which overtook both Abimelech and the men of Shechem (verse 23). This evil spirit God sent to punished Abimelech and the men of Shechem for the evil they had done to the 70 sons of Gideon. Their blood cried out from the ground for vengeance until God responded and laid it at Abimelech, and the men of Shechem's feet. Know this, that sooner or later, God will make a righteous judgment for the shedding of blood. If found guilty, God will return judgment on those in support of it and on those who deny or do nothing to stop it. The Shechemites, who favored and supported Abimelech's bloody projects by making him king after all he had done, God judged and punished along with Abimelech (Judges 9:56-57). Any partnership based on bloodshed done wickedly cannot last, no matter who they are.

God's righteous judgment upon Abimelech and the Shechemites

came when Shechem rebelled under Gaal. Gaal was probably one of the descendants of the Canaanites, pretending to have descended from Hamor, the father of Shechem, and former prince of that country (Judges 9:28; Genesis 34:2). He hoped, due to the state of the public mind and their disaffection to Abimelech, he would cease power, and thus restore the ancient government as it was under Hamor, the father of Shechem. Too often, men rebel against a wicked ruler, but as in this case, they choose another who was just as corrupt. So, they only increased their distress and hastened their ruin.

To assure victory, the Shechemites celebrated their unwise and dangerous decision. By entered into the house of their god, they ate, drank, and cursed Abimelech. They called on the name of their God, only this time to do away with the very same men they asked their God to support three years earlier. It was at this point that Gaal stood up perhaps because he was caught up in the moment, or in a drunken fantasy of self-exaltation, and started to boast, saying, "Who is Abimelech, and who is Shechem, that we should serve him? If only these people were under my authority! Then I would remove Abimelech." So, he said concerning Abimelech, "Increase your army and come out" (Judges 9:28-29)! O how often we find that boasting, pride, and self-esteem are empowered by drink and as a result, they are forerunners of defeat, degradation, and contempt (Ref. Proverbs 16:18). How often does the evil heart of man ask God for things that are not in his best interest? How often do men, when those requests go unanswered, resort to actions purely out of a selfish heart to achieve those said interests? How often, once obtained, do they cause more hurt and destruction than good? Remember, "the heart is deceitful above all things, and desperately wicked who can know it" (Jeremiah17:9). Is it not a blessing that we have a God who loves us enough to withhold unwise requests?

> "If a son asks for bread from any father among you, will he give him a stone? Or if he asks for a fish, will he give him a serpent instead of a fish? (12) Or if he asks for an egg, will he offer him a scorpion? (13) If you then, being evil, know how to give good gifts to your children, how

much more will your heavenly Father give the Holy Spirit to those who ask Him?"

Luke 11:11-13

Zebul, the governor of Shechem during Abimelech's absence (Judges 9:30-34), hearing the boastful words of Gaal sent messengers to inform Abimelech of the ongoing events. Once Abimelech heard of this betrayal, he came quickly to dispose of the threat posed by Gaal. One interesting side note here is the meaning of the name Gaal. Gaal means loathing, contempt, or outrage. Who was the son of Ebed? Ebed means servant. In other words, the Shechemites put their confidence in a deplorable, contemptuous disgrace of a man who was the son of a servant. In essence, the men of Shechem traded one bramble for another.

The lesson we can learn from this is two-fold. One is that

> "Your wickedness will correct you, and your backslidings will rebuke you. Know therefore and see that it is an evil and bitter thing that you have forsaken the Lord your God, and the fear of Me is not in you, says the Lord God of hosts."
>
> Jeremiah 2:19

> "And therefore, they shall eat the fruit of their way, and be filled to the full with their fancies."
>
> Proverbs 1:31

And two is that any friendship based on sin is hollow at best, and it will never lead to Godliness (Ref. 2nd Samuel 13:3-5, 32-33). In other words, betrayers are betrayed by the betrayers among them. Let me show you what I mean. Zebul first pretended to be Gaal's friend. Second, he informed Abimelech of the plans of Gaal and the Shechemites. Third, he stayed with Zebul as a friend would do until the army of Abimelech arrived. Forth, when Zebul saw the approaching army, he betrayed Gaal by deceit. Fifth He then ridiculed him as a man who had no sense and therefore unfit for the job at hand because he was like a fool who would believe anything. A man who was so gullible. So silly and so cowardly that he perceived danger where there was none and one who was ready to fight a shadow. Notice: "when Gaal finally saw the Abimelech's army, he said to Zebul, Look, people are coming down from the tops of the mountains!" However, Zebul said to him, "You see the shadows of the mountains as if they were men" (verse 36)! This ploy was meant to detain him from taking action and thereby giving a more significant advantage to Abimelech's army. It worked Abimelech's army eliminated Gaal and his men! Finally, when Gaal perceived that in fact, it was the army of Abimelech, Zebul mocked him with what he had said but a day or two before, in contempt of Abimelech (Judges 9:38): "Where indeed is your mouth now, with which you said, 'Who is Abimelech, that we should serve him?'" Proud and haughty people change their attitudes quickly in the face of truth and to fear those whom they have despised and challenged. Gaal had, in his boasting, challenged Abimelech to "increase his army and come out;" (verse 29), but now Zebul, in Abimelech's name, challenges Gaal: "Are not these the people whom you despised? Go out, if you will, and fight with them now." (Ref Judges 9:38)

Abimelech, without mercy slew all the men of Shechem beat down their city and sowed it with salt (Ref. Judges 9:45). He then burned to death a thousand more men and women who fled for sanctuary in the temple of Baal-Berith, their false god. The same sanctuary and god he embraced and used to gain support three years earlier. The sowing of salt in small quantities renders land extremely fertile; however, large amounts it destroys all vegetation. Over-salted ground is barren, incapable of producing vegetation Ref. Job 39:6; Psalm 107:34. Hence the sowing of an enemy's land with salt was a custom in certain nations to express permanent desolation. Once Abimelech destroyed the land, he marched to Thebez, nine miles east, and took the town; but while trying to burn the tower door, an upper millstone struck him on the head. Success often renders men reckless, and when they are arrogantly confident, often they are very near to destruction. They may escape the greatest apparent dangers, and then fall in ways never considered (Judges 9:56).

"Thus, God repaid the wickedness of Abimelech, which he had done to his father by killing his seventy brothers.

(57) And all the evil of the men of Shechem God returned on their heads, and on them came the curse of Jotham the son of Jerubbaal (Ref. Proverbs 15:25; Luke 1:52)."

Judges 9:57-58

The life of Abimelech came to an end very much like the great general Sisera (Ref. Judges 5:26); that is, at the hand of a woman. According to verse 53, a certain woman cast the upper part of a millstone upon Abimelech's head. Which did not bring immediate death, and to save face (his pride), Abimelech called for his armor-bearer to draw the sword and to slay him? As a result of Abimelech's death, Israel's regained peace and an end came to this civil war, for "they departed, every man to his place" (verse 55). God's established justice (verse 56-57): preserved the honor of his government, and gave warning to all ages to expect blood for blood. When the wicked work became known, the righteousness of the Lord came apparent by the judgments He executes. Though wickedness may prosper for a while, it will not prosper forever.

The conclusion of this story is a must understand lesson. God will repay the wicked for the wickedness inflicted, not only upon his fellow man but also towards Him. Jehovah is a God that judges the earth and proclaims the sins of men in their punishment. The historians, neither the Israelites nor the readers of this story, cannot overlook the direct action of God. The historian makes it open and understandable "Thus God repaid (verse 57)." They saw it for what it was; the recompense of God upon the wicked. God's payment was the judgment on Abimelech and the fulfillment of the curse of Jotham upon the Shechemites. Notice once again what the historian wrote about the final event in Abimelech's life.

"Thus, God repaid the wickedness of Abimelech, which he had done to his father by killing his seventy brothers. (57) All the evil of the men of Shechem God returned to them, and also upon them came the curse of Jotham, the son of Jerubbaal."

Judges 9:56-57

There is one last lesson I wish to share before concluding this chapter. God shows us the road to destruction and the seven steps that lead to it. Listed below are those seven steps in the hopes that you will, with all diligence, avoid them. Check out how many of these evil practices Abimelech was guilty of committing. We know what his final fate was, so let that be a lesson we take to heart and learn to avoid the same fate.

1. *Conceit* – Matthew 26:33. To be wise in one's own eyes (cf. Proverbs 3:7; 26:5, 12; Isaiah 5:21; Romans 12:16; 1st Corinthians 8:2; Galatians 6:3).

2. *Slothfulness* – Matthew 26:40. Is to indulge in inactivity; or idleness (Proverbs 18:9, 19:15, 22:13, 24:30-31, 26:13; Ecclesiastics 10:18; Matthew 25:26; Romans 12:11; 2nd Thessalonians 3:11; Hebrews 6:12).

3. *Rashness* – John 18:10-11. Too much haste in resolving or in undertaking a measure, implying a disregard of consequences or contempt of danger; applied to persons (cf. Proverbs 19:2, 21:5, 29:20; Ecclesiastics 5:2; Acts 19:36).

4. *Indecision or half-heartedness or luke-warmness* – Matthew 26:58. The lack of firmness in determinations of the will; a wavering of mind; irresolution (cf. 1st Kings 18:21; 2nd Kings 17:41; Hosea 10:2; Matthew 6:24; Luke 9:62; James 1:8, 4:8)

5. *Evil associations* – John 18:18. The act of making union; or connection with the unrighteous (cf. Exodus 23:2, 33, 34:12; Psalms 1:1; Proverbs 1:15, 4:14, 22:24, 23:6, 24:1; 1st Corinthians 5:9-11; 2nd Corinthians 6:14; 2 John 1:10).

6. *Open Denial* – John 18:25. An assertion to the contrary, a declaration or fact stated is not true; contradiction (cf. Matthew 10:33, 26:34, 26:69-70; Mark 8:38; Acts 3:14; Philippians 3:10, 18; 2nd Timothy 2:12; Titus 1:8, 16; 2nd Peter 2:1; 1st John 2:22).

7. *Blasphemy* – Mark 14:70-71. A man is guilty of blasphemy, when he speaks of God, injuriously; when he cold-heartedly ascribes such qualities to Him as do not belong to Him, or robs Him of those which do. The law sentenced blasphemers to death, Leviticus 24:12-16. 1st Kings 21:10; Acts 6:11 (cf. Psalms 74:18,

109:18; Isaiah 52:5; Matthew 9:3, 15:19; Mark 3:29; Romans 2:24; 2nd Timothy 3:1-2; Titus 2:5; James 2:7, 3:10).

JEPHTHAH — RISING ABOVE ONE'S BACKGROUND AND PAST

After the death of Abimelech, it was, for the most part, peaceful under the leadership of two judges about little is known, Tola and Jair. There is evidence, however, (Judges 10:1), that some deliverance was necessary from outside oppression, due to the unprecedented rebellion of the Israelites against God. They started serving no less than seven false Gods, which included Baal and Ashteroth (v. 6). The apostasy of this time included much more than the mere recognition of Canaanite deities. According to verse 6, Israel worshiped the gods of no less than five foreign nations. These would have included Hadad, Baal, Mot, and Anath, and in Moab, Chemosh was the prominent deity (1st Kings 11:33). In Ammon, they worshiped Molech (1st Kings 11:7, 33), in Zidon; they worshiped Ashteroth, Astarte, or Venus, and the Philistines looked toward Dagon and Baal as well as other Canaanite deities for fertility and guidance. The spiritual trends observed in Israel at this time were meant to merge their acknowledgment of Jehovah with their worship of their false gods. This syncretism or the combining of different beliefs, while blending practices of various schools of thought, was an abomination to Jehovah, for it involved the total abandonment of true and sole worship of Jehovah in favor of other national false deities. It could only bring the wrath of God upon them.

> "Then the children of Israel again did evil in the sight of the LORD, and served the Baals and the Ashtoreths, the gods of Syria, the gods of Sidon, the gods of Moab, the gods of the people of Ammon, and the gods of the

Philistines; and they forsook the LORD and did not serve Him. (7) So, the anger of the LORD was hot against Israel; and He sold them into the hands of the Philistines and into the hands of the people of Ammon. (8) From that year they harassed and oppressed the children of Israel for eighteen years – all the children of Israel who were on the other side of the Jordan in the land of the Amorites, in Gilead. (9) Moreover, the people of Ammon crossed over the Jordan to fight against Judah also, against Benjamin, and the house of Ephraim, so that Israel was severely distressed. (10) And the children of Israel cried out to the LORD, saying, "We have sinned against You because we have both forsaken our God and served the Baals!"

Judges 10:6-10

As we have seen too often repeated in the book of Judges, idolatry seemed attractive at first. But after eighteen years of oppression and warfare, the Israelites had to reconsider the advantages of such commitments. The result of these unholy commitments was that God made them subject to two other nations the Philistines to the southwest, and the Ammonites to the east. We see the awesome power of Ammon in verse 9 by the territories they had conquered. They penetrated Israel to the center of its territory. Desolation, conquest, and slavery once again led Israel to cry out for Jehovah's help, whom they knew had been faithful to them in times past. They suddenly realized that idolatry had betrayed them and that heathen idols were entirely impotent to help them. A mere recognition of sin was not enough this time (Ref. verse 10). God wanted repentance, a once and for all doing away of all foreign gods, and a total, unqualified commitment from His people that they would obey His commandments.

This time, before the Lord agreed to help His people, He responded to their cries with a straight forward and explicit rejection designed to get them to see the futility of following false Gods and hopefully cement their faithfulness to Him. God asked them why they called upon Him since Israel had turned to the gods of Canaan, Syria, Moab, and Zidon in past times of crisis. So why He asked do you not look to those gods for deliverance now? Verse 14 records the awesome words of God, "Go and cry unto the gods which ye have chosen let them deliver you in the time of your tribulation." (Ref Judges 10;14) These words could not help but pierce their very hearts. They realized that prayers to any false deities brought no benefit. This realization compounded by their utter helplessness and sorrow of heart made them turn heavenward, crying to Jehovah for help.

If anyone ever questioned the greatness of God and His intense love for His people, look to this story. For nowhere is there more evidence of God's greatness and love than in this particular narrative. Israel cried out to their God, and the Bible records that *"his* (God's) *soul was grieved for the misery of Israel"* (verse 16). Human compassion and concern would have been long since exhausted if it had encountered the kind of rebellion that God had experienced at the hands of His children. God's mercy and love endures forever. Notice; in Israel's great distress, God also grieved on account of His children's misery and through His mercy and love which endures forever, He answered their cries and sent forth a deliverer.

Brethren, what a God we serve! Have you ever felt that your sins have caused you to walk away from God, and you feel so lonely, helpless, and desperate that you have nowhere to go or no one to turn? Then remember that even in your deepest despair and hopelessness, God still has a heart that desperately wants to help you. Despite the spiritual condition of Israel at this time, when they cried out to God, and God saw the despair in their hearts, even His soul grieved on account of their misery, and He sent help, He sent deliverance. He will do the same for you if your heart is pure! Why? Because God's heart and soul grieves on account of your misery!

In Judges 10:17-18, we can see the complete frustration of Israel's leaders as the Ammonites began to regroup their forces, which were at this time in control of most of Gilead. The princes of Israel looked at one another and found that they had no one that could bring them victory and freedom. Once again, we see that the leaders turned to man to solve their problems. Notice verse 18, they were willing to offer Kingship to anyone who could bring victory. Even after all the deliverances God had brought, they still had it in their heads and hearts to establish an earthly monarchy. They still had not learned God desired a Theocracy!

God, in His grace and mercy, brought Israel's princes the news of a man that had the qualifications to deliver them from the distress their sin had caused. His name was Jephthah, which means "one whom God sets free or one who opens." Jephthah's history is almost a parallel, only opposite to that of Abimelech. Let me show you what I mean. Abimelech left his father's house of his own volition to plan treason and murder to become Israel's king. A position not rightfully his; In Jephthah's case, the opposite is true; his brothers wrongfully drove Jephthah away to keep him from his father's inheritance. Abimelech appealed to the citizens of Shechem to help him in his awful ambition; Jephthah, on the other hand, after the "elders of Gilead discarded him," those same elders pleading with him to receive that which was rightfully his. Abimelech had committed unprovoked and cruel murder with his hired band of mercenaries; Jephthah withdrew to the land of Tob, and once there gathered around him some mercenaries, in the same way, that David did in similar circumstances (1st Samuel 22:2). Unlike Abimelech, however, who collected these mercenaries to destroy his father's house, Jephthah, like David, agreed to go war against their common enemy. We can conclude this from verse18, which tells us that before the war between Gilead and Ammon, Jephthah had acquired fame contending against Ammon.

Jephthah had the qualifications needed to meet the Ammonite challenge. His reputation as a warrior and leader preceded him. That is why the elders of Israel sought him out and requested that he become their captain and their leader (Judges 11:5-6). See how God prepares men for service; he designs and makes their trials work for their advancement and preparation. Jephthah's rejection and condemnation by his brethren gave him the occasion to exercise and improve his military expertise, which grew his reputation, which his brethren heard about and offered him a chance at retribution and reconciliation. This opportunity came as somewhat of a surprise to Jephthah in the light of their previous treatment of him (Judges 11:7). The elders, however, were not concerned about his background or even his morality at this point, they were only interested in one thing, and that was they desperately needed a man with military expertise to set them free from their oppressors (verse 8). They were willing to make Jephthah commander over them. Jephthah speaking with little to no confidence in their proposal, was willing to accept the responsibility but only on the condition that "If you take me back home to fight against the people of Ammon, and the Lord delivers them to me, shall I be your head?" (Ref Judges 11:9) In other words, if I win, will I become your king, and will God then rule Israel.

The question has two purposes. One is for affirmation – "if God delivers them, will you make good on your promise" (paraphrased)? The second is for acclamation – not his own but God's. Let me once again rephrase a bit for clarity. "If, by the blessing of God, I come home a conqueror, tell me plainly shall I be your head? And, if God delivers you, and set you free, shall you then turn again to Him (Ref. Judges 11:9-10)? The same question applies to those who desire salvation by Christ. "If He saves you, will you be willing that He rules over you? For on no other terms will Jehovah save you. If He makes you happy, will you allow Him to make you holy? They immediately give him a positive answer (Judges 11:10), for there was no time for debate for the situation was to pressing and immediate, and the qualifications of Jephthah were to plain. "We will do according to thy words; command us in war, and thou shalt command us in peace." So, with this agreement established, Jephthah and the elders met together before the Lord in Mizpeh, and the agreement covenanted (Judges 11:9-11).

It is interesting to note that Mizpah or Mizpeh as some translations have it means, "outlook or watchtower." It is the name Laban gave it at Galeed, the "heap of witness." It was the memorial altar on which his covenant with Jacob and the boundary landmark between them sealed their covenant (Genesis 31:48-49; 31:52). This place held a great significance to both parties.

Jephthah was a man with an excellent working knowledge of Israel's past, seen in his response to the demands made by the king of Ammon. He must have had a precise and clear understanding of the significance of the place because he used it to enhance the strength of his agreement. Brethren, this is an excellent lesson for all who call themselves Christians to learn and apply. To know the past, your own, and the historical facts presented in the Bible is of absolute necessity when trouble presents itself. (Ref. Matthew 4, e.g.,) George Santayana, a twentieth-century famous western philosopher, once said, "Those who do not remember the past are condemned to repeat it."1 Brethren, we do not need to repeat our exercises in futility.

It is also interesting to note just how often our immediate needs outweigh and overshadow all other aspects of our lives. The real test of your love for Christ will come when you stand facing this type of tribulation, and you must choose between what is most important to you God or things.

At first, they cast Jephthah aside because of his past, now because of their great distress, they ignored Jephthah's past and offered him their obedience and the Kingship. Their first impulse was to choose a man with the right qualification, a man who fits their needs. Seeking for a man with the right qualifications is not wrong or even unwise; the sin was that they did not seek God's counsel first! They chose Jephthah based on their earthly wisdom.

> "Woe to the rebellious children," says the Lord, "Who take counsel, but not of Me, and who devise plans, but not of My Spirit, that they may add sin to sin."
> Isaiah 30:1

God's great mercy and grace demonstrated themselves despite their foolishness and sin. God gave them the right man despite choosing him based on wrong motives. Brethren take special note; this is the exception, not the rule!

How often do we do the same thing in similar situations? We find ourselves in extreme circumstances, and seeing no way out, we, without counsel from the Omniscient one, choose a person to save us based on his earthly qualifications, looks, personality, experience, etc. Sometimes like in the case of Jephthah, it works out, but most often, there is a resulting failure that brings oppression and pain. In either victory or defeat, the sin remains the same – our first course of action should be to seek the counsel of the all-knowing one, God Almighty, the Omniscient One, for His solutions are always right. Remember, "If any of you lacks wisdom, let him ask of God, who gives to all liberally and without reproach, and it will be given him" (Ref. James 1:5).

The story of Jephthah tells us of a man who rose above his background and rejection but held no ill-will toward those who had wronged him. He was neither vengeful nor bitter. But when a national emergency arose, the people of the land called upon him for help, and Jephthah displaying a true spirit of compassionate forgiveness rose to their defense.

Jephthah's introduction to us was one of "a mighty man of valor" (Judges 11:1), the same term used by the angel when first addressing Gideon (Judges 6:12). He was a wild, daring, Gilead mountaineer. He was an experienced and brave warrior who did not shrink before the responsibility thrust upon him. He completely understood that success depended totally upon God. But as he often demonstrated, understanding our dependence on God and applying its principles are two different things. Regardless of the personal cost, he was a man you could count on, as a man of integrity. He was a man who, due to his humility and compassion, elevated himself above his perceived shortcomings. He was a man devoted to God, but there are serious questions about Jephthah's relationship with God. As we take a closer look at his relationship with God; severe deficiencies become apparent, these insufficiencies cost him severely.

Jephthah's first act was not to marshal the armies of Israel together and confront the Ammonites, who at this time were enjoying unparalleled success against Israel. Instead, his first intent was to negotiate a settlement of the dispute (Ref. Judges 11:12). Those that behave themselves Godly and stand in righteousness can take comfort against those that charge them with injustice and wrongdoing. Our righteousness will answer for us in times to come (Genesis 30:33) and will put to silence the ignorance of foolish men (1st Peter 2:15).

Jephthah sent messengers to the king of Ammon, asking what the issues were in their conflict with Israel (verse 12). According to the king of Ammon, Israel had no legitimate right to the territory which they occupied on the east bank of the Jordan. The king of Ammon knew something of the history of Israel's conquest of the land, for he referred to the Israelites exodus out of Egypt, and their settlement in the

Transjordan Valley. His request was a simple one: restore those lands to us without reservation (verse 18). Jephthah replied to the king of Ammon, showing him that he, too, knew the history of Israel's exodus from Egypt and ultimate settlement in the land.

Beginning with verse 14, Jephthah used four arguments to answer the charge made by the king of Ammon.

1. *Jephthah pointed out that the land which Israel possessed has initially been in the hands of the Amorites, not the Ammonites* (cf. Numbers 21:21-30; Joshua 13:25; Judges 11:14-23).

2. *Jephthah used a religious argument* showing that it was the God of Israel who gave his people that land (cf. Deuteronomy 2:24). Even the pagans recognized that when victory came by a deity, the victors had full right to possess that territory. Notice verse 24, "Will you not possess whatever Chemosh your god gives you to possess?" Let us be aware of this one feature regarding the honor and respect that we owe to Jehovah, as our God. We are to maintain possession of that which He gives us to manage. Once received, we must use them for Him, keep them for His sake, cherish and respect them for they are God's alone, and part with them when He calls for them and not before. He has given them to us to hold, not to covet, for we must covet only God (Ref Matthew 25:14-46; Luke 19:12-27; 1st Timothy 6:20; 2nd Timothy 1:14; 1st Peter 4:10).

3. *Jephthah used political precedent.* He raised the question that if Balak (verse 25), an earlier king of Moab, did not fight against Israel on the grounds of land rights, why then should the king of Ammon do so this late in history? It is true that Balak resisted Israel in that territory, but only because of his hatred of the nation, not because he was attempting to make a formal claim on that territory.

4. *Jephthah used time as an argument* (Judges 11;26). It had been 300 years since the basis of your claim took place why in all that time, when it was well within your power to reclaim it and possess it, did you not make a claim or ever fight to recover the land which you claim is yours?

Here are some lessons that we must learn from Jephthah and the way he handled this dispute:

1. *That Jephthah did not delight in war,* though he was a mighty man of valor, and a worthy adversary. His first consideration was not of war. He sought to prevent war and find a peaceable solution. War should be the last remedy, not to take part in until all other methods have failed. War should be the last resort of Kings. The sword of justice, as well as the sword of war, should not be considered until all contending parties have first exhausted all other means (1st Corinthians 6:1-2).

2. *That Jephthah only wanted justice.* If the children of Ammon could convince him that Israel had done them wrong, he was ready to restore the rights of the Ammonites. If not, it was plain by their invasion that they did Israel wrong, and Jephthah was prepared to maintain the rights of the Israelites. A sense of justice should guide and govern us in all our undertakings (Ref. Zechariah 7:9, 8:16; Micah 6:8; Matthew 23:23).

3. *That Jephthah used logic,* tact, and intelligence and understanding in trying to deal with the king of the Ammonites, not emotions; he then concluded his argument by doing the best thing of all. He informed the king of the Ammonites (no name given) that the "self-existent and eternal; Jehovah," which is the Jewish national name of God, a name that the king of Ammon knew well, would judge what was right and true. If you decide to go to war over this, God will choose between you and us by giving the victory to the side whose cause is just.

4. *Any dispute or appeal should first be made to God He would judge righteously.* He will always determine the outcome. If someone violates or denies our inalienable rights, God should decide what is right and punish that which is wrong. As the sword of justice, God will judge the lawless and disobedient persons (1st Timothy 1:9), God as the sword of war is for rebellious and disobedient princes and nations. In war, therefore, our eyes must always be Godward.

The unavoidable now came to pass. The king of Ammon decided to fight for his cause and let the gods decide. How often do men put their faith in God, believing that their cause and actions are just? Too often, however, being egocentric is the basis for one's actions. How often do the results of such actions humiliate or, worse yet, destroy those who act accordingly?

God honored Jephthah for his actions, notice that "The Spirit of the Lord came upon Jephthah" (verse 30). We have seen this statement before in our study of the Judges. The Lord extraordinarily raised the Judges for a specific purpose; whether that purpose was to be a Judge, savior, or prophet. Just in the book of Judges, we see the phrase *"The Spirit of the Lord came upon"* used regarding Othniel, Gideon, Jephthah, and Samson. And now Jephthah who was anointed and appointed by the Lord not only for that position and purpose but also the Lord made him the newest judge of Israel. The Spirit of the Lord coming upon him was the qualifying sign given as evidence that Jephthah was God's chosen vessel.

We now see the first significant sign that Jephthah's relationship with the Almighty was not what it should have been. Before beginning the war, Jephthah vowed a foolish and unwise vow to the Lord.

> "If You will indeed deliver the people of Ammon into my hands, (31) then it will be that whatever comes out of the doors of my house to meet me, when I return in peace from the people of Ammon, shall surely be the Lord's, and I will offer it up as a burnt offering."
>
> Judges 11:30-31.

By using the words "whatever comes out (NKJV), or "anything that comes out (Literal Version)," "whatsoever comes forth" as the Jewish Publication Translation and the KJV puts it, Jephthah could not have been thinking of a head of cattle, or one of his flock; because the expression "comes out of the doors of my house to meet me" is an expression that does not apply to an animal-driven out of the stall just at the moment of his return, or to any animal that might run out to meet him.

Jephthah's vow was, doubtless, an over enthusiastic outburst of a sincere heart, but there was a great need for thoughtfulness and caution in it. If we vow a vow to God, we should think long and hard of what we are about to vow and then express our intent in the plainest of terms. It is not wise for a Christian to bring himself into bondage by rash pledges and thoughtless declarations. Moses warned God's people that "if a man makes a vow to the Lord, or swears an oath to bind himself by some agreement, he shall not break his word; he shall do according to all that proceeds out of his mouth" (Ref. Numbers 30:2). Jephthah's case should be an example of the consequences of a vow made through intense emotion and in thoughtless haste.

There is no doubt that Jephthah intended to impose on himself a very difficult vow, which would not be the case if he had been merely thinking of a sacrificial animal. Think about it, "What kind of vow would it be if some great prince or general would say, "O God, if you will give me this victory, the first calf that meets me is yours." If Jephthah had an animal sacrifice in mind, he certainly would have vowed the best of his flocks. This fact alone leaves us with a great mystery of what Jephthah must have been thinking when he made this unwise and thoughtless vow. There can be little doubt that when Jephthah declared that he would dedicate the first thing that came out of his house to meet him that he intended to leave the choice of the sacrifice to God himself.

In Jephthah's eagerness to smite Israel's enemies, and to thank God for the victory, Jephthah could not think of any particular object, significant enough to dedicate to God; he, therefore, left it to Providence, Whatever, therefore, God would send out of his house to meet him, he would offer it as a burnt offering to Him. But whether Jephthah thought it would be his daughter or any family member cannot be determined either positively or negatively.

What does this story of Jephthah's vow teach us?

1. *Jephthah was ignorant about the presence, purpose, and person Jehovah* (11:29-39). He thought that he had to "make a deal" with God to employ His help. He viewed God no differently than how the Ammonites saw their gods. The result was that Jephthah

made a thoughtless and ill-conceived "vow." Our Lesson – know God like He wants to be known – intimately (John 10).

2. ***Jephthah's ill-conceived and thoughtless vow caused hardship for him, and his family*** (especially his daughter), his friends, and all of Israel. Israel lamented for Jephthah's daughter for many years. Judges 11:39-40 tells us that this lament became a custom in Israel for four days yearly. Our Lesson – Be extremely careful about the words you use and who you involve in those words (Proverbs 13:3; 29:20; Matthew 5:37; James 1:26).

3. ***That Jephthah was ignorant of Biblical truths*** The Bible forbids human sacrifice (Leviticus 18:21, 20:2-5, Deuteronomy 12:31; 18:10). Our Lesson – we must know and use God's word, for it gives us all we need to survive in today's world, and it will sustain us in the world to come (Matthew 22:29; Luke 11:28; John 5:24,8:31; Philippians 2:16; 2nd Timothy 3:16; James 1:21; Revelation 1:3).

4. ***Jephthah was ignorant about what pleases the Lord.*** He thought that God is one whose help came as a result of Quid pro quo. But that is not the God of the Bible. Our Lesson – we cannot earn God's favor, nor can we deal for it. God's favor is free (Romans 3:24, 5:15, 8:32; Ephesians 2:5, 8-9).

5. ***Ignorance of the presence, purpose, and the person of God results in hopelessness*** (Judges 11:29-40). Our Lesson – Know God intimately – He will be the lamp to your feet and the light to your path (Ref. Psalm 119:105). Meaning; He gives you direction, guidance, a future, and a hope (Ref. Jeremiah 29:11).

6. ***Jephthah not only did not know the Word of God; he didn't know the God of the Word!*** Our Lesson – we as last day Christians need to understand the importance of knowing the Lord in His fullness as Scripture presents Him (John 1:1,14, 5:39-40, 14:6-7, 20:31; Acts 17:11).

7. ***Most times, what we do not know hurts us.*** Ignorance is not always bliss. In Judges 10-12, we saw the devastation that such ignorance causes. We saw the consequences of zeal without Biblical knowledge. Our Lesson - through the ignorance of Jephthah, we see the importance of knowing God – intimately.

He will guide us and give us true light to our blessed future, one free of trouble, hurt, and devastation. (Leviticus 5:17; Jeremiah 5:4; Hosea 4:6; Matthew 22:29; Romans 10:2-4; Ephesians 4:17-19). Knowing God does not mean you will not experience trials and tribulations, but in Him, there will always be victory and escape.

8. *Jephthah was ignorant about basic communication skills.* He made a bad situation worse because he did not take the time to listen to the Ephraimites. Compare Gideon's response to the Ephraimites (Judges 8:1-3) with the way that Jephthah responded to them (Judges 12:1-6). Our Lesson - ignorance of basic communication skills results in loneliness, love lessness, hardship, and trouble (Judges 12:1-7; Matthew 5:37; Colossians 4:6; Titus 2:8). Be kind one to another (Ref. Ephesians 4: 31-32).

9. *Jephthah's extremely high regard for his vow made it crucial for him to perform it.* Our Lesson – we must have this same intense sense of our obligations to God as Jephthah did. Our obligations to God must rank higher than all other considerations: "I have opened my mouth unto the Lord (in a solemn vow), and I cannot go back" (Judges 11:35; cf. Numbers 30:2; Deuteronomy 23:21; Job 22:27; Psalm 50:14; 76:11, etc.).

10. *Jephthah's daughter's pattern of loyalty and obedience is noteworthy and in need of copying!* She was immediately obedient, pious, and patriotic (verse 36). Our Lesson – is to emulate the grateful and honorable sense she had of the divine, His goodness in giving victory over Israel's enemies and God's deliverance from them. Jephthah's daughter's thoughts were not for herself but only for what her father vowed to God and that it might be honored. Notice her words; "My father, if your word was given to the Lord, do to me according to what has gone out of your mouth because the Lord has avenged you of your enemies, the people of Ammon" (Judges 11:36). "Greater love has no one than this than to lay down one's life for his friends" (John 15:13). As Abraham's son willfully submitted to his father's will even at the cost of his life, so did Jephthah's

daughter. Our Lesson – God would have obedience rather than sacrifice (1st Samuel 15:22; Proverbs 21:3).

In concluding this chapter, let's re-emphasize what I believe are the two most important lessons we can take from Jephthah's rash and thoughtless vow:

(1) we must avoid making rash vows especially to God. We must carefully ponder every course we desire to pursue and consider any potential consequences in each. And

(2) we must be willing to fulfill our vows once we have made them. Whether in marriage, business, or any other area of life, we must do what we have said that we will do!

SAMSON — PART ONE: SHALLOWNESS DESTROYS FAITH

We now begin our study on the man God used to break Israel's seventh cycle of sin, the last cycle of sin recorded in the book of Judges. It once again begins with God declaring that His people did evil in the sight of the Lord (Judges 13:1). As a result, the Lord delivered them into the hands of another oppressor, this time the Philistines.

The Philistines were people who inhabited the shoreline plains between Gezer and Gaza in southwestern Palestine. According to the Old Testament and discovered archeological monuments, the Philistines worshipped two Babylonian gods, Dagon (1ˢᵗ Samuel 5:2) and Ashtoreth (1ˢᵗ Samuel 31:10). This powerful and warlike tribe made frequent incursions against the Israelites. There was almost a perpetual war between them. They often held the tribes, especially the southern tribes, in degrading servitude (Judges 15:11; 1ˢᵗ Samuel 13:19-22). These hostilities did not cease until the time of Hezekiah (2ⁿᵈ Kings 18:8) when they were entirely subdued.

To confront this threat God, rose up the thirteenth judge found in the book of Judges – Samson, whose name means "awe-inspiring and according to (Josephus Ant. 5:8, section 4) Samson means "strong." When we look at the life of Samson, the judge God called and ordained to deliver His people, and one thing stands out; he had a propensity for worldly pleasures. The story of Samson clearly and vividly warns all believers of the danger of trying to do God's will while at the same time being superficial and shallow-minded in his reverence to God. True Christianity is the one lifestyle where total commitment to God and His cause is the only method of success. A lifestyle where one's carnal nature and God's calling are incompatible, and therefore, any attempt at keeping both alive, will result in catastrophic failure.

Judges chapters 13-16 tells the story of Samson warring against an arch enemy nation called the Philistines. The Hebrew word for Philistine means "migrants or immigrants." A migrant mentality is one that moves from one region to another or from one thought to another. This definition not only describes the Philistine nation but the lives of faith that God's people were exhibiting at the time of Samson. Being of a migrant mind lends to the idea that it is easy to follow God and be part of the world at the same time. All you need to do is accept Jesus as your savior and trust in Him. Then all is well because that is all God requires. Sorry, it does not work that way! Having a migrant mind leads to disaster and death, just like it did for Samson.

Accepting Jesus as your savior is only the first step on a journey that demands complete dedication and commitment which will take the rest of your life. In other words, we must recognize Jesus' lordship in our lives. Brethren, we must come to the realization that God gave His all for us, and He now requires us to give all to Him. You can delight yourself in complete dedication and committed to God, or you can delight in the things of this world and end up in disaster, but you cannot commit to both! You cannot be double-minded (Ref. James 1:8, 4:8).

> Do not be unequally yoked together with unbelievers. For what fellowship has righteousness with lawlessness? And what communion has light with darkness? (15) And what accord has Christ with Belial? Or what part has a believer with an unbeliever? (16) And what agreement has the temple of God with idols? For you are the temple of the living God. As God has said: "I will dwell in them and walk among them; I will be their God, and they shall be My people." (17) Therefore "Come out from among them and be separate, says the Lord. Do not touch what is unclean, and I will receive you." (18) "I will be a father to you, and you shall be My sons and daughters, says the Lord Almighty."
>
> 2nd Corinthians 6:14-18

Having a "migrant mind" describes what many Christians have today. Think of how many "church butterflies" you have seen in your Christian walk. You know who they are; they attend your church for a few weeks or months get bored and leave for another church, and so on. Why, because they are looking for something new and exciting, something that will pique their interest. They are people always looking for the latest thing or the next revival – these people have no solid roots, no foundation. They cannot develop a solid foundation because they do not stay in the same place long enough to grow one. These people have a "migrant or immigrant mind" and will never be able to develop spiritually. They, like the Israelites described in Judges regularly, fall into the "Cycle of Sin."

As we continue our study of Samson, there is an exciting fact overlooked in this seventh cycle of sin. There is a part of the cycle of sin missing. We have seen that the cycle of sin has four distinct parts.

1. The Children of God start out serving the Lord, but at the same time are doing what is right in their own eyes. They are migrant or double-minded.
2. The enslaved children of God are again in misery because they are now serving other gods.
3. The Children of God cry out to God for deliverance on account of their oppression.
4. God rises and anoints a Judge who delivers Israel from their oppressors.

In the cycle presented to us in Judges 13-16, however, the third part of the cycle is surprisingly absent. Nowhere in this story do we see the children of God crying out for deliverance. Isn't that extremely strange seeing that they have been in bondage, oppressed, dominated, and under servitude for 40 years, the longest period of oppression found anywhere in the book of Judges? Though it is not evident that the Philistines had entirely subjected the Israelites, they often vexed them and made inroads upon God's people. It is quite evident from Judges 15:11 that Israel was, in fact, under Philistines supremacy. So why was there no one crying out to God for deliverance? Could it be that the Israelites were now satisfied and content with the way things were? Or could it be that they had grown accustomed to it, and as a result, there was no more fight left in them?

There is no information given in the Biblical text about any slavery, mass destruction, domination, or pronounced evil of any kind inflicted on God's Children. It appears that there was a sort of relationship and commerce between the two people (Ref. Chapter 14). God's people seem to be content with their lives; they had food; they were able to farm their land and conduct trade (Ref. 15:11). It just wasn't really that bad, at least it was much better than it used to be, so they accepted their servitude. God's people just threw up their hands and surrendered to the forces of evil without a fight. As long as it did not hurt, they just went along with it and found a way to survive. They accepted the situation; they made no waves. They were friendly, understanding, and received the change and differences. Does this not remind you of what the church is doing today? Superficial and shallow-minded. But this is not what God designed His Children or His Church to be. God's design is not for us to serve two masters (Ref. Matthew 6:24; Luke 16:13)! The Church of Jesus is to be light and salt to the earth. It is to be aggressive and life-changing, not passive and compromising. Our Gospel is profitable for doctrine, for reproof, for correction, for instruction in righteousness, this is impossible if we are compromising to all forms of evils and different gods and beliefs (Ref. 2nd Timothy 3:16). Wake up and stand for our beliefs, fight Church!!!

God's children are not to be under subjection to anyone. God wants us to experience peace beyond all understanding and to live a life of fulfillment and joy. For "the Lord will make you the head and not the tail; you shall be above only, and not beneath, if you heed the commandments of the Lord your God, which I command you today, and are careful to observe them" (Ref. Deuteronomy 28:13). We are to be lenders, not borrowers (Ref. Deuteronomy 15:6). We are to be the judges and rulers of this world, not slaves to fleshly or spiritual despots (Ref. 1st Corinthians 6:3). We are Children of the "Most High," a chosen generation, a royal priesthood, a holy nation, and His special people, who are to proclaim the praises of Him who called us out of darkness into His marvelous light (1st Peter 2:9). We must stand against the whiles of the enemy, that is why God has given us His armor, His word, His Spirit, His Gifts, His weapons, and told us to go and fight a good fight, set captives free, deliver the oppressed, preach the Gospel of peace (Ref. Matthew 28:18-20; Mark 16:15-18; Ephesians 6:10-18; 1st Timothy 1:18, 6:12; etc.). But that was not happening at that time, nor is it happening today. God had had enough of their slave mentality, so he sent them a warrior judge in an attempt to show His people the way to freedom from oppression and bondage. That warrior judge's name was Samson.

Samson was one of the most renowned of the Hebrew judges. Samson was from the tribe of Dan; his father's name was Manoah. He was unique because God foretold his birth and manner of life before his birth. An angel of the Lord appeared to Samson's mother and announced a two-part prophecy concerning her future son (Judges 13:5). The first is that He would be a Nazarite from birth; he was the first Nazarite for life named in the Bible. The word "Nazarite" means "sanctified, holiness or devotion." It means to be set apart or separated unto the work of God. Being a Nazarite entailed three main commands.

1. They could not drink or eat fruit from the vine. (No wine, grapes, etc.)
2. They could not go near a dead body, nor defile themselves by touching anything 'unclean.'
3. They could not cut their hair all their days.

An interesting side note is that there are only three people mentioned in scripture who were Nazarites from birth – Samson, Samuel, and John the Baptist. All of these men were born to barren women. Does this not present another aspect of God other than He gives life to the dead, and makes the barren, fruitful? I believe it does! All of us have had times that appear 'hopeless' just like these women, but God brings out of our chaos a divine order because He can create something from nothing. When God created the heavens and the earth, Genesis tells us that the earth was without form and void. Without form or void means the earth was in chaos and in that state had no value or purpose. It did not take God any time at all to create, out of this chaos, earth's glorious and perfect operating system, which we all enjoy today. The understanding and faith in God's power and ability should give hope to every downtrodden and defeated believer. Let us turn to God in submission when we are in a state of chaos and give Him our full faith. He will create a divine order for us and provide us with hope and a perfect solution. Brethren, (5) Trust in the LORD with all your heart and do not depend on your understanding. (6) In all your ways acknowledge him, and he will make your paths straight. (Proverbs 3:5-6 ISV).

The second part of the prophecy was that he should only "*begin*" to deliver Israel out of the hand of the Philistines. This phrase "He would only begin to deliver ' is the first and only time used in Scripture to describes God's chosen vessel's ministry. Since when did God's chosen judges, only "*begin* to deliver Israel"? (Ref Judges 13:5) Did Othniel, Ehud, Gideon, etc. only begin to deliver Israel? No! As we shall soon see, Samson would only partially deliver Israel from bondage because He could not entirely deliver himself from his earthly and physical desires. The simple fact is that a man cannot lead others where he refuses to go himself!

There is perhaps another reason why Samson could only begin to deliver Israel out of bondage, one that we mentioned earlier. That is that deliverance was something the Children of God did not want. This lack of desire might seem strange, but it seems that after 40 years, Israel got quite comfortable under subjection to the Philistines. Remember, no one was calling out to God for deliverance at this time! A phenomenon strangely repeated by many believers today. Could it be that we, too, are comfortable being under subjection to spiritual Philistines? That is a question for your heart and God to work out – not for me to answer.

Spiritual growth demands change, and as we all know, spiritual growth and change are hard and quite painful. Many choose not to travel down that road. However, complacency is comfortable and easy. Too many Christians prefer to follow this wide and easy road, thinking that it leads to heaven. Question; does this road lead to heaven? Jesus tells us, No, it does not! Jesus warns us to "Enter by the narrow gate; for wide is the gate and broad is the way that leads to destruction, and there are many who go in by it. (14) Because narrow is the gate and difficult is the way which leads to life, and few find it." The way to life is narrow. It is not "the great highway" that people feel comfortable and easy to travel. No, The way to death, on the other hand, is broad. Multitudes are on it. It is the great highway in which people are comfortable following. They fall into it quickly and without effort, and go without thought. If they wish to leave and travel by a narrow gate to the city, it would require effort, thought, and determination and total commitment. So, says Christ, "diligence" is needed to enter life (Ref. Luke 13:24). All must strive, to obtain it, and thus, the narrow way, which is unfrequented, and solitary only a few find.

The life of Samson now begins. Manoah's wife finally gives birth to a little boy. Can you imagine the joy they experience in this miracle of God? Remember, after years of trying to have a child without success, it was an Angel of the Lord who came to them and said she would give birth to a deliverer.

The childhood of Samson is a mystery. Nothing of his childhood comes to light other than what we see in Judges 13:24-25.

> So, the woman bore a son and called his name Samson; and the child grew, and the Lord blessed him. (25) And the Spirit of the Lord began to move upon him at Mahaneh Dan between Zorah and Eshtaol.
>
> Judges 13:24-25

This small comment about his childhood tells us volumes about his future, however. The scriptures announce that the "Lord blessed him" and endued him with graces and gifts, which were necessary for the work he was called, along with all the evidentiary proofs that showed Samson was under the protection of the "Most High." These endowments caused him to increase daily in stature and extraordinary strength. In other words, God never sends someone to do a job without giving him the proper tools, wisdom, strength, and direction to complete it. As evidence of this, verse 25 proclaims that "the Spirit of the Lord began to move upon him" (Samson). (Ref Judges 13:5) Where God gives His blessing, He gives His Spirit to qualify that blessing. Those indeed in whom the Spirit of grace begins to work receives God's blessings.

Can you imagine the hope these godly parents had in Sampson? They demonstrated all their expectations and hopes in his calling,

Samson means "Little Sun" or "Little Servant." He that would shine like the sun, or he that would be a light bearer of Israel. What about all those who by word or by observation learned of this miracle child. In this upcoming light bearer of Israel is where their hope and expectations could only come. Can you imagine their hope and expectation for this gift of God? Could they think that finally there is someone who will be a spiritual model for us; a true mighty man of strength, stature and a man sent from God to show us the way of salvation. Much in the way that Israel experienced centuries later with John the Baptist. But as is always the case when we put our hopes, dreams, and expectations in the hands of man, we get disappointed and hurt.

Gideon was a man like this. He was a great leader and hero. He did many brave exploits. The hope of Israel was upon his shoulders, and in a small way, they realized it, but the story of his leadership ended in failure. Why? Because he wanted what other people had. He was greedy; he lusted after money and things. And as a result, God's children never realized the fullness of what God had for them. In like manner, and perhaps the saddest example of this principle is Samson. He had the potential to become a great leader. But he failed. Why? Once again, he wanted what other people had. He lusted after money, women, and possessions.

In Samson, however, there was an undermining sin that he never dealt with, one that caused him to think that because he was God's servant, called and blessed and possessing great strength, he could do anything, have everything and defeat any foe. It was the sin of pride and arrogance. These sins are what ultimately destroyed Samson, and still has the same devastating effect on believers and non-believers today.

When any man is so arrogant to believe he can have or do anything and still live for God, have God's blessing, and defeat any foe, it inevitably leads him down the road to destruction. Arrogance proudly declares, "I can have it all," but God is calling us to give all away. Pride is saying, "I can do it all," but the Bible says in John 15:5 without God, we can do nothing. Arrogance proclaims, "I can defeat any foe," but God is saying, "I am your shield, your exceedingly great reward" (Ref. Genesis 15:1; Matthew 5:12). "Yet in all these things, we are more than conquerors through Him who loved us. (Ref. Romans 8:37). Did you notice through whom we are more that conquerors? Not in ourselves! But through Him (Christ)!The mentality of pride and arrogance is worldly. Being worldly is ultimately destructive and devastating to one's soul. Samson stands out as a man of striking contrasts. He indeed was a man of faith consumed by frivolousness. A man called by the Spirit and led by the flesh. Notice;

1.   He a Nazarite from birth (Judges 13:5), but continually associated himself with evil (Judges 14:1-3).
2.   God blessed Him and moved him by the Spirit (Judges 13:25; 15:14), but he continually gave into carnal desires (Judges 16:1-4). Here in order are the steps of Samson downward, which led to his inevitable destruction and death.
     *   Self-confidence: "I will go out" (Judges 16:20)
     *   Self-ignorance: "He did not know" (Judges 16:20)
     *   Self-weakness: "The Philistines laid hold on him" (Judges 16:21)
     *   Self-darkness: "They put out his eyes" (Judges 16:21)
     *   Self-degradation: "They brought him down to Gaza" (Judges 16:1—3, 21)
     *   Self-bondage: "They bound him with fetters" (Judges 16:21)
     *   Self-drudgery: "He became a grinder in the prison-house" (Judges 16:21)
     *   Self-humiliation: "Call for Samson, that he may make us sport of him" (Judges 16:25, 27)
3.   His actions were often foolish and unwise (Judges 15:4), but possessed undaunted courage in battle (Judges15:1-4).
4.   He was mighty in physical strength (Judges 16:3, 9, 13, 14), but mighty weak in resisting temptation (Judges 16:15-17).
5.   To summarize his life – he had a noble beginning but a noticeably poor end (Judges 16:30).1

We can easily define as worldly Samson's actions. Being worldly by definition is living for the things of this world at the exclusion of spiritual precepts and truths. It is unfortunate that the way Christians describe "being worldly" often depends on their traditions and training. We think that not being worldly means not doing certain things. Or not going to certain places. Now, as Bible-believing Christians, we know that some things are entirely against a Holy life and defined in scripture. Many Christians who go around describing things as "worldly" describes actions that did not exist in the world of the first century. All we need to discover the true meaning of worldliness is to look at the definition given by the apostles. Believers in the early century received letters from the apostles, John, and James, which clearly warn us of the danger of being worldly. Fortunately, God has preserved for us those letters. So. should not our definition of worldliness be based on how these writers defined it?

In 1st John 2:15-17 the apostle John declares to Christians

"Do not love the world or the things in the world. If anyone loves the world, the love of the Father is not in him. (16) For all that is in the world – the lust of the flesh, the lust of the eyes, and the pride of life – is not of the Father but is of the world. (17) And the world is passing away, and the lust of it; but he who does the will of God abides forever."

Simple enough of a definition. It is much easier said than done, no doubt, but simple to understand. In John's mind, 'being worldly' is 'living as the unbeliever lives.' Think about what kind of life that is. Reread 1st John 2:16. Love not the world means to pursue your victory by rising above the world and all it has to offer, seeking only those things from above. Why? Because, if any man loves the world by seeking happiness in it, he does not love God! The lust of the flesh (the pleasures of the outward senses), whether of the taste, smell, or touch; the lust of the eye (desires of imagination, of that internal sense) whereby we relish whatever is grand, new, or beautiful, or the pride of life (the pomp found in clothes, houses, furniture, equipment, or manner of living). All of which procures honor and therefore gratifies our pride and vanity, which directly includes the desire to be looked up to or praised and indirectly includes covetousness.

John, here in verse 16, uses the Greek phrase "*alazoneia bee'-os,*" meaning "pride of life." "*Alazoneia*" is a word that means "empty or braggart talk." "*Bee'-os*" means "sustaining life, resources, wealth, goods." "*Alazon*" will heap praise on one's self, even to strangers. He tells of all the money that he does not have or does have! It is an entirely selfish, greedy, and a proud way of life.

With that said, it is essential to know that all the worldly attitudes listed in verse 16 are not from God, but from the ruler of this world. Remember, the desires of this world, along with the world itself, will pass away. That is, everything that can fulfill one's earthly desires will vanish away? But he that does the will of God, who loves God and not the world, will abide forever in the enjoyment of what he loves. Those who love that, which passes away, will pass away with them forever.

Worldliness is lusting after the things that will please the flesh, things that will please the eyes, or the things that our pride tells us will satisfy us and those things that we are proud to possess. Lusting, after all, is the opposite of being content in all things, for it brings great rewards (Ref. 1st Timothy 6:6; Philippians 4:11 and Hebrews 13:5). Notice, especially 1st John 2:15. We spoke of it earlier. You cannot desire both the love of the world and the love of God. It is either, or!

Samson lived a worldly life. His desire to please himself while controlling his own life. He spent his time with people who did not know God (Ref. Judges 14:10, 17), he lusted after women, and never learned to control his temper, or his pride and most importantly he forgot where his source of strength came. The evil desires and lack of moral fiber of the Philistines wore off on Samson as a result of his continual association with them. Notice how he spoke to his father in the presence of his Philistine companions. "I have seen a woman. Get her for me." What attitude does that demonstrate to you?

Samson saw, Samson lusted, Samson arrogantly demanded, and Samson pompously insisted, (Judges 14:1-3) is but one example. Still, his entire life story shows the same arrogant attitude, which is evident in the fact that all three of Samson's loves were women of his long-established enemies, the Philistines. His worldly views controlled him. He thought that nobody could overcome him or was smarter than him, so he used hard questions for fun (Judges 14: 12-18). He played with the enemy (Ref. Judges 16:4-16.). He never took them seriously. Perhaps the worst example of his awful arrogance and pride was that his passion and its gratification blinded him, notice He never had a thought of insecurity or danger. His daring of the enemy to destroy him was the result of it. Look at his playful, teasing attitude in the first three attempts made by Delilah, each one getting closer to the truth. Was it not apparent to any reader what Delilah's intention was? However, Samson so lacked in suspicion or concern of anything harmful happening to him that he believed no matter what happened "I will escape like I did before" (Ref. Judges 16:20). How arrogant! This game with Delilah led to what could be the saddest commentary in the Bible. *"He (Samson) did not know that the Lord had departed from him* (Ref. Judges 16:17-20). That is what 'being worldly' means and its result! I wonder how many of us, right now, this moment, "do not know that the Lord has departed from us? Are you sure! Are you unconcerned or lack suspicion of what the evil one is trying to do in your life that you are not taking the consequences of your actions seriously? Or are you so worldly that you believe that nothing can happen to you because you say that you are a child of God and he will protect and save you no matter your commitment level. Do you have the same mindset about your relationship with God, as Samson did? He indeed was a man of faith consumed by frivolousness — a man called by the Spirit and led by the flesh.

Brethren, we must remember that we are speaking of a man who knew God. Samson was a man with many spiritual advantages. Samson's life is a sign of warning for all Christians who think that complete dedication to Christ and His ways is not necessary. Be ye warned!

Let us take a quick look at some of Samson's spiritual advantages.

1. He came from a good home – His parents were Godly. They wanted to know God's plan for their son's life. Before he was born, they prayed about him. Notice some of their requests
    A. Teach us what we should do for the boy that will soon be born (Judges 13:8).
    B. What will be the boy's rule of life (Judges 13:12)?
    C. What will be his work (Judges 13:12)?

The original message of the Angel contained this interesting and curious information. Why only begin to free Israel from its enemies? (Judges 13:5) Manoah wanted confirmation. Accordingly, in Judges 13:13, the Angel refers to and expands upon the information he gave Manoah's wife earlier.

There are several wonderful lessons contained in this story of Samson's announced birth. Let us examine them.

➢ Manoah prays that God would send the same blessed messenger again, to receive further instructions concerning the management of this Nazarite child. He feared that his wife might have forgotten some part of the angel's information and instructions due to her excitement of finally having a child. He wanted to make no mistakes. "Lord, let the man of God come again unto us, for we desire to be better acquainted with him." (Ref Judges 13:8) The first lesson is that those that have heard from heaven cannot but wish to hear more and again meet with the man of God. Notice he does not go or send his servants to comply with and find out what the man of God said, but he seeks the messenger upon his knees. He was the one who prayed to God to send him; he wanted to meet him face to face; and as a result, He finds him.

➢ Manoah's main desire is in the questions asked of the Angel. "What will be the boy's rule of life and his work?" (Ref Judges13:12) We can translate this as "what manner of life will he lead," and "what will be his exploits?" Good men are more concerned and desirous to know the duty that they are to do rather than of understanding the events that shall befall them; for commitment is ours, events are God's. God will not fail to guide those that are sincerely longing to know their duty, and apply themselves in pursuit of His ways (Ref. Psalm 25:8-9).

➢ When the messenger of God appeared again, Manoah's wife swiftly goes and gets her husband. Undoubtedly, she earnestly asked the blessed messenger to stay until she could return with him (Ref. Judges 13:10-11). She did not desire him to go with her to her husband, but she went to bring her husband to the Angel of God. What that tells us is that those who would desire to meet with God must meet with Him where He is, not where we want Him to be.

➢ Those that have personal experience with the things of God should hastily and always invite others to come and discover the same experiences (Ref. John 1:45-46, 4:16).

➢ Samson, from the time of his birth, knew his religious protocols, especially regarding his calling as a Nazarite (Ref. Judges 16:17). His spiritual knowledge of its rules should have been a help to him, a straight path to follow, with warning signs all around. God had also given Samson special promises (Ref. Judges 13:5). He knew them well, and when needed, he should have remembered them. He was responsible to God for that knowledge (Ref. James 1:22-25). Notice the clear warning in these verses; Religious tradition is no good if we do not love God enough to obey Him. Samson made promises to God, but he did not keep them; which shows his worldliness.

➢ He had true experiences with God because God has touched him before through the power of the Holy Spirit (Ref. Judges 14:6, 19; 15:14). But he continued in his ungodly ways, seeking the same things as the world seeks, and showing no remorse because of his actions in obtaining them.

➢ He was a man who had experienced the reality of answered prayer. There was a time where Samson was so weak and thirsty that his life was in danger, so he cried to God for help, and the Lord provided for his need immediately (Ref. Judges 15:18-19); which was a sign from God that He was with Samson and God was there to help and encourage him. But despite God's abundant mercy and grace, he still lived in self-centeredness. Once again, a sign of a worldly attitude.

These lessons are for all of us. Serious dangers are lurking when one thinks that they would never be like Samson because their love for God is great, their Biblical knowledge strong, and their religious traditions intact. But the Bible warns us to be careful; "let him who thinks he stands take heed lest he fall (1st Corinthians 10:12); and Romans 11:20b; "Do not be proud of it (your heritage) instead, be afraid (GNB)."

So, where did Samson go wrong? What started him down the slippery slope to destruction? Did he not fall into the same "Cycle of

Sin" as the Israelites consistently did over the past 200 years? Absolutely! We can see his first step downward in Judges 14:1-3; cross-reference this story with 1st John 2:15-16, which we have already looked at, but is worth looking at again.

> "Now Samson went down to Timnah and saw a woman in Timnah of the daughters of the Philistines. (2) So, he went up to his father and mother, saying, "I have seen a woman in Timnah of the daughters of the Philistines; now, therefore, get her for me as a wife." (3) Then his father and mother said to him, "Is there no woman among the daughters of your brethren, or all my people, that you must go and get a wife from the uncircumcised Philistines?" And Samson said to his father, "Get her for me, for she pleases me well."
>
> Judges 14:1-3

Samson goes down to Timnah, a town in the southern part of the hill country of Judah, about 8 miles west of Bethlehem. Timnah was a town occupied and controlled by the Philistines. The Biblical text gives no reason for Samson's desire to go down to a Philistine controlled area, but verse 13:25 does say that the "Spirit began to move" on Samson, which implies that the Spirit was still controlling him. If that is true, we can extract from it a significant association. Samson, led by the Holy Spirit, seeks an occasion to confront the Philistines, which we know was his calling. His friendly and personal association with them, however, is a strange method of accomplishing his call, but the truth is Samson was himself a riddle, a paradox. He did that which was great and good, by doing that which was worldly and evil. Samson was a man God designed not to be a pattern for us to follow, but a type. A type of man who, typified sin for us, and appeared in the likeness of sinful flesh, that He might condemn and destroy sin in the flesh (Ref. Romans 8:3).

Once Samson saw a Philistine woman who pleased his eyes, and due to his overwhelming fleshly lust wanted to have her. Notice how he went about it. He goes to his parents with a harsh and irreverent attitude and demands of them; "I have seen a woman...now, therefore, get her for me as a wife" (verse 2). Now cross-reference verse 17 in 1st John 2. Can you see the mistake Samson is making? There are two things we can notice right away. One is that this is a worldly action. It was weak and foolish. Ask yourself, should a child of God who is not only an Israelite but a Nazarite at that, one who is in a unique way devoted to the Lord, covet someone who is, in this case, a worshipper of Dagon or in our case an idolater or at least an unbeliever? Shall one called to the army of God be intimate with his sworn enemy (Ref. 2nd Corinthians 6:14-16)?

Samson, knowing the intimacy and grace of God, saw this woman, and she pleased him well (Judges 14:3). It does not appear that he had any reason to think her wise or virtuous, or in any way likely to be a help-meet for him; all he saw was her beauty. Her beauty was the determining factor, and therefore nothing else mattered. She must have her. Christian, anyone guided only by his eyes, and governed by fleshly lust in determining a spouse, must afterward be aware that they might have a beautiful ungodly Philistine in their arms.

Samson's parents did well in trying to dissuade him from unequally yoking himself with the unbeliever (Ref. 2nd Corinthians 6:14). Let those who profess Christ understand, an attraction with the profane and unbelieving, brings death to the door seeking you! Hear and apply Samson's parent's reasoning: "Is there no woman among the daughters of your brethren, or all my people, that you must go and get a wife from the uncircumcised Philistines?" (Ref. Judges 14:3) Let me put this in modern terms. Why don't you search for a spouse who is following your faith; if you are a believer search for a spouse who is a believer, if you are not a believer search for a spouse who is not a believer. Do not be unequally yoked. It can only bring disaster to both of you. Why do you think God gave the command to His people not to intermarry with any other nation (Ref. Deuteronomy 7:2-3; 1st Kings 11:2)?

Samson's parents remembering what the Angel of God had spoken to them many years prior regarding Samson's call must have considered that God brought forth this strange request, and He must have had a special reason for it. It certainly would have been improper for Samson to insist that they give him this woman, and for them to deny granting it. Their loving compliance with Samson's unwise and potentially dangerous request is an example to parents everywhere about being unreasonable when they strongly disagree with their children's choices. Nor should they deny their consent, especially without hearing from God or for some worthy cause. For in the same way as children must obey their parents in the Lord (Ephesians 6:1), so parents must not provoke their children to wrath, lest they be discouraged (Ephesians 6:4). For to outright deny a child as many parents have already learned, usually results in the child doing what he wishes anyway. This action also leads the child to disrespect their parents. Samson, on the other hand, in subjection to his parent's authority, asked for their consent, though he did it harshly and irreverently, out of lust and having no respect, he didn't wait until he got their approval.

If only Samson had listened to his godly parents, his life would have been different. Let me show you what happens when we do not consider wise counsel, especially Biblically wise counsel. In Judges 14:8 as Samson was returning to the Philistines to collect his wife, he sees a swarm of bees that had built a hive inside the carcass of the lion. One Samson had previously killed the last time he went down to this Philistine stronghold. At that time, Samson might have done well to ask himself why He was having this fight with the lion in the first place. Be that as it may, maybe he should have taken it as a sign that going down after his Philistine woman was wrong and dangerous, and that this lion was there as a sign from God; a stop sign, if you will. Think about it! Remember, God orders the steps of a righteous man (Psalm 37:23).

Now let us get back to the beehive in the carcass of the lion. What a glorious picture that exemplifies that even when death surrounds God's children, God brings forth life, and amid bitterness and hardship, God produces sweetness and provision. Even in the middle of a dead and decaying world, we see God raising a sweet life-giving source of nourishment that anyone can come and partake of when they wish to escape their horrifying circumstances.

The beehive and its honey are emblems of those sweet blessings that come from God's grace. He should have extended it to the people of Christ through His defeat of Satan, who is the roaring lion who seeks to destroy (Ref. 1st Peter 5:8). Does not this event metaphorically illustrate the calling of the modern-day Church? Are we not put here as a life-giving source amid a dead world to give nourishment and life to those in need of it? We surely are!

But keep this in mind as well. The devil loves to counterfeit God's grace. Many mature Christian can testify that not everything that comes our way in the form of a blessing is of God (Ref. Genesis 3). The bees are a symbol of the chastisement that the Lord brings upon his people for disobedience. Three passages in the Bible refer to the offensive power of bees (Ref. Deuteronomy 1:44; Psalms 118:12; and Isaiah 7:18). Here in Judges 14:8, we see that Samson saw the honey; the honey was a desirable blessing to the eyes, but in this particular case, it was not of the Lord. Why? Because for Samson to partake of the Honey, he had to violate his Nazarite vow by touching the Lion's dead carcass. That should have been enough reason for him to realize that this was a trap set by the enemy. The swarming bees Samson had to overcome was the second indication that this blessing was not of God. For the bee in the Old Testament, illustrate pagan people that would come against Israel (Ref. Deuteronomy 1:44; Psalm 118:12; Isaiah 7:18). Through these bees, God attempted to stop Samson from going after the desired honey and breaking his vow by the use of a swarm of bees. Samson should have realized this and backed away. Once again, however, his pride, lust, and his dependence upon his physical prowess won out, and he proceeded to make the wrong decision and take a gift that was not of God.

So, what should we learn from this? We, as children of God, must first learn a basic rule of conduct. "Put on the Lord Jesus Christ, and make no provision for the flesh, to fulfill its lusts" (Romans 13:14). Every decision in a Christian's life should have this foundation. This command, however, has two parts. If we try not to fulfill the lusts of our flesh in our strength, we end up in Romans 7 – where the good you want to do, you do not do, but the evil you don't want to do that you would do! That is where the other part of this command comes in. Notice what comes first in this command. "Put on the Lord Jesus Christ. The words rendered "put on" are the same words used in Romans 13:12, and are commonly employed in reference to "clothing" or "apparel." The phrase to "put on" in this reference means to take up his principles, to imitate his example, to copy his spirit, become like him.

This command contains the whole of our salvation. It is a strong and beautiful expression for the most intimate union with Christ. It vividly expresses the reality of all the graces which are in him. The apostle does not say, put on purity and sobriety, peacefulness and benevolence, but he says all this and a thousand times more by saying, "Put on Christ." We must learn to walk close to the Lord and ask Him to live through us. Doing this is always the first part of the formula. But we must also do the second part in conjunction with the first. In other words, do not put yourself into situations where you know you could fall! Do not trust yourself or your strength or conviction! A patient once said to his doctor that he had broken his arm in three places. To which the doctor replied, "Well then, I'd stay out of all those places." Good advice! Do all you can to avoid temptation.

The rest of the story of Samson up to and including his capture, imprisonment, loss of eyesight, humiliation, the ridicule he threw in the face of Jehovah, and the resulting exaltation of the Philistine god Dagon, was the result of the same cause which we have just discussed. Samson was proud, arrogant, and worldly! His desire was not for the things of God, but he loved the world and the things in the world.

> "If anyone loves the world, the love of the Father is not in him. (16) For all that is in the world – the lust of the flesh, the lust of the eyes, and the pride of life – is not of the Father but is of the world. (17) And the world is passing away, and the lust of it; but he who does the will of God abides forever."
>
> 1st John 2:15-17

There is an illustration I remember reading, which will make a point of this lesson stand out. The ring-tailed monkey common to the island of Madagascar is a squirrel monkey. It is very difficult to catch. It is exceptionally agile; many hunters have tried in vain to catch this little monkey. But the Zulu's have been catching them for years! For they know that the monkey has a significant weakness – melon pits! What the Zulu's do to capture it is to make a narrow slip in a melon, just wide enough for a monkey to slide his hand in sideways. The monkeys cannot resist. They push their hand in, grab the pits, and suddenly find that they can't get their hand out of the melon once they have made a fist to clench the pits. Their desire to eat those pits is so strong that they do not let go of them– and there they stay trapped! Well, Samson, with his particular type of desire, was like these Monkeys, and he never learned to let go of his worldly lusts! Those lusts were the trap that caused his downfall, humiliation, and ultimately his death.

Samson became so proud of who he was and worldly in his thinking that He caused pain and despair to fall on everyone associated with him. It affected his life, his testimony, his family, his nation, and his God as well. We must realize three things about Samson that are lessons for us to heed.

1. *He did not obey God* – Remember he was a Nazarite from his birth. He knew what that meant, and he acknowledged it. Therefore, he should have followed them with all due diligence.

    a. *He must not drink alcohol* (Numbers 6:1-8). Samson must not have thought that this promise was important. He went to parties where there was alcohol. Most probably, he was drinking it along with the Philistines he was trying to impress and associate with (Read Judges 14:10, 11, 17, 18). Our lesson – be aware, the danger of any alliance with Philistines [unsaved] is often not apparent at first. In the long run, however, these alliances have a habit of wearing us down. Early in Samson's life, it caused him to become angry, kill thirty Philistines, and eventually lose the woman he desired. In the end, it caused his captivity, the loss of his eyes, the exaltation of a false god – Dagon, his ridicule, humiliation, and ultimately his death.

    b. *A Nazarite must not touch a dead body*. Samson was a man of war who killed many. But beyond that, remember the Lion? He killed a lion on his way to Timnah. Upon his return, he saw that bees had built a hive filled with honey inside the carcass. What did he proceed to do? He reached into the lion and took some of the honey (Ref. Judges 14). Lesson One – Not all blessings are from God, for there is pleasure in sin, and it can temporarily satisfy. The Bible does not speak of the 'passing pleasure of sin' without reason (Ref. Hebrews 11:25). It does speak, however, of the 'hardening' and 'deceitfulness' of sin (Ref. Hebrews 3:13). Though sin promises much, in the end, it only leaves emptiness, hurt, and death. Learn from Samson, and do not let your curiosity and your fleshly desires lead to compromise.

c. *He must not cut his hair.* We all know the story of Samson and Delilah and Samson's betrayal and capture by Delilah and the Philistines (Ref. Judges 16). Our lesson – we must not play games or take chances with sin, for your salvation is at stake.

But there was another rule Samson knew about and refused to obey. He was not only for a Nazarite, but God told his people do not marry people from other nations. Samson refused to obey God in this matter as well (Read Judges 14:1-3; Exodus 34:16; Deuteronomy 7:3 and Joshua 23:12-13.). Disobedience is where being worldly begins. We refuse to accept the control of God's word or to follow its instructions.

2. *He did not love the people of God* – Samson's insistence that he wanted women from other nations rather than his own clearly shows his failure to love God's people. Even his friendships and associates were of the Philistines. How does this show a love for his people? Out of all the Judges recorded, it is essential to note that Samson was the only judge who did things on his own without calling on his people for help. Why? Arrogance, pride, and self-dependency or because he did not care about his people! If he did care, he would not want to hurt them by his actions or by the choices he made.

3. *He did not give honor to God* – God had a purpose for Samson. He wanted Samson to begin to rescue his people (13:5). But Samson became a failure. He should have brought honor to a holy God. Instead, his evil life brought dishonor to his God. The enemy declared: 'Our god helped us to defeat Samson our enemy' (16:23). No! Samson's disobedience to his God gave victory to their false god.

Centuries later, Paul wrote about this same subject. Paul was angry about believing Jews that were dishonoring God due to their behavior. Paul told them that their morals were terrible. Their religion was just words, and it had no meaning in their lives (Ref. Romans 2:24). "And the name of God is blasphemed among the Gentiles because of them" (Ref. Romans 2:24) Plus, the word 'Jew' had become a bad word. People thought of words like 'wicked,' 'selfish,' and 'greedy' to describe the Jewish people and their religion. Notice Romans 2:25: "Being circumcised [referring to the Jews] is worthwhile only if you obey the Law. But if you do not obey the Law, you are no better off than people who are not circumcised [Gentiles]" (CEV). Brethren, our goal in life should be to please God in every thought and deed. Why? Because He loved us enough to come to earth to save us, and He loves us enough to continue the good work He started in you until the day of Jesus Christ" (Ref. Philippians 1:6).

Samson, like so many of us, put his life into categories. One category we will call "things that God does not care about" or things that are "unimportant." The other category we will call "things we believe are important to God." Once those categories are part of our lives, we live our lives accordingly. The simple truth, however, is that God does not have a category called "Unimportant." In God's eyes, "all scripture is given by inspiration and is profitable for doctrine, for reproof, for correction, for instruction in righteousness: (17) that the man of God may be perfect, thoroughly furnished unto all good works" (2nd Timothy 3:16-17). In other words, you cannot departmentalize God's word by obeying one command and not the other. But despite our unholy and ungodly categorizing, God's unlimited grace still abides with us. In Samson's case, God even allowed him to keep his supernatural strength, whereby fulfilling his calling. Why? Because "all the promises of God in him are yea, and in him Amen, unto the glory of God" (2nd Corinthians 1:20)! God, despite knowing our sinful nature and the judgment that comes along with it, gives the power and guidance of the Holy Spirit to remove those items in the "unimportant" category and help us to place them into the "important to God" category. The "important to God" category starts with changing us into His image. "Sanctification. "is what the Bible calls this process. The faster we allow this to happen, the faster we can live the greater life promised to us in Him.

To finish this portion of our study on Samson's life, let us take a look at what his capture, humiliation, and death can teach us. Judges 16:20, as stated earlier, contains the saddest commentary in the Bible. *"He (Samson) did not know that the Lord had departed from him."* (Ref. Judges 16:20) There comes a time in all believers' life if we continue to be disobedient to God, where we must finally reckon with His rejection, where extended mercy is no more, and we do not recognize that the Lord has departed from us. It is inevitable that the more we disobey, the farther we remove ourselves from God.

Samson never saw where his disobedience, his unwise alliances, and his worldliness would lead. He thought that no matter what he did, there would be no consequences – God would always be there as before. In his self-confidence, Samson figured he would go out and shake the Philistines off like he had before (Ref. Judges 16:20). How unfortunate it is that men, are not aware of their helpless condition till they learn it the hard way. Samson didn't even know that his strength was gone, or even worse, that the Lord had abandoned him. How many have lost the favorable presence of God, and were not aware of it. They provoked God to withdraw from them, but they did not sense the loss, nor did they suppose that God would do so. Samson's possession of his extraordinary strength came from the presence of the Spirit of the Lord (Ref. Judges 13:25). Now the Spirit of the Lord had departed from him, and so did his strength.

The practical lesson in this story is that the destruction caused was by the presumption of self-dependence. With the strength of the Lord gone, Samson was at the mercy of his enemies; and mercy is not something you can expect from the devil. They first put out his eyes, and then he became the ultimate slave (16:21). No one ever starts with the intention of losing their strength and spiritual sight. Samson certainly did not know it would come to this, but it is the inevitable result of worldly compromise and disobedience,

Samson realized his awful mistake in the end. Look at his situation; he was a prisoner. Sampson lost his eyes, so he could not determine his direction in life; he had to depend on God for guidance or be a slave to his enemies. He made flour from grain (16:21). Sampson had no hope, no end in sight, and he had only discouraging thoughts of a life that could have been and dreams of a better one. He brought dishonor to himself, his family, and his people, and most importantly, to his God. He did this by being worldly, arrogant, and proud in his thoughts and actions. These things that were true about Samson are just like it is in everyone without a relationship with God. God desires that each one should come to his senses, repent, and by the grace of God start anew. God grace abounded in Samson's life, and God offered him a second chance. God demonstrates His mercy and grace throughout Samson's time in captivity, by allowing Samson's hair to grow again despite Samson's broken vow. Thank you, Lord, Hallelujah! What does this teach us?

1. First is that it is probable that Samson reflected on his folly, and became sincerely penitent, and renewed his Nazarite vow. His hair grew along with and in conjunction with his repentance, and his strength grew along with his hair. Brethren let us be careful, however, in our exegesis and not misinterpret the truth of this event. The growth of Samson's hair was not the cause of his strength. It was only the physical evidence or the badge of his consecration; it was no more than a token that God accepted him once again. God's grace does not cast away His servants. It is one of the wonders of divine love, and it holds on with mercy's unending intensity even when his children prove unworthy of it. The way God showed his unmerited favor was in the fact that the Philistines did not notice the growth of Samson's hair. Remember, the Philistines were well aware that it was when they cut Samson's hair. his supernatural strength disappeared, and they captured Jehovah's invincible warrior. There could be several reasons for the Philistine's lack of regard for the growth of Samson's hair.

    A. It could be that perhaps the philistines were willing that his great strength should return so that they would be able to extract more work out of him, and seeing that he was blind, they were in no fear of him for he could not focus that strength without their direction.

B. Another might be that they genuinely believed Dagon brought Samson to them. To this false deity, they ascribed their success (verses 23-24): "Our god has delivered Samson our enemy, and the destroyer of our country, into our hands." Did you notice who it is that was getting the praise? Not Jehovah! But Dagon, the god of the Philistines. What this shows is that when we, the Church, become like the world, the god of this world gets the glory, and we dishonor Christ. Christians, we must never allow that to happen!

C. Also, it could be that the Philistines knew that it was Delilah that betrayed Samson, for they had paid her for doing it, better still they attributed Samson's capture to their god who they believed used Delilah as the tool to capture him. Therefore, they were secure in their belief that Dagon's power would once again protect them. This idea makes little sense when you consider the destruction to life and country that Samson, their super-powered, invincible enemy, had caused them over the past 20 years. What makes more sense is that the Philistines never noticed Samson's hair growing back. God probably blinded the eyes of the Philistines from noticing the growth. This blindness is a true demonstration of God's immeasurable power, unlimited grace, and endless forgiveness toward His people, even when they fall. This type of blindness is neither beyond the Biblical record nor beyond God's capabilities. The Philistines experienced the same kind of blindness, as did the residence of Sodom and Gomorrah (Ref. Genesis 19). Like Sodom, so fell the Philistines.

Samson's life should teach us something. As long as Samson remained a Nazarite, he was unconquerable. He was a man consecrated to God who did not remain so. Samson was a man of faith consumed by frivolity, an arrogant man with divided loyalties and subject to compromise. The story of Samson teaches us that there are severe dangers in being independent, arrogant, proud, and worldly, one consumed only with one's self. Evils are inevitable when we become isolationist (Ref.

Ephesians 4:1-3), or involved in mixed or foreign marriages (Judges 14: 3; Ref. 2nd Corinthians 6:14-1`8), or caught up in immoral sexual relations, but especially in playing with temptation. In the history of Samson, we notice all these unwise and evil activities. He, of all the judges that we are privy to know their lives, though he was invincible and independent, not needing anybody or anything to help him in any way. Samson never called the armies of Israel together, never tried to unify the nation, and never asked assistance in fighting the Philistines. What he did, he did in his God-given immeasurable strength. We know nothing about any good he did for Israel. Nothing about his judgeship, his court, his wisdom, or military leadership, nor are we told anything about the manner of Israel's life under his authority. He was an independent who cared more for himself, his needs and wants than his God, his calling, or his people. So, can there be any wonder why his life ended so tragically, and his calling was only one of beginnings not of endings (Ref. Judges 13:5). Brethren, we might think that we could never be like Samson or fall into the same temptations, but the Bible warns us to be careful, for we could fail too (Ref 1st Corinthians 10:12). "Do not be proud; be afraid" (Ref. Romans 11:20)!

Let us now look at the way Samson overcame his circumstance, his past, and his shortcomings and how he defeated his enemies. I believe that we can glean four things from Samson's last days on earth. These four things, when offered as a pure and selfless offering to God, will earn you a place in God's heart.

1. **He overcame by understanding that God's adversity is God's university.** Even with the loss of eyesight, he saw beyond his circumstances and allowed God to use him for his betterment. For great is the calamity that can produce unspeakable good. If it leads one to repentance and faith in Jesus Christ, though his grave is with the wicked, his resurrection will be with the just.

2. **He overcame by God's unlimited grace.** Here again, are those wonderful words of hope. Nobody has to feel despair. "But Samson's hair began to grow again" (16:22). God always gives another opportunity to those who, in faithful prayer, ask for it.

God's grace is so great that He will not refuse to accept us. Our part is only to acknowledge our sins, ask forgiveness, and repent.

3. **He overcame by prayer** (Judges 16:28). "O Lord God, remember me, I pray! Strengthen me, and I pray, just this once, O God that I may with one blow take vengeance on the Philistines for my two eyes!" When we realize our mistake, we should pray immediately. God has promised that he will forgive us and help us (1st John 1:9). It is important to note here the fact that in all the recorded history of Samson that this prayer is only the second one. The first is in Judges 15:18. Also, note that both Sampson's prayers come at a time when he thought he was going to die. Prayer is conversing, communion, and communication with God. We are to pray unceasingly (Ref. 1st Thessalonians 5:17). Pray about all things, not only when we are in need, or a life and death battle. Prayer is our preparation or our boot camp if you will, for the hardest times of our lives.

4. **He overcame by his death.** Samson's prayer ended with 'Let me die' (Judges 16:30). By his death, he defeated his enemies. Samson stretched out his arms one to a pillar, which formed the sign of a cross, and like Jesus, Samson would die, and like Christ, Samson would be victorious, through his death! Samson realized that to reap God's rewards, and one must live for God and be willing to die for Him as well! If Samson had chosen to die to his selfish desires and allow God to work through him earlier, it would not have come to this. But here in his last moments, Samson came to the end of self and died obeying the Lord instead of his selfish lusts. Choosing death to self-brought utter disaster to God's enemies. "So, the dead that he slew at his death were more than he slew in his life" (Ref. Judges 16:30). What a lesson for those in Christ! We, as Paul said, are to reckon ourselves as dead to sin and alive in Christ! (Ref. Galatians 2:20, Romans 6:6, 11)

God heard Samson's prayer. Samson gave his life. He helped to achieve God's purposes. He brought honor to God. As a result, God gave Samson a place among the elite men of faith (Hebrews 11:32). Christian, do you wish to find the only way to escape from being worldly? Jesus spoke to those who wanted to. He said: "Whoever desires to come after Me, let him deny himself, and take up his cross, and follow Me. (35) For whoever desires to save his life will lose it, but whoever loses his life for My sake and the Gospel's will save it" (Mark 8:34-35).

Samson learned this lesson the hard way, and we do not have to! Samson's life is a type of many Christians today – worldly, proud, arrogant, set in their path, believing that they can do anything because God's grace abounds. Samson's last days on earth, however, sounded the alarm. We must be alert to the ways of the enemy; be aware of the dangers associated with pride, frivolity, compromise, and worldliness. in the last days, terrible times will come, and compromise will become the norm. The Bible tells us that many will fall away from the faith and follow after their lusts and that the time will come when people will no longer put up with sound teaching, but according to their desires because they have itching ears, they will heap up for themselves teachers. They will turn their ears away from the truth and turn them aside to fables (2nd Timothy 4:3-4). Against these things, the Apostle Paul exhorts us to run the race of salvation with endurance, putting aside every weight and fixing our eyes on the Lord Jesus Christ.

> "And do this, knowing the time, that now it is high time to awake out of sleep; for now, our salvation is nearer than when we first believed. (12) The night is far spent; the day is at hand. Therefore, let us cast off the works of darkness and let us put on the armor of light. (13) Let us walk properly, as in the day, not in revelry and drunkenness, not in lewdness and lust, not in strife and envy. (14) But put on the Lord Jesus Christ, and make no provision for the flesh, to fulfill its lusts."
>
> Romans 13:11-14

Now you might think I have been a little hard on Samson. After all, he did make the 'hall of faith' (Hebrews 11:32). There are things that we should commend Sampson for, and the problem is that when we examine the life of Samson, what remains is the "what if" question.

What if – Samson demonstrated complete dedication to God? What if – Samson would not have been disobedient desiring the Philistine woman? What if, Samson did not break his Nazarite vow? What if, Samson would have never associated with Delilah? Etc. A.B. Simpson the founder of the <u>Christian and Missionary Alliance</u> expressed his thoughts about Samson life like this: Samson was "a marvelous example of what God might have done with a thoroughly separated man, and what self-indulgence and sin can do to hinder the glorious promise and the gracious purpose of God."

SAMSON — PART TWO: A PORTRAIT OF TODAY'S CHURCH

The story of Samson though historically factual vividly portrays symbolically, the problem that has raised its destructive head in the modern-day Church. When we look at the state of today's Church, we see a body of believers not sure of its calling, message, convictions, desire, family ties, or direction. We see a church with divided loyalties, a church walking the fence between God's true calling and the best methods to use to keep the Church productive. We see churches following any system that will achieve the wants, desires; pleasures, and actions or thought patterns that will accomplish the parishioner's vision for it, even if that means compromising their faith, calling or doctrines. The Church, like Samson, will soon experience a rude awakening if it does not alter its ways and come to grips with the specific reasons for its calling. The Church must start acting in harmony with the precepts demanded by the specific calling placed upon her.

Once we have discovered our God given calling, it becomes utterly imperative to act within the framework of that calling; anything more or less will weaken God's anointing upon that ministry. Imagine a Person called, trained, and equipped to be a sniper, but desires to practice medicine instead. He puts down his rifle and picks up a stethoscope. He opens up an office and starts treating patients. The catch is. he is not adequately trained, or equipped to be a doctor, nor is the blessing of God upon him to act in that manner. That is what happens when a man of God does not realize what his true calling is. Or when he decides not to operate within God's calling. How effective do you think he would be?

Ask yourself, would I want to be under this man's care if you desired to be at your best and healthiest? I think not.

Unfortunately, there are many well-meaning Christians who are following men just like this sniper/doctor hoping for the best. Many called men and women of God start out doing all they can for Christ when they should be letting Christ do all He can in them. They are unaware of His exact will for their lives, and with uncontrolled zeal, they err in their ministry path. A minister must know his precise calling! So, he can do what God has called him to do and nothing less. Know His will for your life before you go anywhere or do anything in His name. Remember the seven sons of Sceva who were trying to do God's work without knowing Christ or His calling (Ref. Acts 19:14-16). They failed miserably, and they ran away beaten, wounded, and humiliated. Losing to the devil's devices or schemes is what has happened to countless men and women of God who tried to do the work of God without knowing the direction or calling God has given them. Brethren, please do not add your name to that list. If you work within His calling, your effectiveness will be without measure. Remember, the world was changed immensely by only 12 men who knew Christ intimately and understood the specific work God told them to do (Acts 17:1-6), and they turned the world upside down (Ref. Acts 17:6).

On the other hand, when believers are only interested in getting by, or in how easy and cheep the effort and expense will be or are complacent because at this point and time things are going well, they do not need a minister of higher quality, calling or anointing. You know what I mean; they are delighted just to be sitting in the pew and hearing a quaint little sermon with no anointing or life-changing potential. They are not interested in getting to know Christ any better because they believe they have already received their "get out of Hades free card," and that's all they want anyway. A large number of believers just described, choose to watch over the House of God and do so with much worldly success, the problem with this is their churches are dead, spiritless and powerless. For too many believers will, for the most part, only choose a leader according to their desires, not the desires of God. They think they can gain the blessings of God with a minimum of inconvenience, cost, or effort. They do not want the annoyances of total commitment, and they will choose a leader who will give them the comfort that goes along with their fleshly likes and pleasures.

> "For the time will come when they will not endure sound doctrine; but after their own lusts shall they heap to themselves teachers, (4) having itching ears; And they shall turn away their ears from the truth, and shall be turned unto fables (5) but you be watchful in all things, endure afflictions, do the work of an evangelist, fulfill your ministry."
>
> 2nd Timothy 4:3-5

It is also true that many in the Body of Christ do not know how to tell the true blessing of God. Nor do they care if the Church they are attending is the correct one for them and their family. Many Christians do not care enough to discover these things because they are content and happy with the way things are. The Church fits their earthly standards, and they do not know, nor do they want to know Jesus intimately enough to ask Him and discover His will regarding their lives, their church home, their proper place of worship, nor, most importantly, their calling or ministry. Let me make this point more transparent, "every believer is called to ministry, in one form or another!" Do not forget it or dismiss it as untrue (Ref. 1st Peter 2:9). Lord, how many of us are languishing in a place where our true potential evades us, and our blessings are restricted due to lack of commitment. Oh God; help us find that commitment and discover our true calling, service and potential!

Consider this. What do you think will take place when the sniper slash doctor minister finds that his practice has no real power and is not flourishing? Might he use some gimmicks, advertising, or maybe some impure, perhaps deceptive methods to keep his practice going? Might he hire some professional with expertise in marketing? Look around at the Church today, really look and see if this is not the effforts used by many churches. . I could give you dozens of examples of well know "ministers" (I am using that term very loosely) use this exact formula. One well-known example is a world-recognized news agency discovering that a famous TV preacher, was, bringing the same person on stage in various states, praying for him and having him get out of a wheelchair claiming miraculous healing each time Why? To attract followers, that would attend his meetings, to buy his tapes his books, and increase his revenue. By the way, the man is still on TV despite the Revelation of his deception; because 'Tolerance' is in, 'truth' is out, and compromise is the name of the game! Brethren, this is why the Church is in-effective, and so ridiculed, and why people reject the salvation message. They do not see the real and genuine because what is fake overshadows it.

So, the question becomes, "What is our calling? Jesus, when asked by the scribes regarding the greatest commandment, Jesus said, "Thou shalt love the Lord your God with all your heart, and with all your soul, and with all your mind. Jesus added that this is the first and great commandment." But it is not the only one. Jesus continued by saying, "And the second is like it: 'You shall love your neighbor as yourself' On these two commandments hang all the Law and the Prophets" (Matthew 22:36-40). Do you notice what the center or foundation of both commandments is? Love! Love God – Love Man! He also said, "If you love me, keep my commandments" (John 14:15). In 1st John 3:18, we read, "let us not love in word or tongue, but in deed and truth." Genuinely loving God means honoring Him, and paying close attention to His desires and the truths expressed in His Word. The Bible warns, "Be doers of the word and not hearers only, deceiving yourselves." (James 1:22).

Let me make the answer to the question of "What is our calling" very simple. Our first calling (which includes all ministers and ministries) is to love God with all your heart, soul, mind, and strength, then love man second – both unconditionally! If we achieve that, there is no need for other commandments. The man that truly loves his neighbor will not plot or do harm against him; he will not injure nor defile his bed, nor rob or deceive, covet or steal from him. He will not damage his character or bear false testimony against him. But, on the contrary, the man who truly loves God will bestow upon him all the good he is capable of in the same manner as he wishes to receive, He will tell his neighbor about the way Christ demonstrated His love for him and why. He will lay down his life for him if necessary. Therefore, in true Godly love, we find the completion of all the Law. True Godly love eliminates the need for any Law.

If we can understand that, it is not hard to see what the most significant single problem was with Samson and is now with the modern-day Church. Their love for the Lord and other men is not with their whole heart, mind soul, and strength. Their love followed not after the Lord but after selfish desires, and their actions are indicative of their agenda. As a result of this, Samson, like the modern Church, is experiencing a significant loss of power. Again, Samson, just like the contemporary Church, did not do what God called him to do, and he went places where he was not supposed to go and acted in opposition to God's divine precepts. These actions resulted in his loss of power and accompanying signs, which was the ultimate evidence that the Lord was no longer with him. What is even the most disturbing thing of all is that he did not know that the Lord had left (Ref. Judges 16:20). I wonder how many of us even know that the Lord has left them or their Church?

Here comes a character test moment! Ask yourself, do you want to be the best Christian you can be? If the answer is a heartfelt yes and divine love and power is not evident in your life or Church, then should you not be searching for a group of believers that are demonstrating their faith in Christ properly? The cost, no matter if it is in dollars, distance, or church convenience, is inconsequential. Find that Church, plant yourself there, and if it does not have all the aspects you need, work to develop them. Do not be like many in this latter-day who "have a form of godliness, but deny the power of it; even turn away from these. (6) For of these are those creeping into houses and leading silly women captive, the ones having been heaped with sins, being led away by various lusts, (7) always learning, but never being able to come to a full knowledge of the truth." (2nd Timothy 3:5-7).

Have you ever asked yourself, "What exactly does 'have a form of godliness, but deny the power of it' really mean?" Could "have a form of godliness" be referring to the people who profess religion, who are in some way connected to the Church, and who are zealous in maintaining "a form of religion?" Samson demonstrated this same "form of religion." Samson was a man who was known for his calling and God's anointing; he professed to do the work of the Lord but lived a life that denied

God's power and influence. Remember claiming that his strength was in his uncut hair (Judges 16:17), and not in his Nazarite commitment to the Lord God of Israel. Are you known as a Christian because of your church affiliation or because of Christ in you?

There is no doubt that the same apostasy that existed in Samson's Day still existed in the Church of the first century. We know this by Paul's reference to it in 2nd Thessalonians 2 and 1st Timothy 4. Take note of all the actions listed in these two chapters that were part of the apostate way of life. These actions will also manifest again just before the coming of the Lord Jesus Christ. The first-century apostate church practiced many of these actions but tolerated them, the same as our modern-day Church. All that remains unfulfilled on the list given in these chapters is the revealing of the "son of perdition" the "man of sin," whom many scholars believe is alive and living somewhere on the earth today.

> MANY CALLED MEN AND WOMEN OF GOD START OUT DOING ALL THEY CAN FOR CHRIST WHEN THEY SHOULD BE LETTING CHRIST DO ALL HE CAN IN THEM.

But what about denying the power thereof – it means to be in opposition to the real power of God; by not allowing it to exert any influence in one's life. It imposes no restraint on passions and carnal activity. It means, except in the form of religion, living one's life as if there were no restraints. Living without constraints is common in the world and the Church. The most common aspect of those who adhere to this "form of religion" is that they demonstrate no evidence that there is any true piety in their heart, or that a genuine relationship with God has any actual control over their souls. It is much easier for people to observe forms of religion than it is to bring the heart under God's controlling influence.

The reason I have full confidence in this hardline is because of the question Jesus asked his disciples, "When the Son of man comes (referring to His second coming), will He find faith on the earth" (Luke 18:8)? Remember, miraculous signs will follow them that believe (Ref. Matthew 16:17)! This question in Luke 18:8 Jesus asked under the backdrop of His upcoming death. In Luke 18, we have one parable, illustrating the need of continual dependence (The Parable of the

Persistent Widow) upon God, and another related to the conditions of our acceptance by God (The rich young ruler). Sometimes do you not wonder just how dependent on the mercy of God you are? What a fatal choice the rich young ruler made. He failed to see that the One calling him to a full surrender of his soul and substance was the One, who, although a king, became a servant, and who being rich – became poor. Is there anything keeping you back from completely surrendering to Christ? Get rid of it right now!

With the shadow of the cross darkening the path of the Lord Jesus, we find Him solemnly warning His disciples of the upcoming trials. They, just as we, must expect to share the same bitter cup. To many of us who wish to know Him in the power of His resurrection, must first know him in the fellowship of His suffering's, by conforming to His death (Ref. Philippians 3:10-11). We pray, "Oh God give me the power;" but we do not want the sufferings. The error in this is that it does not work that way. It did not work for Samson; it did not work for any of the men of faith, nor will it work for us. Again, this is another reason why the modern Church, for the most part, is so weak and powerless. They do not want the sufferings, and as a result, they will not get the power. Worldly compromise and gimmicks have now replaced the real power of God in most of the church world.

Brethren, do not be amazed by this hardline – Paul warned Timothy of this "Gospel compromise" becoming prevalent in the last days, as did Peter and Jesus Himself.

> "The Spirit clearly says that in later times some will abandon the faith and follow deceiving spirits and things taught by demons... (3) For the time will come when they will not endure sound doctrine, but according to their desires, because they have itching ears, they will heap up for themselves teachers; (4), and they will turn their ears away from the truth, and be turned aside to fables."
>
> 2nd Timothy 4:1, 3-4

"Knowing this first: that scoffers will come in the last days, walking according to their lusts, (4) and saying, "Where is the promise of His coming? For since the fathers fell asleep, all things continue as they were from the beginning of creation."

2nd Peter 3:3-4

"Then they will deliver you up to tribulation and kill you, and all nations will hate you for My name's sake. (10) And then many will be offended, will betray one another, and will hate one another. (11) Then many false prophets will arise and deceive many. (12) And because lawlessness will abound, the love of many will grow cold."

Matthew 24:9-12

As already shown, Samson is an Old Testament symbol of the modern-day Church living in a state of "Gospel complacency." Sampson was living apart from any control of the Spirit of God. We (the Church) like Sampson, are to be the shining light in these final dark days of history. We are to be the great champion of freedom. We, like Samson, are to perform many feats of heroic strength that no man can equal. We are to be the mighty, invincible force that conquers all enemies of the cross. But we, again like Samson, have lost touch with our source of strength. Just as God cut Sampson off, so are we. Some might say it was a result of Delilah having his hair cut. I beg to differ; the cutting of his hair only illustrated a much deeper problem. God had spiritually cut him off long before the loss of his hair. Samson should never have been involved with pagan women, especially Delilah. God had told Israel to stay away from foreign women because He wanted Israel to be pure and holy, set apart for Him, for only through Him total peace and joy would come. But Samson rejected God's Law and His will for his life. The cutting of his hair dramatically illustrated that he had separated himself from the Lord earlier, and the most alarming fact is that he didn't even know it (Ref. Judges 16:20). And regrettably, so it is with us. We have intermarried with the impure, unequal, and unholy. We have rejected many of God's Law and compromised His precepts. We have convinced ourselves that a loving God did not mean a lot of what He said, or that the Bible is not God's truth, but much of it is allegorical. We want to believe that all it contains is out of date moral rules contained within fables that do not apply in modern times. Therefore, we pick and choose what we want to believe based on our convenience; and as a result, we like Samson do not realize that the Lord is far from us, and we often do not even know it! Ask yourself, where is the Gospel's world-changing power? Is God's power evident in our lives and the life of the Church? If not, is it not time to turn back to following Christ and all his ways without compromise or question?

Do we not see compromise and alliances with the Philistine (unbelievers) enemy today? Of course, we do! Be aware of these compromises because they will lead to a one-world religion. The alliances the Church is making today are leading the way to a compromised, worldly, end time 'religion' which holds vague concepts of 'God' without the power of Jesus' victory on the cross. 'Tolerance' is in, 'truth' is out! Is a sin with enormous proportions and devastating consequences.

> "But know this, that in the last days perilous times will come: (2) For men will be lovers of themselves, lovers of money, boasters, proud, blasphemers, disobedient to parents, unthankful, unholy, (3) unloving, unforgiving, slanderers, without self-control, brutal, despisers of good, (4) traitors, headstrong, haughty, lovers of pleasure rather than lovers of God, (5) having a form of godliness but denying its power. And from such people turn away! (6) For of this sort are those who creep into households and make captives of gullible women loaded down with sins, led away by various lusts, (7) always learning and never able to come to the knowledge of the truth."
>
> 2nd Timothy 3:1-7

Do not these verses accurately describe the world around us, and many Christians we know? This writer's purpose is not to demean you, your Christian friends, or the universal Church. It is, however, to open your eyes and make you think about some things that can and will change your life for the better and make you a more powerful, active, and loving representative of Christ. If we are living in the "last days," is not this passage in 2nd Timothy 3:1-7 an accurate description of our world and the Church? Can't you see God gave us this verse as a warning for us to see, and God wants us to have more than Gospel complacency and compromise? If you believe that the Church is right where it is supposed to be, doing what it is to do, then this chapter will not be of concern to you. So, skip it! If, however, you believe that God wants to do much more with His children, than take heed to what you have read and continue reading. Perhaps you will pick up a tip or two that will help change and increase your role in God's army in these last days.

If you have decided to read further, then the question becomes not whether the universal and institutional Church is good, bad, or indifferent, or whether or not there are real Christians in those churches! The question is, will you be able to adhere to your faith when the great falling away and apostasy hits? Or should you be doing something today so that you are ready for what will become much more devoid of hope and fruitless in the near future (Ref. 2nd Thessalonians 2:1-4)? End-time prophecies run throughout the Bible, and they conclude in the Book of Revelation, which was a letter written specifically to seven churches in Asia and preserved for people of all ages. God recorded and preserved the warnings given to the seven churches for the benefit of all who read them. Seven times in Revelation 2 and 3, we hear the same warnings: (the number seven in Scripture symbolizes completeness or perfection); "He, who has an ear, let him hear what the Spirit is saying to the churches." These warnings are not agreeable to the ears. They are challenging, 'to say the least" Christian believers need to expand their comfort zone and ask hard questions that require hard solutions and situational actions that would produce change. The Bible tells us that in the last days, many Christians will fall away from the faith, which begs the questions, what should we do so that truth does not include me? What should we do to stand firm in Christ? What should we do to enhance our relationship with Christ, other Christians, and other Churches? Does God have something better for me? Is He leading me in to do things that may be different than what I have been doing? What will conditions be like in the last days for the "end time" Christian, and do I have the faith to hold on to Christ through it?

You want the answers to these questions; Then you need to hear the voice of Christ and do what He tells you to do. Study to show thyself approved unto God; meditate upon His word at all times, carry it with you, and most importantly live by it. Why? Because Jesus is the answer to these questions and many more! The stakes are extremely high, your life and the lives of all those you love are in the balance. Many, even the elect, will be deceived. There will be a great falling away – not *"might be"* a great falling away. OH, No! There *"will be"* a great falling away, brother will turn against brother and mother against daughter, and they will give up those they love to the religious leaders thinking they are doing God a favor (Ref. Matthew 10:21). No matter what you believe or how much you pray for this not to happen, it will most assuredly happen! It is God's word. God's word is the truth, and every jot and title are truth.

Scripture has already confirmed that there will be a great falling away in the "last days." According to Bible prophecy, there will be signs that will make us aware of the upcoming "Gospel compromise." Refer again to 2nd Timothy 3:1-7 and the book of Revelation, chapter 2 and 3. The signs found in Timothy and the letters recorded in these two chapters of Revelation reveal signs, attitudes, and actions attributed to the great falling away. Generally speaking, most Christians today demonstrate these signs, attitudes, and actions found in one or more of these seven churches, and the warnings listed by these seven churches describe the state of our modern-day universal Church. These seven letters represent the Lord's evaluation of the condition of His Church, both from a historical and contemporary point of view. The Lord gives us a grave warning repeated seven times in Revelation chapters 2 and 3. The warning is, "He, who has an ear, let him hear what the Spirit is saying to the church." (Ref Revelation 2:7. 2:11, 2:17, 2:29, 3:6, 3:13, 3:22,13:9 If anyone Has an ear let him hear. Let us take a few minutes to find out what these letters tell us about the condition of the Church today?

We know from reading Revelation 2:1 that Jesus is walking among the churches. Is there anyone that would disagree that this is also the case today? Of course not; it would be the correct response from anyone with an objective evaluation. Let us notice what Jesus is telling these churches, which again represent the actual state of those churches as well as the contemporary state of today's Church. The Lord presents to each Church four aspects of their condition.

1. A commendation (the things they have done well)
2. A criticism (things he finds wrong with them)
3. Instruction or exhortation (to do something about it)
4. A promise for each Church (blessings brought forth by obedience)

Notice when you read Revelation 2 and 3 that there is a remnant of overcomers in each Church. This remnant shows us that no matter how bad their condition or the condition of the world around them, some small remnant will continue to obey God and God will preserve that remnant

There are a few more exciting things to note about these churches. In two of the churches, Ephesus and Pergamos, God brings up the Nicolaitans and says that he hates their deeds. The Nicolaitans were a religious sect that committed condemned acts. Refer Revelation 2:6, 15. They were almost identical, with those that held to the doctrine of Balaam. Their beliefs were:

➤ Characterized by covetousness
➤ Involved in the perversion of Grace – salvation by Grace plus works
➤ Fleshly in nature
➤ Exalting their followers and diminishing God's authority
➤ Presumptuous and arrogant especially regarding the powers of darkness
➤ A pick and choose group who chose what Scriptural warnings to adhere to
➤ Like sounding brass and tinkling cymbals, they are without any discernable influence
➤ A group who lacked the fruit of the Spirit
➤ Sensual in nature attracting those who so desire it
➤ Boastful

> ➤ Pandering to people's wants, desires, and egos
> ➤ A clergy not under submission to the Lord but submitted only to the laity

As a whole, the comments and criticisms given to each Church are the same regarding churches throughout history. But there is no other church that so epitomizes the Western Church of the last days than Laodicea. They were busy doing the works of the Lord. They think everything was great. They are materially wealthy and in need of nothing. You ask them how they are doing, and they tell you fantastic. God is good. Everything is wonderful, and the Church is bursting at the seams. Their finances are all in order, and they are so happy, just like their T-Shirts, bumper stickers, and Christian music declares. Many modern churches are clueless, just like that of Laodicea.

They are so blind that they can't even see they are naked. And worst of all, notice where Jesus is in regard to this church. He is outside the Church (Revelation 3:20), knocking on the door trying to come in. Jesus is unimportant and uninvolved, banished, and unwanted. He is outside the building. His name is a marketable commodity used to attract members.

How could this possibly happen? In a vain attempt to continue, it compromised its stance against sin, which produced a lack of commitment. Like Samson, the Church has become very worldly. They now provide the same type of music, weaker messages; they have much more tolerance, more inadequate standards of conduct, create unwise and forbidden alliances, etc. Think about it. Does not this illustrate Samson's life? He was a Nazarite, separated, and consecrated to the Lord. His God-ordained calling was for bringing freedom to an oppressed people. God gave divine power and special weapons to Samson to fight with (e.g., a jawbone of a donkey) and, when used under the anointing of God, destroyed the enemy no matter the enemies' power and number.

Is this not a perfect description of the calling Placed on God's universal Church? Samson, however, lusted after that which God did not permit, a Philistine woman and also a prostitute (Judges 16:1-4). He directly disobeyed his father; he compromised his faith and placed the Lord outside of his thoughts, and he ignored the Lord's precepts. The evil association with Philistine women ended up with Sampson's losing his eyes and his ultimate demise under the deceptive hand of Delilah. Will that be the Church's future as well? Or has it already started? Can the modern-day universal Church truly see what true sin is? Or do they care what it is! Can you honestly say that the abundance of churches of today are alive and full of life? If you think they are, it is your blinded eyes that you are using. There is no way! If you disagree, take note of their lack of influence and respect in the world today that the Church possesses.

Looking at Judges 16:5, we see the words of the enemy. As you read them, keep them in mind because they show Satan's intent regarding God's children. "And the lords of the Philistines came up to her and said to her, "Entice him, and find out where his great strength lies, and by what means we may overpower him, that we may bind him to afflict him; and every one of us will give you eleven hundred pieces of silver." (Ref Judges 16:5)

Samson's alliance with Delilah was the trap sprung by his enemy to strip Samson of his strength. Our enemy 'Delilah' (Satan) uses the same tactics today to strip the Church of its power, by using "Gospel compromise," worldly alliances, and false religion. The enemy's tactics and objective has never changed. Why should it? For as long as the Church has been around, these tactics have been extremely effective in obtaining Satan's objective. Hopefully, God's people will start to recognize this evil strategy and stand firm against its influences.

There is no place in this story of Samson and Delilah that Delilah was at all subtle. She came right out and asked Samson for a way to destroy him. When she thought he had told her, she blatantly demonstrated her intent. Samson found himself tied up and warned of an upcoming attack by the Philistines in precisely the manner he revealed to Delilah. Brethren, this happened not once, but four times. The fourth time he told her the truth, and the philistines subdued and imprisoned the man of God. You would think that Samson would see that she was trying to harm him after the first time. I am sure that some of you might come up with some excellent reasons why Samson allowed this to happen like maybe he was love blind, or maybe Samson wasn't the sharpest tack in the box! But I believe it was the pride and arrogance of Samson that made him think he could play with the enemy and go unharmed. Samson's self-confidence and pride in his strength caused him to believe that he would go out and shake the Philistines off like he had previously. He didn't even know that his power was gone or even worse that the Lord who gave him that strength had left Him. In like manner, the Laodicea church, in their pride, made decisions that blinded them to their lack of spiritual power and wellbeing. Nor did they see that they had cast Jesus outside of the Church.

With the strength of the Lord gone, Samson was at the mercy of his enemies. And compassion is not big on the enemy's agenda. They put out his eyes, Samson became a slave, forced to do work for the enemy. I don't want to push the analogy too far, but it is worth noting that the Church of Laodicea is referred to as blind, having departed from their commitment to Jesus (Ref. Revelation 3:17). She has lost her ability to see or discern anything spiritually! Now no one ever starts with the intention of losing their strength and sight, physical and spiritual. Samson certainly did not, but it is, nevertheless, the inevitable result of worldly compromise. By the way, notice who was getting the praise for Samson's capture and his physical condition according to Judges 16:26-29. Not the one true God, but Dagon, a false Philistine god. When God's Church tries to compromise its beliefs, it becomes like the world, and it is the world's gods that get the praise, while dishonor falls upon Christ, our Lord.

So, is there hope? Of course, there is! During his time of captivity and obvious remorse and repentance, God's Grace came upon him – Samson's hair started to grow again, but first, it involved him getting back to the first principles of his calling. According to Judges 16:28, after Samson came before all his enemies so that they could make sport of him – Samson prayed. "O Lord GOD, remember me, I pray! Strengthen me; I pray, just this once, O God that I may with one blow take vengeance on the Philistines for my two eyes!" (Ref Judges 16:29) And Samson took hold of the two middle pillars which supported the temple, and he braced himself against them, one on his right and the other on his left." God seeing Samson's repentant heart endued Samson with power once again, and Samson was victorious, this time in his death!

Samson finally learned the ultimate lesson, and so must we. To succeed in Christ and our calling, we must die to ourselves and let Christ live through us. Paul put it this way: "I have been crucified with Christ; it is no longer I who live, but Christ lives in me; and the life which I now live in the flesh I live by faith in the Son of God, who loved me and gave Himself for me" (Galatians 2:20).

Finally, Samson was willing to die and again, so must we! Of course, it didn't have to cost him his life. If Samson had chosen to die to his selfish desires and allow God to work through him earlier, it wouldn't have come to this. But in Samson's last hour, he came to the end of his arrogance and pride and gave himself wholly unto the Lord's will. Samson died, true enough. But what this shows us is that all our choices good and bad carry with them consequences we must face. But Samson's died obeying the Lord instead of his selfish lusts, and his decision received honorable mention in the Hebrew "Hall of faith." What a lesson for those in Christ! Christians, as Paul said, are to "reckon themselves to be dead indeed to sin, but alive to God in Christ Jesus our Lord" (Romans 6:6, 11)

Samson is a wake-up call for the modern-day Church. It is a call to be alert to the ways of the enemy, especially in these last days. For it is a call against compromise and worldliness. We know that in the last days difficult times will come and many will fall away from the faith and follow after their lusts. We also know that a time will come when people will no longer adhere to sound teaching. And because of these things, the Apostle Paul exhorts us to run the race with endurance, fixing our eyes on the Lord Jesus Christ. Let us remain faithful to His word, even if others turn away, and upon His return, those that endure to the end will hear those precious and envied words "well done my good and faithful servant." (Ref. Matthew 25:23; Luke 19:17).

In conclusion, let me share with you some further insights into the life and death of this man of God, which in turn can directly influence the modern Church.

1. **In Samson, we see the danger of being a loner**. Everything Samson did, he did alone. He judged Israel for 20 years and never sought help from others, nor did he ask it. "Though one

may be overpowered by another, two can withstand him. And a threefold cord is not easily broken" (Ecclesiastics 4:12). not forsaking the assembling of ourselves together, as is the manner of some, but exhorting one another, and so much the more as you see the Day approaching (Hebrews 10:25)

2. **In Samson, we see the danger of not being aware of underestimating our sinfulness.** Samson figured he had things under control regarding his fleshly lusts, but his desire for wrong associates, love, romance, and sex led directly to his destruction. Samson was the great conqueror who never allowed God to conquer him. "Pride goes before destruction, and a haughty spirit before a fall" (Proverbs 16:18).

3. **Samson's pride and arrogance deceived him into thinking that he could keep going back to tempting and dangerous places.** Just about every time he went to the land of the Philistines, he fell into moral compromise. He should have been aware of this danger because of his knowledge of God's commands and have at least learned from his first experience. Instead of putting himself in tempting and dangerous situations, he should have fled from youthful lusts (Ref. 2nd Timothy 2:22) like Joseph did (Genesis 39:12). His relationship with Delilah should never have developed. But he, instead of breaking his illicit relationship with Delilah, he allowed this relationship to destroy him. Read Hebrews 11:24-26.

4. **His last and most significant victory over God's enemies came after he became broken, humiliated, and blind.** He could no longer look to himself but had to look to the Lord. Before this, we don't see Samson as a man of prayer, but here only for the second time, do we see him praying. We must pray without ceasing (Ref. 1st Thessalonians 5:17). Know what you are and who Christ truly is!

5. **Samson is a compelling picture of wasted potential.** He could have been and should have been one of the greatest men of God in the Old Testament, but he wasted his potential through "Gospel compromise." Do not let this happen to you! "Abide in Me, and I in you. As the branch cannot bear fruit of itself, unless

it abides in the vine, neither can you, unless you abide in Me. (5) "I am the vine, and you are the branches. He who abides in Me, and I in him, bears much fruit; for without Me, you can do nothing. (6) If anyone does not abide in Me, he is cast out as a branch and is withered; and they gather them and throw them into the fire, and they are burned" (John 15:4-6). Does this not describe the life of Samson? Does it not also describe the experience of much of today's Church as well?

ELI – A MAN OF GOD WHOSE PRIORITIES WERE OUT OF ORDER

E li, a man whose name means "The Lord is exalted" or "My God," was a descendant of Ithamar, the fourth and youngest son of Aaron the High Priest. He was a kind man by nature, and was beloved and highly respected by all who looked to him for spiritual guidance. He was the High Priest at Shiloh, where the Ark of the Covenant rested in the Sanctuary. It was at Shiloh where Eli made his residence, and therefore Shiloh became the center of Jewish religious life. He was the first man to serve both as High priest and judge of Israel at the same time. At the age of fifty-eight, Eli became judge of Israel right after the death of Samson in the year 2830-31BC approximately. He held this office for forty years, until his death at the age of 98 (1ˢᵗ Samuel 4:18).

There are few Biblical characters in whose character we cannot find some great and glaring fault. There is usually a spot or wrinkle of some kind in everyone; however, for the most part, Eli was a good man whose life was pure and righteous. His character was one of distinguished piety, seen by his meek submission to God's divine judgment upon him and his sons (1ˢᵗ Samuel 3:18), and in his supreme regard for the Ark of God (1ˢᵗ Samuel 4:18). Eli was a highly respected member of the priesthood.

The first mention of Eli in the Bible is when Hannah came into the Sanctuary praying for a son. Hannah was the wife of a prominent Levite, Elkanah. She had been childless for many years and vowed that if God blessed her with a son, she would consecrate him to the service of God all his life. As the woman was silently praying, Eli saw her lips moving and mistook her as intoxicated and questioned her piety. Notice Eli was a man who was zealous for the things of God and severe in his criticism of those who broke the commandments of God. Notice the attitude in which Eli reproved Hannah, who he thought was drunk, "How long will you be drunk? Put your wine away from you!"

Perhaps in Israel's time of apostasy it was not a strange thing to see drunken women at the door of the tabernacle, Eli could easily have suspected Hannah to be one of them. When sin is so prevalent and permeates every aspect of society, it would not be uncommon to see sin in everyone. Look around, and you will see and feel the same conditions today. Suspecting sin in Hannah was Eli's mistake; he judged the situation without knowing the facts. His attitude towards Hannah should have been one of observation and the gathering of information. If his own eyes had already become dim, he should have asked those about him to investigate the matter. His error became worse because he was the priest of the Lord, who should have had compassion on the ignorant (Ref. Hebrews 5:2). Eli's mistake in believing people guilty and expecting sin in everyone brings reproach on those so accused and their accusers. Love commands us to look for the best in everyone, and it forbids us from thinking evil toward anyone. In contrast, Eli's lack of this same zealousness in reproving his sons was a major character flaw. Eli's leniency towards his sons, not only as their father but as the high priest of Israel, resulted in sorrow in his declining years, for it forced God to kill Eli's two sons and Eli for bringing religious indifference in Israel.

Hannah, on the other hand, humbly explained to Eli that she was not drunk; she was silently praying to God for a son. Eli seeing the truth and knowing that he had erred expressed his prayerful wish that God would grant her heart's desire. God honored Eli's request and Hannah's. Within a year, she gave birth to a son, and she named him Samuel, who became a great prophet and Eli's successor as judge.

After weaning Samuel Hannah stayed true to her promise, she took Samuel to Shiloh, where she turned him over to Eli, who brought him up in the service of the Lord (1st Samuel 1:24-28). Hannah's presentation of Samuel to Eli begs a very intriguing question. Why would Hannah present her first-born son to Eli for the service of the Lord, knowing that Eli's reputation as a father figure was extremely questionable due to his two sons who were known to be extremely corrupt and evil? The answer lies in who the vow was made. Notice:

> Then she made a vow and said, "O Lord of hosts, if You (the Lord) will indeed look on the affliction of Your maidservant and remember me, and not forget Your maidservant, but will give Your maidservant a male child, then I will give him to the Lord all the days of his life, and no razor shall come upon his head."
>
> 1st Samuel 1:11

The vow was to the Lord nit eli. Hannah gave her greatest treasure, her most sought-after prize to God, and that treasure was her son, Samuel. Even though she loved him with all her heart and soul, she had promised to give him to God. What is your greatest treasure? Are you willing to lay it down and give it to God? How about your loved ones? Are you ready to give all you are and have to God? Do you remember what Jesus said? "For where your treasure is, there your heart will be also" (Matthew 6:21). Hannah and Elkanah were devout God-fearing parents. Hophni and Phinehas, Eli's sons, were wicked. They abused the people who came to worship the Lord at Shiloh. For Elkanah to go up year after year to worship the Lord, knowing that Eli's sons were likely to be abusive is a testament of his devotion to God demonstrated his faith and dedication to the Lord Jehovah. Hannah was the same in her commitment. She, despite knowing the reputation of Eli's son and Eli's obvious error in raising them, still fulfilled her vow to God. She offered Samuel to God for a lifetime of service, believing with all her heart that despite being under the supervision and direction of Eli, God was still in control. Why; because she knew God as faithful and true; She knew Him as El-Berith, the "God of Covenants." She knew the Lord was trustworthy, for she experienced what the Lord God had done in her own life.

When we seek the Lord to help us in spite of outward circumstances, all those that come against us, and all fear, doubt, worry, and depression, we too will find that our hearts rejoice in the Lord. Hannah said in 1st Smuel 2:1 that her "horn is exalted in the Lord. I smile at my enemies because I rejoice in Your salvation." A "horn" is a symbol of strength. Before seeking the Lord, Hannah was anything but strong. She was bitter in her soul. She couldn't eat; her husband brought her no joy. Even the church had let her down. Not so the Lord! In Him, she found comfort and strength. In Jehovah, Hannah found the answer to her spiritual emptiness. She gained victory over her enemies and joy in His presence. She knew, perhaps for the first time, the Holiness of the Lord and discovered that there is no one like Him. Immoveable, immutable, her Rock, Jehovah Shalom, her God of peace, and this knowledge convinced her to fulfill her vow without fear or doubt. She knew that God would raise Samuel to be a faithful and true servant of God.

God's grace toward Hannah was the fulfillment of Her vow to the lord as well as toward Eli. God knowing Eli's sin and failures regarding his two sons Hophni and Phinehas, gave Eli a chance to make amends. In his old age, he was to raise Samuel in the fear and admonition of the Lord. Eli took this opportunity wholeheartedly and with dedication and determination, and he succeeded! Under Eli's guidance, Samuel grew up in a pure religious atmosphere and soon showed himself a worthy pupil. Young Samuel faithfully followed Eli's instructions. Eli was prouder of him than of his own two sons who, unfortunately, did not follow in their father's footsteps. Eli's two sons served as priests, even though they were worthless men (1st Samuel 2:12). When they offered the sacrifices to God, rather than taking their authorized share of the offering, they took as much as they wanted (1st Samuel 2:13-14; cf. Leviticus 7:29-34). Also, they showed their utter contempt for the priesthood and God Himself by taking this portion before it became a sweet odor to God (1st Samuel 2:15; cf. Leviticus 3:3-5, 16). This contempt carried over to the Tabernacle of Jehovah as well, for they committed adultry with the temple prostitutes working in the Temple (1st Samuel 2:22).

By taking advantage of their privileged position through bribery, corruption, and sexual promiscuity Hophni and Phinehas dishonored the priesthood in the eyes of the masses; consequently, the people despised the offerings which they made to God (1st Samuel 2:17), and their faith in the priesthood. The conduct of these men brought the worship of the Lord into disrespect and scorn. The young Samuel, on the other hand, was a man after God's own heart; he was faithful, just, and extremely virtuous; he never allowed one word from his mouth to "fall to the ground," which is a metaphor for "not one word of his mouth was worthless" (1st Samuel 3:19). And due to his character, "all Israel from Dan to Beersheba knew that Samuel had been established as a prophet of the Lord" (1st Samuel 3:20).

1st Samuel 2:22 tells us that "Eli was very old, and that he had heard everything his sons did to all Israel…" Eli, therefore, rebuked his sons, but not strong enough, for they did not change their ways. He did not discipline them with the severity that their evil deeds merited. He should have not only exercised the stern authority of fatherhood but also rebuked them as the High Priest and judge of Israel. Their actions warranted immediate dismissal of their duties and banishment from the priesthood. Instead, Eli only mildly reasoned with his sons saying: "Why do you do such things?" (Ref. 1st Samuel 2:23) What he should have said was something like, "Your actions are shameful, scandalous and blasphemous, and they must stop. Your actions bring dishonor and scorn to God, our people, and the priesthood; therefore, you are dismissed from your office as Priests of the Most-High God until your evil ways cease!" But he did not! The lack of authority used toward his sons, whether it is because he loved them or because he feared them more than he did God, brought dishonor and ridicule upon God and His priesthood. Eli's sons disregarded this weak and fruitless protest, for their hearts were cold and callous, and their disregard for their father showed that they no longer respected him or his divine position.

Eli, as high priest and judge over Israel, was in a position of authority and responsibility for the worship which He offered to God. He should have dismissed his sons as priests, but instead, he continued to let them serve, "he did not restrain them" (1st Samuel 3:13). He wanted to be kind to them, but it was a false and mistaken kindness. A sharp rebuke and corrective actions would have saved them from ruin. Eli had only to be firm and resolute in his corrective actions. As a result of Eli's weakness of conviction, his rebukes fell on deaf ears, and as a result, "the Lord desired to kill Eli's sons (Hophni and Phinehas)" (1st Samuel 2:25).

Brethren how true this is of most Christians in their efforts to be a witness. We are the epistle written in our hearts, known and read by all men." (2nd Corinthians 3:2). In other words, "Actions speak loader than

words,[2]" especially in the things of God. How often does our witness for
Christ fall on deaf ears because our convictions are weak, our lifestyles
do not reflect God's glory or holiness, or we do not take the commands
given by God seriously and let evil things go unchallenged. The Bible
tells us that all scripture is for reproof and correction (2nd Timothy 3:16).
This verse is not only speaking of our reproof and correction but that it
reproves and corrects all who hear it. How are they going to hear and,
therefore, be capable of reproof and correction, if we do not tell them
(Romans 10:15)?

I am afraid that many of us are guilty; in the same way, Eli was, for
lacking the moral fiber to withstand sin, to reprove and correct those
who are doing evil. Here are some areas in which we sin similar to that
of Eli and many of us I'm sure are not even aware that we are guilty of
doing them:

1. **We lack righteous anger toward sin.** We have become
   guiltless as a people. We allow doctrines that depart from the
   truth to go unchecked rather than to stand against them. As
   we have just seen, it is a sin not to withstand evil. Look around
   you. The American people tolerate the Gay Rights Movement
   and the endorsement of lesbians as priests, and Abortion.
   We seldom support the people who openly oppose them. For
   example, our church brethren kept silent while the Supreme
   Court debated Roe vs. Wade making nothing more than
   minor weak protests, and we all know the result of that lack
   of righteous anger. And many modern church organizations
   are now supporting and accepting Gay ministers as well as the
   right of women to murder an unborn child. Many churches
   are now tolerating men who preach another Gospel but cannot
   tolerate the men who stand opposed to these false teachers.
   They accept a watered-down and liberal Gospel but walk away
   from the truth that convicts them of sin. They are willing
   to receive the promised blessings of the Gospel, primarily
   financial, but at the same time dismiss the effort and cost
   that goes along with receiving them. We need to wake up to
   the fact that we are becoming more and more susceptible to a

"peace and prosperity " approach toward the Gospel. We lack the stomach for a fight and the backbone to withstand the advances of sin. In other words, 'Tolerance' is in, 'affirmative actions for God's truth' is out.

2. **We do not honor the Lord first.** Eli also sinned in that he did not remove his sons as priests; he honored them above God. Similarly, some parents honor their children above God. I have seen cases precisely like this where the reaction of the parents was to bad-mouth the elders and quit attending services in defense of the evil their children do. For example, just last week, my daughter, who teaches at a Christian school called being upset that the parents of one of her students who she caught cheating on an exam, came into class. In front of the other students, teachers and the principle cursed her out for writing their daughter a reprimand. The parents proceeded to rip up the reprimand, pulled the child out of school, and have not returned to the school or church since. They told the elders and the pastor that they decided that the school and the church were not right for their family. It was later the school found out that after the parents tried several other schools and churches, none of which were satisfactory, they ended up homeschooling the child.

3. **We fail to discipline sin properly.** Modern psychiatry has tainted us with the philosophy that teaches us that restraining our children in what they wish to do causes them to grow up inhibited. Consequently, we see children of Christians parents who disrespect anyone or thing that they consider to be unpleasant; they talk back to their parents or otherwise act any way they please. Parents who do not discipline their children are as guilty of sin before God as their children and more so. Proverbs 15:9-10 tells us that

"The way of the wicked is an abomination to the Lord, but He loves him who follows righteousness. (10) Harsh discipline is for him who forsakes the way, and he who hates correction will die." And that "the rod and rebuke give wisdom, but a child left to himself brings shame to his mother."

(Proverbs 29:15)

4. **We fail to bring up a child in the way he must go** (Proverbs 22:6). By committing to parents, the training of their children, God has given them the ability to form their future character, and He will hold the parents responsible for the influence their children exert. As Abraham trained up his children, in the way of the Lord, in the paths of justice and judgment, so should we. Train them up, not in the way they want to go "For the heart is deceitful above all things, and desperately wicked; who can know it" (Jeremiah 17:9)? But in the way, they should go! Train them in the way in which, if you love them, you would have them go. Train them in ways for their profit and advantage. Parents have to bring those who are under their care up in the nurture and admonition of the Lord (Ephesians 6:4).

But how do we do this in the face of today's constant and uncompromising liberalism; when for six to eight hours a day, our children are taught values that are in direct opposition to Biblical principles? Being the father of 4 children, I freely admit it is not easy; in fact, it is almost impossible, note the word almost. But with God, all things are possible (Ref. Matthew 19:26; Mark 10:27). But let us remember that "greater is He that is in me than he that is in the world" (1st John 4:4). School, peer pressure, and worldly friends have only limited time with our children. We have the majority of it. Therefore, we must pray with them and for them, bring them up under grace, and the ministry of the word and prayer. Instruct them on how to develop a personal relationship with God, teach them their duty to God and man, and, most importantly, set for our children good examples of a holy life with holy actions and conversation. Teach them according to their understanding and maturity so that they can receive the instructions given them. Why? Because if you train them properly, "when your child is old, he will not depart from it" (Proverbs 22:6). There might be, at least for a time, some exceptions to the rule, but God's word is truth, it cannot be wrong. For where there is proper education on what is morally right and wrong, those taught will not easily forget, nor will the Godly principles wear off. Men ordinarily do not forsake the good they have experienced and depart to evil. When children have matured, their hearts, once adequately seasoned with the grace of God, are more likely to put to practice that which they understood and experienced as a child.

Properly raising his children in the ways of the Lord is where Eli failed, and as a result of this failure, God looked down on Eli's actions and proceeded to send a "man of God" to Eli. Eli's sin was that he had honored his sons above the Lord, (1st Samuel 2:29) because he did not stand for God and rebuke his sons (1st Samuel 3:13). Since Eli was in a position to remove his sons from serving as priests, he sinned because he did not stand up for God and against his son's actions and remove them from their office as priests. He lacked the righteous indignation, which Jesus manifested when He cleansed the Temple (John 2:13-17). A. C. Grant said in the International Standard Bible Encyclopedia, "The character of Eli, while sincere and devout, seems to have been entirely lacking in firmness. He appears from the history to have been a good man, full of humility and gentleness, but weak and indulgent. He is not a strong personality; Eli's sin was for the way he treated his sons' misconduct, and three things resulted from his lack of righteous indignation toward God and His commandments.

1. All the descendants of Eli would die at an early age. His descendants would lose their priesthood.
2. Hophni and Phinehas would die on the same day. Death was the judgment ordered for their sins.
3. God would bring forth a faithful priest who would do according to what was in God's heart and mind.

There are two essential inescapable lessons seen in this event.

1. God distributes honor and dishonor upon whom he wills. He can exalt the meanest or the humblest to greatness.
2. when we deal with God, we must always expect him to deal with us as well, more favorably than we deserve (Ref. Psalm 18:25-27).

Approximately 8 to 10 years after this pronouncement, the word of the Lord came to Samuel in the night. We all know the story of how one evening, while lying in bed in the Tabernacle at Shiloh, Samuel heard a voice calling his name. He sprang up and ran to the aged Eli, thinking he had called him. But Eli told him to go back to bed, for he had not called him. God came to Samuel three times before Eli became aware that it was a Divine summons. He told the lad that when he heard the voice again, he should reply, "Speak, O Lord, for Thy servant hears." Samuel did so, and the Lord spoke to Samuel concerning Eli and his house.

The message Samuel received was a somber one:

> "Behold, I will do something in Israel at which both ears of everyone who hears it will tingle. (12) In that day, I will perform against Eli all that I have spoken concerning his house, from beginning to end. (13) I have told him that I will judge his house for ever for the iniquity which he knows, because his sons made themselves vile, and he did not restrain them. (14) And therefore, I have sworn to the house of Eli that the iniquity of Eli's house shall not be atoned for by sacrifice or offering forever."
>
> 1st Samuel 3:11-14

It happened that the Lord revealed to Samuel the judgment that would soon fall on the house of Eli. The next morning, Eli demanded that Samuel tell him the message that he received from the Lord (1st Samuel 3:17). Please note Eli's burning desire to know the will of God. Eli's burning desire to know the will of God deserves imitation today. When Samuel related the word of the Lord to Eli, Eli said, "It is the Lord; let Him do what seems good to Him" (1st Samuel 3:18). Eli accepted the Judgment of God, knowing that it was a confirmation of that which he had heard once before. Eli's submission to the will of the Lord reminds us of the prayer of Jesus in the Garden of Gethsemane. "O My Father, if it is possible, let this cup pass from Me; nevertheless, not as I will, but as You will" (Matthew 26:39). Eli quietly submitted to the will of the Lord. He was not like so many who become bitter toward the Lord and complain about their lot in life. Instead, Eli submitted to the Lord's will, even though he did not like it. Eli's duplicity towards his sons once again showed that in spite of God's second warning, Eli could not bring himself to crack down on his sons.

This warning was the second prophecy of God's judgment against the house of Eli and was virtually the same as the first. This second pronouncement begs some questions. Why so long between the two judgments? Why the second pronouncement? And why did Eli not fall before God in repentance asking for mercy when either the first or second pronouncement came? Much in the same way as David did regarding the prophecy of the death of his first-born child 100 years later, or what Hezekiah would do approximately 400 years later, regarding the prophecy of his death?

Let us now take these questions one by one.

1. **Why so long between the two judgments (13 years approximately)?** The prophet Amos tells us that "Surely the Lord God does nothing; unless He reveals His secret to His servants the prophets" (Amos 3:7). Over and over throughout the Bible, we see this exact truth. Before the Lord imposes judgment, He sends a prophet (a "man of God") to announce the judgment, which is about to fall upon a sinful people or nation. In this case a "man of God" was sent to arouse Eli's conscience, by pointing out to him, first the grace manifested in the choice of his father's house as the keepers of God's house (Ref. 1st Samuel 2:27-28), and, second the desecration of the sanctuary by the wickedness of his sons (1st Samuel 2:29). When God makes declarations concerning the future, he furnishes the evidence of their accomplishments to produce universal conviction. This conviction is to manifest repentance, and secondly, to reestablish holiness in his people. We must remember that the divine intervention of God is a commentary on His word, and the more we see the operation of His Word, the more we shall know the reality of God. When men manifest a readiness to receive God's instruction, He will communicate to them the knowledge of His will. Though it may be trying, the result is that God's people will receive an excellent reward for their obedience. In the case of Eli, 13 years have

passed, and no repentance or change has manifested. Therefore, God's judgment must take place!

2. **Why the second pronouncement?** Whereas the first prophecy was one of announcement, awareness, and conviction in the hopes of producing repentance, the second was one of confirmation, certainty, and ultimate judgment. Eli and his son's day of grace was over, and their judgment sealed. What an awesome warning to those who trifle with holy things, and who turn the grace of God into licentiousness as these men did. Remember, their sins were not only affecting Eli and His sons but all of Israel. They were dishonoring to God and His precepts. Giving cause to all who saw these acts of desecration to follow their form of religious practices turning the hearts of many to lasciviousness. Under wicked religious leaders, the people become exceedingly wicked and thus ripe for divine judgment; and when ripe, others who are wicked help bring those judgments to pass.

3. **Why did Eli not fall before God in repentance, asking for mercy when either the first or second pronouncement came?** We know that God is merciful, and His mercies endure forever (Ref. Psalm 118). Eli had experienced firsthand the unending grace and mercy of God. He had seen it as we have said earlier, by the grace manifested in the choice of his father's house to keep His sanctuary (1st Samuel 2:27-28). By the mercy bestowed upon him to raise another son in the fear and admonition of the Lord, Eli, experienced a long and productive priesthood. But why he did not fall in repentance before the Lord, no one knows, for the Bible does not say. Any explanation on this writer's part would be mere conjecture than truth. But perhaps, Eli felt he deserved the punishment, and therefore, he just accepted it as the inevitable judgment of God upon his wrong decisions and inactions. Here is the problem with that explanation. The message came through Samuel, why? Could it be because God wanted to bring him to repentance and save him, and not his sons, whom he had determined to destroy (Ref. 1st Samuel 2:25)? Might it have been a means of stirring him to do his duty and

in doing so, prevent the judgment? One thing is known for sure; God's effort did not have any effect on Eli. There was no repentance, and God's judgment came to pass.

When the will of God is known, true piety will lead a soul to consent to it, Eli by accepting what God said as truth and accepting that God does must be right and good then following God's will for him tells us something about Eli? Eli was wrong regarding his sons, but he was right with God. We must admire Eli's pure submission and imitate it, but at the same time, we must remember a lesson that Eli seemed to have forgotten; Jehovah is a God of mercy and will forgive our trespasses (1st John 1:9). Remember, you can delay or alter God's pronounced judgment. For example, Hezekiah's pronounced death (2nd Kings 20:1–6); God's destruction of Nineveh (Jonah 1:2, 3:4–10); or God's impending judgment upon Sodom and Gomorrah God's pronounced judgment changed. In the judgment of Sodom and Gomorrah, God changed the conditions of His judgment five times in response to the intercessory prayers of Abraham (Ref. Genesis 18). If we choose to forget God's mercy and not ask for it, we commit as large a sin as any other; for in so doing, we have denied the very character of God.

For approximately 24 years after the second pronouncement of Eli's family's upcoming judgment, the Jews lived in peace. But then the war started once again, and Israel and the Philistines faced off between Ebenezer and Aphek, a battleground northwest of Jerusalem at the border of Philistine occupied territory near the Plain of Sharon in Ephraim's territory. At the first encounter, 4000 Israelites died on the battlefield (1st Samuel 4:2). In desperation, the people had Hophni and Phinehas, bring the Ark of the Covenant to the battle to raise hope and lead them to a victorious battle. It did not work for God was not with them, 30,000 more Israelites died, which included Hophni and Phinehas. Their deaths fulfilled the prophecy given first by the unnamed prophet and then by Samuel. As a result of the Philistine victory, the Ark of the Covenant became the possession of the Philistines.

Eli was now 98 years of age and extremely overweight; he sat on his porch, watching and waiting for news of the battle. His heart trembled for the Ark of God (1st Samuel 4:13). Finally, a messenger came to report, and when Eli heard that the Philistines captured the Ark of the Lord, Eli then fell over backward, broke his neck, and died. It is vital to note Eli did not die when he heard of Israel's defeat or that both of his sons had died. But Eli fell backward and died when he heard the news of the capture of the Ark of the Covenant. It seems that Eli had finally learned that honoring God above all else is paramount for a man of God. Eli's concern for the ark shows his genuine love for the Lord.

Too many today fail to manifest this kind of concern over matters pertaining to the Lord and His Church. Petty problems at home bother us more than internal issues in our church. We stay at home from worship for the slightest reason. We have limited or no concern when we hear that false teachers are ravaging the flock. What God requires in today's Christians is more of Eli's interest in matters pertaining to God. We need Christians who are concerned for the lost and are willing to work in leading them to salvation. We need men who love the Lord enough to shed tears over matters pertaining to His Church. We need men and women who love the Lord enough to prepare themselves to serve in His church. We need Christians who will without compromise stand for God without flinching or compromise, who will stand unmovable in the face of moral decline and practices. Christians who will stand on 2nd Timothy 3:16-17 and wholeheartedly do what it says. "Every Scripture passage is inspired by God. All of them are useful for teaching, pointing out errors, correcting people, and training them for a life that has God's approval. (17) They equip God's servants so that they are completely prepared to do good things (GW).

Let me share with you're a story that will demonstrate to you the hypocritical face of most churches and Christians today.

In a small Texas town (Mt. Vernon), Drummond's Bar began construction on a new building to increase their business. The local Baptist church started a campaign to block the bar from opening across the street from the church with petitions and prayers.

However, work progressed right up till the week before opening when lightning struck the bar, and it burned to the ground. The church folks who had been praying for months that the bar would not open, and went as far as to pray that it would burn down, were rather smug in their outlook until the bar owner sued the church because the church was ultimately responsible for the fiery demise of his building, either through direct or indirect actions of the church. The church vehemently denied all responsibility or any connection to the building's demise in its reply to the court.

As the case made its way into court, the judge looked over the paperwork. At the hearing, he commented, "I don't know how I'm going to decide this case. It appears that we have a bar owner who believes in the power of prayer, and an entire church congregation that does not."1

Eli's descendants continued in the office of High Priest until the time of Solomon. At that time, Abiathar, who was of the same lineage as Eli, was replaced by Zadok, thus bringing an end to Eli's line as High Priest (1st Kings 2:22, 35). Zadok was the fulfilment of the prophecy given by the unknown prophet and repeated by Samuel against the house of Eli (1st Kings 2:27). Let us take the lessons we have seen from Eli and learn from them. Let us not make the same mistakes which he made, but let us emulate only his positive attributes. "For whatever things were written before were written for our learning, that we through the patience and comfort of the Scriptures might have hope." (Romans 15:4).

Let me bring out one last warning for all who might misinterpret the 24 years God waited before carrying out his judgment upon the house of Eli as God being lacks in His promises. Or perhaps that the 24-year delay had nothing to do with God's promise, but was just a coincidence. "For all the promises of God in Him are Yes, and in Him Amen, to the glory of God through us (2nd Corinthians 1:20). Also, Nehemiah speaking of the Jews sinful attitudes during the time of the wilderness journey said;

> "They refused to obey, and they were not mindful of Your
> wonders that You did among them. But they hardened
> their necks, and in their rebellion, they appointed a
> leader to return to their bondage. But You are God,
> Ready to pardon, Gracious and merciful, Slow to anger,
> Abundant in kindness, and did not forsake them."
> Nehemiah 9:17 (c.f. Psalm 103:8; 145:8)

Those with whom God deals require His mercy and grace. He favors them when they are guilty, and He is not slow to show compassion for their condition; neither is he reluctant to lift them out of it by His grace. Mercy pardons sin, grace bestows favor, in both, the Lord abounds! Mercy and Grace is His way! He made it known to Moses when He said, "The Lord, the Lord God, merciful and gracious, longsuffering, and abounding in goodness and truth" (Exodus 34:6), and in that way, He will abide forever. Also, King David said, "The Lord is merciful and gracious, slow to anger, and abounding in mercy" (Psalm 103:8). He can be angry, He can deal and does deal with the guilty out of righteous indignation, but He lingers long, with loving patients. He waits long to give time for reflection, repentance, and the opportunity for the acceptance of His mercy. God's patient mercy and grace are the way God deals with the vilest of sinners and with His children much more so. Towards His children, however, His anger is short-lived and will not reach into eternity, and when His passion manifests in fatherly discipline, He does not do so quickly. From this, we should learn to be slow to anger just as He is; if the Lord is longsuffering in spite of our great annoyances, how much more should we endure the sins of our brethren!

Now notice the last phrase, "Abundant in kindness (or mercy)." Abundant in Hebrew is "rab"; it means "overflowing, abounding, exceedingly full of." God abounds in kindness, and so, He needs to be, or we would soon experience God's righteous anger. He is God! Our sins would soon drown His love if it were not abundant and overflowing. Above the mountains of our sins, the floods of His mercy rise. As the verse of the old hymn "Jesus, Lover of my soul" by Charles Wesley says, "Plenteous grace with thee is found, Grace to cover all my sin; Let the healing streams abound; Make and keep me pure within."

God invites everyone to experience His pardoning mercy. Those who hear the Gospel partake of His inviting mercy, and all saints live by His saving mercy. His upholding mercy preserves us, we live in peace by His consoling grace and will enter heaven through His infinite and everlasting mercy. Come now, you are all invited to partake of God's Abundant Mercy today!

SAMUEL – A MAN OF PRAYER WHOSE RIGHTEOUSNESS PREVAILED

He Lived God's Way

Samuel was the earliest of the Hebrew prophets after Moses and the last of the judges. His name means "Asked of God" or "Heard of God," He was the son of Elkanah of Ephraim and Hannah (1se Samuel 1:1). Samuel was Hannah's first-born, and he was born in Ramah (1st Samuel 2:11; 7:17). Samuel was a Nazarite from his birth (1st Samuel 1:11), the characteristics of which were:

1. Abstinence from intoxicating drinks
2. Showing sober-mindedness and diligence
3. Self-denial and separation from sensual indulgence
4. Showing submission – "Not my will but thine" (Ref Luke 22:42)
5. No cutting of the hair – Indicating the complete dedication of all the power of the head to God
6. Avoidance of contact with a dead body – Indicating absolute purity of life (Numbers 6)

Samuel's call to service came not because of war or oppression due to outside foreign powers, like the other judges. His calling came as a result of a far worse conflict, national religious abhorrence, and apathy, which came as a direct result of wicked men, perverting God's precepts and profaning the sanctuary, in debauchery equal to that of Canaanite temples (1st Samuel 2:12-17). Therefore, God used the cry of a barren righteous woman for a son that she would dedicate to Him from birth.

When Samuel was around twelve years of age, approximately 7-8 years after his dedication to the temple, he received his first revelation of the Lord, which was a clear message of doom against Eli, the reigning High Priest and Eli's two sons (1st Samuel 3:11-14).

Samuel's ministry was fourfold.

1. **As a prophet** (1st Samuel. 2:27-35; 3:19-21; 8:22). His faithfulness was a rebuke to the unfaithfulness of Eli. To the end of his days, Samuel proved the office of prophet, and his ministry was from God. Under the impact of his pure and courageous pronouncements, Israel renounced her idolatry and shook off the yoke of the Philistines.

2. **As an intercessor.** Samuel was born in answer to prayer, and his name constantly reminded him of the power of prayer and of the necessity of maintaining holy intimacy with God. Samuel deemed it a sin not to pray (1st Samuel 7:5-8; 8:6; 12:17, 19, 23; 15:11).

3. **As a priest.** Although Samuel was only a Levite and not a priest by ancestry. God's word regarding Samuel, "I will raise," implies an extraordinary office (1st Samuel 2:35; 7:9, 10; 13:8-10; Judges 2:16). Samuel exercised priestly functions by the following actions:
   1) By intercession (1st Samuel 7:9)
   2) By offering sacrifices (1st Samuel 7:9, 10)
   3) By benediction (1st Samuel 10:17, 25)
   4) By anointing kings (1st Samuel 10:1; 16:13).

4. **As the last judge of Israel**. Samuel "judged Israel all the days of his life." Even after the government of Israel had changed from that of a theocracy to a monarchy, Samuel still acted as a circuit judge, going from place to place giving divine judgment upon moral and spiritual questions, and maintaining in the hearts and lives of the people the law and authority of Jehovah (1st Samuel 7:15-17).

Samuel had taken up residence in Ramah, where he made his headquarters. Young men gathered to him and formed the earliest of the schools of the prophets. It was at Ramah where he married and became the father of two sons. Their names are suggestive of Samuel's piety and walk with God, the name of the one being Joel meaning "Jehovah is God," and of the other Abiah, "Jehovah is my Father." We also see his devotion to God demonstrated amid the massive corruption in Israel's religious life. With the Ark of the Covenant being in Kirjath-jearim and the remnants of the Tabernacle in Shiloh, approximately 20 miles away and with the discontinuance of the sacred rites and feasts, Samuel was still able to walk with God and preserve a devout religious life.

Samuel was giving himself to the great and noble work of Israel's national and religious reconstruction. Samuel had now seen about 40 years of peace, but these years included disunity and anarchy. There was no army or militia to keep the foreign nations at bay, no worship of Jehovah, and the Jews were guilty of looking to the Ark for help in times of oppression and not God. Therefore, Samuel's mission consisted of 4 major goals. They were:

1. **The work of reconstruction** – For approximately 20 years, Samuel traveled throughout Israel every year, holding sacrifices, services, and giving comfort to every city. In the hopes of bringing unified worship of Jehovah back to Israel.

2. **The work of ministry** – the evils of idolatry were eating away at the heart of the nation. The people had forsaken the God of their fathers for the Phoenician and Philistine deities. Shrines to Baal and Ashtaroth covered the land. Dirty orgies of shameless impurity were everywhere, and it was evident that only a widespread revival of religion could save the people from rotting away because of the very evils for which God destroyed the ancient Canaanites. Samuel must bring Jehovah back to the forefront. How many of us are guilty of putting Jesus on the back burner of our lives and need to bring Him to the forefront. Where is He in your life?

3. **The work of prayer, the word, and lifestyle** – Samuel was preeminently a man of prayer. He is known on the subsequent pages of Scripture as one that called on the Lord and a man with a

sterling reputation and lifestyle ones whose words were always pure and true. (1st Samuel 3:19, 9:6-9; Psalm 49:6; Jeremiah 15:1).

4. **The work of bringing unity** – The national unity needed recovery from the anarchy in which it was experiencing. For in their condition, it would be useless to think of holding the land against any inroads the neighboring warlike nations would attempt. As long as each tribe was content with an isolated existence, repelling its enemies, and being indifferent to the condition of its neighbors and the country at large, chaos resulted. Even though each tribe was proud of its history and independence while fulfilling its distinctive mission, Unifying Israel was essential for its future independence and integrity. Israel, as a nation, would not survive without it.

Unity is no less desirable in our age. The divisions found in the Church are her curse and render her impotent before her enemies. It is a sad spectacle to witness the divisions between Christians in the face of a mocking world. We shall never be able to make men believe until we have learned to magnify our points of agreement, even though their method of worship and faith may differ widely from our own.

But before we get too far ahead of ourselves, let us cover what I believe are four transitions a young Christian must go through to achieve maturity.

1. **The transition of the Soul – Salvation** – Early on in Samuel's life, his service was based solely upon his mother's faith in God and her dedicated lifestyle. Samuel, though in service to Jehovah, did not know the Lord's voice, he only knew the importance of the work (1st Samuel 3:7). What he needed was an intimate encounter with Jehovah. Which Jehovah gave him.

2. **The transition of the eyes – Personal witness** – The vision came by night. The Lord stood next to Samuel (1st Samuel 3:10). We must see (a deeper form of intimacy) for ourselves the truth of our faith.

3. **The transition of the Spirit – Surrender** – "Yes, Lord, here am I" (1st Samuel 3:10). Not my will but thine.

4. **The transition of our faith – Obedience** – Samuel, but a boy, told Eli his mentor, who was the High Priest and Judge of all Israel, the hard message given to him by God (1ˢᵗ Samuel 3:18). From faith to faithfulness. We must go beyond believing and proceed to do whatever God commands.

No one can ever grow into a true servant of God without these four transitional steps. Each of these steps takes time, and they come separately in most cases. Salvation comes when one recognizes their wretched condition and the limitless mercy and grace of God the Father. Once a person has come to that realization, they must experience God for themselves. They cannot live on someone else's experience. In Samuel's case, he saw the Lord standing next to his bedside and spoke to Him as a friend. Most of us, however, get to know God not in that way but in a way that is personal and real for us. Exactly how, only you and God will experience, but one thing is for sure, it will be personal and real, something you can always go back to when your faith is weak and your trial overwhelming. It is then that you will be able to say, "I know my God is real, for I have personally met Him. Remember when, etc.…"

Surrendering one's life is the next step. "The spirit indeed is willing, but the flesh is weak," is what (Ref. Matthew 26:41; Mark 14:38) Jesus said. to His disciples when they could not pray with Him in His most terrifying hour (Ref. Matthew 26). Jesus' disciples walked closely with Him for three and one-half years before Jesus made this statement. Surrendering is an ongoing process; it takes time. It is a hard and trying way, but very much worth it! When we learn to surrender to God's will, we start to see the evolution of our faith. Obedience becomes easier each time we obey, and as a result, our faith becomes stronger.

Now let us start to look at some of Samuel's faithful actions and see what we can learn from them. After twenty years of quiet and unobtrusive efforts to reunite all Israel to the worship of Jehovah, it finally became manifest. Samuel had led his people to desire and manifest the old unity, which had made them unbeatable and unstoppable before their enemies. Israel was now displaying a distinct yearning for the worship and presence of the Lord (Ref. 1ˢᵗ Samuel 7). Unfortunately, this display of unity was a result of an enemy uprising, which threatened Israel's very existence. But at the same time, if you remember, the last time this enemy threatened Israel, the Jews were complacent and satisfied and they accepting it. They fought to keep the status quo (Ref. the chapters on Samson). This time, however, (1ˢᵗ Samuel 7:2) all the house of Israel "lamented (cried, yearned or sought) after the Lord" seeking His help. An evident and definite improvement!

In 1ˢᵗ Samuel 7:3 we have a summary of what Samuel spent many days proclaiming to the divided tribes "If you return to the LORD with all your hearts, then put away the foreign gods and the Ashtoreth's from among you, and prepare your hearts for the LORD, and serve Him only; and He will deliver you from the hand of the Philistines." If the Lord Jesus is the center of our hearts and lives, He will inevitably draw us into close fellowship. Jesus becoming the center of our heart's desire had a significant effect on the people in turning their hearts once again to the worship of Jehovah. "So, the children of Israel put away the Baals and the Ashtoreth's, and served the Lord only" (1ˢᵗ Samuel 7:4). What a far cry from the position they took the last time the Philistines were oppressing them, and it showed just how great a job Samuel had done in his ministry calling.

Can you imagine all the emotions running through Samuel? To finally see after 20 years of continuous preaching the importance of returning to Jehovah, a great multitude of repentant Jews standing before him crying out to the Lord to forgive their sins; and asking Samuel to pray that the Lord would grant them mercy. It must have felt like a drink of water to a thirst starved Man at the edge of death.

Long periods of toil with no visible evidence of success for a man of God are not unusual.

Here are some examples.

Abraham 100 years old before he had a son – Genesis 21:1-4
Isaac 20 years before he had a son – Genesis 25:20-26
Jacob had to work 14 years to marry his first love; Rachel – Genesis 29:
Children of Israel 430 years before their bondage in Egypt stopped – Exodus 12:41
Jesus healed a woman with an issue of blood for 20 years– Mark 5:25

The Man at the Pool of Bethesda who waited 38 years for a healing –
John 5:2~
The Man, blind from birth – John 9

There are many more examples than the ones listed. The point is
that Samuel was faithful and steadfast in the work of the Lord, even
though he did not see the results he hoped for, for many years. Samuel
did not become discouraged or slack in his effort; he did not complain
about it or demand of God some proof of his calling. He was a man
who just did what God called him to do and left the results to God. God
rewarded his faithfulness and dedication, as we now see in 1st Samuel 7. I
wonder how many of us cry out to God during those long periods where
all our hard work does not seem to produce any apparent results. How
many of us continue hard and steadfast in spite of the lack of evidence?
Or how many of us would even start to do the work for God knowing
that we would not see any evidence of it in this life?

According to 1st Samuel 7:5, Samuel inaugurated a Jewish reformation
that characterized his 20 years of ministry by convening a great assembly
of all Israel at Mizpah, which was now the political and religious center
of the nation. It was there, in deep humiliation they renewed their vows
and entered again into covenant with the God of their fathers. It was
a period of great religious awakening. Mizpah means "a watchtower,"
and it was a place which has a deep and emotional tie to most of the
Jews where the children of Israel had assembled to choose a leader to
resist the children of Ammon. It was one of the three holy cities, which
Samuel visited as judge of the people (1st Samuel 7:6, 16), the other two
being Bethel and Gilgal. It was here where the people were accustomed
to meet in great national emergencies (Joshua 18:26; Judges 20:1, 3; 21:1,
5). Mizpah was about 4 miles north-west of Jerusalem and located on the
loftiest hill in the area some 600 feet above the plain of Gibeon. Mizpah
has the modern name of Neby Samwil, meaning "the prophet Samuel,"
based on the tradition that Samuel's tomb is there.

Samuel gathered all Israel at Mizpah to pray for them. That day was
for fasting and prayer. The Israelites poured water out before the Lord.
It was a custom, to bring forth the water in a golden vessel and pour it
out at the foot of the altar at the hour of the morning sacrifice. Whether

this was the case here or not, we do not know. The pouring out of water was a memorial of the flowing of water from the rock smitten in the wilderness (Ref. Exodus 17) and the type of the pouring out of the Holy Spirit (Ref. John 7:37-39). It may also be that the pouring forth of the water may have implied that they poured out their whole heart in floods of repentance and tears, for they desired, due to the heaviness of their grief, to wash their land free from the accumulated evil of the past years. It may also be that the people realized their utter helplessness, and they felt as if they were but water spilled on the ground. No matter what the reason, it must have been a very striking spectacle, the entire nation of Israel turning back to true loyal allegiance to the God of their fathers. Should not America do the same today? For we have become even more religiously corrupt, then Israel had in Samuel's time, and our coming judgment is not far off.

Who will be our Samuel today? Who will persuade the professing Christian Church to put away the evil things which mar her testimony! Is it not true that our Christian Church possesses rampant fornication, Gay and lesbian priests, a compromised Gospel, gossiping, and a tranquil response to false doctrines and teachers, financial misuses, and deceptions, along with many other un-godly things? Are these not indications of the extensive corruption of our spiritual life. I wonder what would be the result if the children of God would come together and in true confession and tears cry out to God like the Israelites did for "We have sinned against the Lord" and "the wages of that sin are death" (Ref. Daniel 9:11; Romans 6:23).

The Philistines heard of this assembly, and looked upon it as an unmistakable sign of the returning spirit of national life, and "the lords of the Philistines went up against Israel" (1st Samuel 7:7). Panic spread through Israel, and why not? How clear in their memories were the terrible experiences of Aphek (Ref. 1st Samuel 4)? Would they repeat them and once again be defeated? There appeared but one hope: God must help His people, or they would once again find themselves conquered by the Philistines. Without God's help, what could timid sheep do against these Philistine wolves? How could unarmed peasants do against armed and trained soldiers? How could the newly reviving national life of Israel, withstand these mighty Philistines? Brethren notice the actions of these scared and distraught Israelites; they cried out to Samuel for Him to pray to God, "Cease not to cry unto the Lord our God for us, that He will save us out of the hand of the Philistines." They begged Samuel not only to pray for them but not to cease praying for them, why; because they knew beyond a shadow of doubt that Samuel was a man who had God's ear; and they knew that salvation would only come through the Man-God had chosen (Ref. Acts 2:21, 4:12; Romans 10:13). They also knew that their prayers due to their insolence toward God would not hold any weight with God. Have you ever felt like that? God would not pay you any mind because of your lifestyle.

My brethren, this is the only hope for us as well. Are you ground down beneath the tyrant's heels? And held in subjection to the enemy of your soul? Do you feel like you are in prison with no hope of escape? Does it seem like there is no help or hope of deliverance? Are your actions mirroring the Apostle Paul's when he said, "For what I am doing, I do not understand? For what I will to do, that I do not practice; but what I hate, that I do." (Ref Romans 7:15) If they are, God has some excellent news, put these thoughts and feelings away, pour out all your lack of self-confidence before the cross, receive the forgiveness which He would never withhold from the penitent and believing soul. Then, many of the obstacles, temptations, and sins that are holding you back will disappear, and then the Lord will save and free you.

> "O Israel, hope in the Lord, for with the Lord there is mercy, And with Him is abundant redemption. (8) And He shall redeem Israel from all his iniquities."
> Psalm 130:7-8

> "I will deliver you from the hand of the wicked, And I will redeem you from the grip of the terrible."
> Jeremiah 15:21

This writer's wish is that all believers who are experiencing temptation and are overwhelmed sons and daughters of God would bathe their souls in the purifying waters of the Word of God, and develop a spirit of unwavering consecration, prayer, and faith. For in so doing, the Lord will fight for you, and you will find deliverance and blessings for your soul.

The power of Samuel's prayers was well known throughout Israel. Remember, not one of Samuel's words fell to the ground (Ref. 1st Samuel 3:19). That is why the people had come to believe in him as a man who had God's ear. If only Samuel would pray, they thought, they could count on deliverance. They knew that he had prayed for them; they now begged him not to cease (Ref. 1st Samuel 7:8). But Samuel did more than pray. He offered a whole burnt-offering to the Lord, symbolizing that Israel's desire would be for the divine will of God (Ref. verse 9). There must be consecration before prayer and deliverance. It is not enough to put away sin; we must also give ourselves entirely and absolutely to God. There must also be a heart of pureness and wholeness in what we offer to God. If sin continually overcomes you, realize that there is a flaw in your consecration to God that needs removal. Find out what it is, repent of it, ask God for forgiveness and strength to overcome it, and you will become an overcomer.

We know that the enemy does not cease in his attacks. Even while this holy and glorious rededication service was going on, the enemy was preparing to attack. Notice 1st Samuel 7:10; "Now as Samuel was offering up the burnt offering, the Philistines drew near to battle against Israel." Notice the word "As." As Samuel was offering the sacrifice, the enemy was preparing to attack. Brethren, be aware that even while we are in an excellent church service, or engaged in holy consecration, or celebrating our love for God. Or while we are singing and praising His Holy name, or trying to concentrate in prayer or meditating on His awe-inspiring word, the devil is preparing to attack. Can you not see him creeping up trying to surround you unawares? But God! Hallelujah, "but God" is our refuge and strength, the savior of our souls, the preserver of life, our deliverer, and our mighty strong tower, and it is from under His wings that we must trust. "The Lord thundered with a thunder upon the Philistines that day, and so confused them that they were overcome before Israel" (1st Samuel 7:10b). The Hebrews charged the Philistine host with great fury and defeated the Philistines. Samuel commemorated the victory by erecting a memorial-stone, which he called "Ebenezer (the stone of help)," saying, "Hitherto hath the Lord helped us" (1ˢᵗ Samuel 7:7-12).

Samuel set up this stone on the exact spot upon which Israel had suffered its most significant defeat, which led to the capture of the Ark of the Covenant (Ref. 1ˢᵗ Samuel 4:10-11). Is it not true that when we turn to God, he blots out the disgrace of our most significant failure in the glory of our deliverance and victory? (Ref.1ˢᵗ Samuel 7) Yes, child of God, be sure that the place of your most significant defeat will become the place of your greatest victory, in such a glorious way as to fill your heart with adoring praise. Think how, in the generations ahead, fathers brought their children to look at that great stone, and read the inscription, "Hitherto hath the Lord helped us," telling their children how the Lord forgave Israel and conquered their enemies. What He had done then, He will do now! The forgiveness and grace that God demonstrated will be known in each generation. How do you think it would make you feel when you heard of God's faithfulness in times of trouble and God's complete deliverance on your account? Would it not give you great assurance of His love for you? Of course, it would; and it does! From that moment on, Samuel's supremacy reigned in Israel. The Philistines came no more within the border of Israel during Samuel's judgeship. The hand of the Lord was against the Philistines all of Samuel's days.

The next we read of Samuel is the story of Samuel's great disappointment (Ref. 1ˢᵗ Samuel 8). Samuel, as stated earlier, had two sons. It seems, however, that just like the sons of Eli, grace does not run in the blood, it is not hereditary. An honored and respected father may have disgraceful sons. That is just the way it happens sometimes. Samuel being old (approximately 60 or more at this time), assigned his sons as judges due to his advanced age. We might draw from this that they were to support their father in the administration of justice. Samuel had no intention of laying down his office, and still less of making the supreme office of judge hereditary in his family, for he knew, just like Gideon, that God must assign an office, they are not to be appointed by Man. Samuel probably gave them their commissions, because they were able to help by taking some of the burden of the immense amount of travel off him (Ref. 1ˢᵗ Samuel 7:16). Samuel's sons were no doubt respected because of their father's piety, and they might have become great in the eyes of God and the people if they had been virtuous. But they did not walk in Samuel's ways; they turned aside after dishonest gain, took bribes, and perverted justice (Ref. 1st Samuel 8:3).

Samuel was wrong in making his son's judges even though it was only for support's sake. Great men ought not to injure the Church by appointing individuals into offices based on heredity, friendship, or obligation. For when the Church descends into corruption, the blame must fall upon the men who did the appointing.

Samuel's sons, despite all their upbringing and training, did not walk in the ways of their father but set their hearts upon gain. They took bribes, and perverted justice, in opposition to the command of God. These circumstances (Samuel's age and the wickedness of his sons) furnished the elders of Israel with a reason to request Samuel to appoint an earthly king to judge Israel, with this catch, he had to be just like the heathen nations around them. (Ref. 1st Samuel 8:5, 20) The same nations God had already conquered and removed from His people and the promised land. Now God's people wanted what the heathen nations had and what the Lord had explicitly told them not to seek after because of the abominations it would bring upon them. Seeking after foreign gods is narcissistic, self-serving, and incredibly foolish! They were rejecting God! (Ref. 1st Samuel 8:7) The people's request was the fulfillment of a prophecy given by Moses regarding the requirements of an earthly king (Ref. Deuteronomy 17:14-20).

Do not think for a moment that this same choice never happens today by many believers and in many modern churches. Following foreign Gods is the universal failure of Man's heart. It is always craving for the sensual and visible. Like the children of Israel, with their cry, "Make us gods that shall go before us." (Ref. Exodus 32:1) Man demands something which they may see and handle, and before which they can prostrate themselves. Hence all spiritual worship carries with it a tendency to become materialistic. For example, our churches are full of the pictures and statues of Man christened saints before which the religious burn candles and cross themselves, and as a result of this, the common man cannot enter the Holy of Holies. Ritualistic worship has taken the place of inspiration, time restraints have replaced the sweet presence of the Lord, inspirational music and living-word sermons are now cookie-cutter copies of long-ago messages. Jesus Christ is no longer a part of our services (Ref. Revelation 3:20). Read this verse and notice where Jesus is standing. That is right He is outside the Church knocking, desperately desiring to come in! The people love to have it their way, the churches with such formats are flourishing. On the other hand, in the churches where worship center around a deeper holiness and intimacy with God are rapidly diminishing in size, numbers and importance.

The Book of Hebrews calls for us to enter into a deeper, more productive, and more blessed relationship with the Almighty. What are you wanting; A ritualistic service that satisfies the flesh or a spiritual service where the Lord Himself orchestrates all aspects so that He can saturate and exalt every soul in attendance? Are you looking for a king to rule just like the heathen nations, or are you looking for the King of Kings and Lord of Lords to rule?

Samuel was extremely displeased when they said, "Give us a king to judge us" (1st Samuel 8:6). It was not so much that they had rejected him, but that they had rejected God as their King. Samuel saw that this request amounted to a formal rejection of God's Divine government. They had failed to grasp the greatness that God had chosen for them and had selected a level equal to the heathen nations around them. The same heathen nations that their God had destroyed and removed from them. The one hope that Samuel so faithfully worked for all those years, was unrealized. Samuel finally realized that there could never be the manifestation of his cherished dream of a theocracy in Israel, for if it failed in Israel, it would fail everywhere. But God had other plans. Despite His children's utter rejection, God would, in time, through His boundless grace and mercy set up a Divine Kingdom which would never pass away (cf. Isaiah 9:7; Daniel 2:44, 4:3, 34, 6:26, 7:13-14, 27; Micah 4:7).

It was under these bitter circumstances that Samuel opened his heart to Jehovah Shalom; "the Lord of Peace." the one assured safeguard for all broken hearts and wrecked lives for all who labor and are heavy laden, "Samuel prayed unto the Lord." The Lord told him to "heed the voice of the people in all that they say to you; for they have not rejected you, but they have rejected Me, that I should not reign over them" (1st Samuel 8:7). Israel's rejection of God's rule implies that not only in Samuel's opinion but also according to the counsel of God, the time had come for the establishment of an earthly self-government in Israel. God saw that it was necessary to grant their request for the accomplishment of His own wise and holy purpose, for He knew that their desire was based upon worldly confidence and would fail without His continual intervention. In looking to an earthly king, after the manner of their heathen neighbors, instead of Jehovah, they brought upon themselves many great evils, from which simple faith and obedience to God, would have saved them.

They not only declared to the prophet their confidence in the administration of his office, but at the same time, they implicitly declared God incapable of any further rule over their civil and political affairs. This action demonstrated their mistrust in the Lord and His guidance but also His choice of leadership. In the person of Samuel, they rejected the Lord and His rule. They wanted a king because they imagined that Jehovah, their God-king was not able to safeguard their constant prosperity. Instead of seeking the cause of their misfortunes and lack of faithfulness towards Jehovah, they decided to search for peace, safety, and prosperity in the rule of an earthly king. This desire for a king was a sign of scorn and rejection of the government of Jehovah and was paramount to forsaking Jehovah to serve other gods (Ref. 1st Samuel 10:18-19; 12:7). Many churches today are looking to the same type of rule and system that the heathens have to assure and safeguard their constant prosperity as well.

Let me give you an example of this type of human rule for worship. My wife and I were attending a church service at an Assembly of God church in Pennsylvania. At the beginning of the service, the Pastor stood and addressed the congregation (I suppose for the sake of the visitors). He instructed the congregation that if anyone had a word from the Lord, such as a prophecy, tongues, or interpretation of tongues, they were to call the usher after writing it down on paper, and the usher would bring it to the front. He would then judge it along with the elders, and if it were determined to be from God, the congregation would hear it. This method of judging the Spiritual gifts quenched the Spirit of God from moving. The service was void of any life, but the program schedule went smooth, each phase of the service went off on time, every person had their job down exactly right, every person was where they were to be at the right moment, and we were all dismissed right on time. The entire service took precisely sixty minutes. How much is the body of Christ missing because of this Man ordained and formulated service. Is this not precisely what Peter was warning us would happen in the last days?

> "But know this, that in the last days perilous times will come: (2) For men will be lovers of themselves, lovers of money, boasters, proud, blasphemers, disobedient to parents, unthankful, unholy, (3) unloving, unforgiving, slanderers, without self-control, brutal, despisers of good, (4) traitors, headstrong, haughty, lovers of pleasure rather than lovers of God, (5) having a form of godliness but denying its power. And from such people turn away!"
>
> 2nd Peter 3:1-5

Brethren, the Church has been called to sit with Christ in the heavenly places, but until the Church has the proper balance of being established on solid, Biblical truth, and at the same time knowing the voice of the Lord, we are like the blind leading the blind – not only is it impossible to get to where you are going, but you will in short order, crash. The command to obey His word and obey His voice to receive the full blessing and salvation of the Lord was not new to the Israelites, nor is it new to us. No matter how well we know the Scriptures, error will continue if we do not know the voice of the Lord.

> "Except when there may be no poor among you; for the Lord will greatly bless you in the land which the Lord, your God, is giving you to possess as an inheritance – (5) only if you carefully obey the voice of the Lord your God, to observe with care all these commandments which I command you today. (6) For the Lord your God will bless you just as He promised you; you shall lend to many nations, but you shall not borrow; you shall reign over many nations, but they shall not reign over you."
>
> Deuteronomy15:4-6

"Today, you have proclaimed the Lord to be your God, and that you will walk in His ways and keep His statutes, His commandments, and His judgments, and that you will obey His voice."

Deuteronomy 26:17

"My sheep hear My voice, and I know them, and they follow Me. (28) And I give them eternal life, and they shall never perish; neither shall anyone snatch them out of My hand."

John 10:27-28

Conversely, no matter how well we think we know the voice of God, if we do not know the Scriptures, we will eventually drift into error. Many of the mistakes made by the Church throughout its history are the result of not balancing knowledge of Scripture with knowing the power and voice of God.

Today, a large portion of the body of Christ is deeply committed to the Scriptures, but they are unaware, or in denial regarding the power and voice of God, this ignorance has led them into error. The other major portion of the Church knows the power and voice of God but tends to know little of the Scriptures, which leads to emotionalism and radicalism.

Here are some examples of this type of emotionalism and radicalism.

1. A pastor from Zimbabwe tried not just to imitate the miracle of Jesus Christ walking on water (Matthew 14:22-33) but to even increase its level of difficulty by walking across a river teeming with crocodiles. Sadly, he failed.

Pastor Jonathan Mthethwa of the Saint of the Last Days Church tried to do a "Jesus miracle act" to show that faith can move mountains or, in his case, turn crocodiles into stepping stones on the water.

He then gathered his congregants at the banks of a river known as Crocodile River for a personal demonstration of his faith. However, according to the Daily Post, the Pastor drowned and was seen by his church members devoured by three crocodiles.

"The pastor taught us about faith on Sunday last week," Deacon Nkosi, a member of the Church, said. "He promised he would demonstrate his faith to us today, but he, unfortunately, ended up drowning and getting eaten by three large crocodiles in front of us." He said the Pastor fasted and prayed the whole week before they went to the river in his effort to convince them of the power of faith.

"We still don't understand how this happened," Nkosi added. He said Pastor Mthethwa walked for about 30 meters into the river before the crocodiles appeared from nowhere and attacked him. "They finished him in a couple of minutes. All that was left of him when they finished eating him is a pair of sandals and his underwear floating above the water," Nkosi said.

1. Another African pastor also allegedly tried to replicate Jesus' "walk on the water" miracle a few years back but also drowned as a result. Pastor Franck Kabele, 35, of Gabon, reportedly told his congregation that he could reenact the same miracles Jesus did as written in the Bible.

He invited his congregants to watch him perform the miracle in Libreville, Gabon's capital. He told them that he would cross an estuary by foot, which is usually a 20-minute boat ride. But soon after entering the water, Kabele found himself wholly submerged and drowned.

1. Another failed attempt to replicate a biblical miracle was in Nigeria, where a self-proclaimed prophet claimed that he could also walk into a den full of lions and stay there unharmed just like what Daniel did (Daniel 6) as written in the Bible — ignoring the zookeepers. The prophet reportedly entered a cage full of lions. After entering the lions' den, and died.

2. Another example of this emotionalism and radicalism is an international evangelist (who will remain anonymous) a few years ago, said to his congregation that many do not have faith to believe so, the next day, he went down to the lake to walk on

water. The next day a multitude of people showed up to watch the miracle. He told them that he would so this in order to help them to believe. He stepped out on the water and sunk. He angrily turned to the people and said, that he sunk because; "there are people here that would not believe."

The question to ask yourself regarding these examples is; were these men acting on their desire, or did God want them to do what they did, if you believe the latter you must ask yourself, why did it not work and how is the death of these believers, honor God?

We see the unlimited grace of God in the story of Israel's desire for an earthly king in numerous ways. Here are a few examples.

1. **First**, God knew the hurt that Samuel was experiencing He then comforted him by telling him that "they have not rejected him, but they have rejected Me, that I should not reign over them." How great of an honor it is to have God comfort our sufferings and summon His servants to enter into fellowship with Him when we are in the pain and grief which men bring upon us. Did not Jesus suffer when His own received Him not? When His home town rejected Him and when His disciples all fled in His hour of misery. There is an old saying that says, "cruelty and cowardice go together;" so also do self-sacrifice and tenderness. They are different sides of the same coin.

2. **Second**, to show them the error of their earthly desires, Samuel bore witness against them by pointing out their past wrongs and by proclaiming the requirements of the King who would rule over them. Samuel was to testify to them "the manner or behavior of the king," that which he would claim over them, especially a king who was like all the other nations around them, one of such sorts as Israel desired in place of Jehovah. For example, this requested King would rule over his people with arbitrary and absolute power. He will take your sons and appoint them for his chariots and to be his horsemen, and some will run before his chariots. He will take your daughters to be perfumers, cooks, and bakers. He will take the best of your

fields, your vineyards, and your olive groves and give them to his servants. He will take your male and female servants, your finest young men, and your donkeys, and put them to work for him. He will take a tenth of your sheep, and you will be his servants.

Giving this commentary was in the hope that they would see the results of their request and find it less desirable than the Divine Theocracy God wanted for them. Unfortunately, Man's heart wants what Man's heart desires, even in the face of more discomfort, obligation, troubles, and restrictions. Why is it, that Man in the face of so much evidence to the contrary, believes fulfilling his desires is better than what God knows to be better and more satisfying and can deliver both of those in abundance? Could it be that Man desires to satisfy only his selfish desire with no thought or concern for the larger picture? Or is it that he cannot see the larger picture? That question begs another question, is Man incapable of seeing the larger picture, or does he even want to see it? The answer to these questions is in one's own heart. It is also unfortunate that it is not until the heart experiences pain and troubles that Man considers the possibility that he may be wrong and turns back to God in repentance and changes his ways. That is the future that lies ahead for the Israelites.

Brethren, does your heart cry out for an earthly king (you) to rule your heart and life? One who will reduce the conflicting passions of our nature? If so, beware, lest you choose by the lust of your flesh or the pride of your life (Ref. 1st John 2:15-17). Indeed, many things which men's hearts lust after will be their curse, for sin lies at the door, and its desire is for you (c.f. Genesis 4:7)! Are you making the same mistake as these Israelites? You, like them, your choice will determine your future events.

3. **Third**, God in the face of such a blatant rejection compromised with them and gave them what they desired, but not in the way they wanted it, nor did He give them everything they truly deserved. God couldn't provide them with a man after God's own heart under the spirit characterized by the people (heathenism). They wanted one who, by nature, was one liken

unto the neighboring nations. As they requested – God gave them! How often it happens that God grants us according to the insistence of our hearts and our vehement self-will. He gives us according to our request but sends leanness into our souls (Ref. Psalm 106:15).

Let this writer illustrate the point.

Man's Desire	God's Compromise	God's Desire
God (when Necessary)	God (Sovereign)	God (Sovereign)
↓	↓	↓
King (Earthly)	Holy Prophets	Holy Prophets
↓	↓	↓
People (Free to do as they will)	King (Earthly, but humble)	People (After God's own Heart)
	↓	
	People (Blessed of God based on their commitment and obedience)	

4. **Fourth**, God choose an earthly man to be their king who had a humble and had a contrite heart, a man who could become a faithful man of God and would obey the commands of God. In this case, God chooses a man of stature, beauty, upbringing, and humility. His name was Saul. Saul was a man who was

neither a prophet, or a man after God's own heart, nor was he a man of heathen background. He was the perfect compromise between God's will and man's desire. Saul means "asked for or demanded." God gave him every opportunity and assisted him in succeeding in his calling and mission.

Notice, Saul was:

> In his early years a humble man who practiced self-control (1st Samuel 10:22,27; 11:13)
> Blessed of God for leadership (1st Samuel 11)
> A man anointed and filled with the Holy Spirit (1st Samuel 11:6)
> Anointed as one of the prophets (1st Samuel 19:24)

Unfortunately, like any earthly appointed leaders, despite the blessings of the Lord, they tend to fail. No man in Biblical history had so many chances thrust upon him to make a success of his life, and no man ever so often missed them. Saul not only missed great opportunities; he deliberately abused them. His sun rose in splendor but set in terrible darkness. The downfall of his life was a result of pride, self-centeredness, disobedience, and the abuse of power, leading to moral degradation and ruin. Here are the steps that led him down the path to destruction.

> Called of God to be the first commander of God's inheritance (1st Samuel 10:1)
> Self-will restricted his influence (1st Samuel 13:12-13)
> Disobedience and recklessness (1st Samuel 15:11-23)
> Jealousy prompted him to hunt and kill David (1st Samuel 18:8; 19:1)
> Hypocrisy – He patronized the superstition he had forbidden (1st Samuel 28:7)
> Saw no way out, not even in repentance and committed suicide (1st Samuel 31:4)

What is truly unfortunate is once Saul had destroyed his moral and spiritual life, he decided to destroy his physical life as well. Are you shocked by this, it happens daily in the world around us; and yes, even in the Church.

Samuel, on the other hand, demonstrates another admirable trait that we can emulate. It is his absolute surrender to the Lord, the depth of his obedience, and the care he felt for his people in the face of their outright rejection of God. Samuel saw that the people had made up their minds against God's wishes, despite his pain and hurt but in accordance with God's instructions, Samuel told the people all the words of Jehovah. He then set himself up to do the best he could for them. He did this in obedience to the will of God and for the good of his people. This is remarkable; Samuel is one of the few great men in history who, in critical times, by the sheer force of his character and being convinced of the necessity of the change initiates a new form of government and does all he can in hopes for success (c.f. 1st Samuel 10;1-8).

In doing this, Samuel had to sacrifice his previous convictions and spite his better judgment. He had to pull down the very institution he had worked so hard and for so many years to establish. He had to become second in charge, where before, he was the unchallenged leader. He had to become the conscience of a nation, instead of the decision-maker, the voice rather than the arm of a nation. Samuel knew that there was no alternative and that this new government was the will of God. He, therefore, did all he could for the cause of Christ and became the most devoted and efficient organizer of this new government. There is one last thing about Samuel's actions we must recognize. That is, without these unselfish actions, there would no doubt be a David. David's life, his kingdom, and glory would not have been possible without Samuel's less conspicuous, but far more influential career. All the greatness of which the following century boasts goes back to Samuel as its real author.

There are supreme crises in the lives of all Christians, which take us to the brink of exasperation. Where the people who we have loved suffered with sacrificed for, suddenly and unexpectedly turn away from us. They want something else, something more, and they want to go in another direction. Despite our emotions and better judgment, we realize that we must abandon our ways and aid them. This decision often brings grudging courtesy and false grace. Questions arise in our mind like; why should I make way for others; why should I renounce my rights and refuse to press on my way? Why should I change, or why should I help, for my way is right, theirs will lead to hurt and pain? This belief should not be the case, however, for it is at these times that we should remember Samuel's heroism; let us acknowledge that God's will is leading us in the right way; let us care for the flock over which we have been placed as overseers more than we care for ourselves. Let us adapt ourselves to the new order; and further it with all the grace, truth and strength at our disposal, knowing that the blood of our self-sacrifice will by God's blessing, be the best testimony of our faith.

The remaining Biblical references to Samuel are in the rise and fall of Saul and the anointing of David. There are so many lessons that we can learn from the incidences recorded regarding his life and death that it would take the writing of many books to reveal all of them. There are, however, several great lessons found in our study of Samuel that would when significantly applied enhance our walk with Christ. They are:

1. Samuel's purity of life and ministry
2. Samuel's never-ceasing life of prayer
3. Obedience rather than sacrifice
4. Samuel's last words

1st Samuel 10-12 records the formal anointing of Saul as the first King of Israel at Mizpah; Saul's first and second confirmation as King and Samuel's resignation and final address. Samuel's demonstrates his purity of life and ministry in the way he handled all these events.

Let us start with the anointing and the first inauguration of Saul as king found in 1st Samuel 9, we see Saul and his servant searching for some lost donkeys. They seek them many days and in many parts of the country until they finally come to the land of Zuph (1st Samuel 9:5). Anyone can see the testimony of Samuel's pure life and ministry when Saul and his servant arrived in the area without finding their lost donkeys. Saul wanted to return home, his servant implored Saul to go into the city by saying, "Look now, there is in this city a man of God, and he is an honorable man; all that he says surely comes to pass. So, let us go there; perhaps he can show us the way that we should go" (1st Samuel 9:6). As they entered the city, Samuel met them at the gate because a day earlier, God told him that they would come looking for him (verse 15-16). Once they found Samuel, Saul and his servant spent that day and evening with him. Before departing, Samuel asked Saul's servant to go ahead of them, and Samuel anointed Saul with oil and told him that the Lord had anointed him commander over His inheritance (1st Samuel 10:1).

Anointing with oil was and still is a symbol of the endowment of the Spirit of God as the instrument of divine and spiritual power (Ref. Leviticus 8:12). Before this, there had been no other anointing other than that of the priests and the sanctuary itself (Ref. Exodus 30:23; Leviticus 8:10). Samuel consecrated Saul as king by anointing him, and a monarchy became a divine institution. It stood on par with the priesthood, through which the Lord would bestow on His people the gifts of His Spirit for the building up of His kingdom. In this same way, the priests were to be the moral blessings of divine grace. Samuel consecrated Saul which would be how all the blessings of grace would flow. Through this anointing Saul was set apart from all other Kings of the heathen nations. For, he was "anointed of the Lord" (Ref. 1st Samuel 12:3, five, etc.) to be their captain, leader, and spiritual commander of Israel.

Even though his people rejected Samuel's life's work, Samuel still followed humbly after the will of God with abundant mercy and grace. He gave several proofs to Saul, designed to convince this humble and unbelieving man, of the truth of his words and that the Lord appointed him king of Israel and that the Lord would be with him throughout his rule (1st Samuel 10). The last of the signs was that Saul would meet a group of prophets with a stringed instrument, a tambourine, a flute, and a harp, and they would be prophesying. Then Samuel told Saul that the Spirit of the Lord would come upon him, and he would prophesy with the prophets, and he would be changed into another man. How true it is that when God calls someone to serve Him, He provides a special anointing of the Holy Spirit, which causes the old man to pass away, and a new man created (1st Samuel 10:6). It also demonstrates the importance of seeking the infilling of the Holy Spirit. For when the Spirit of the Lord comes upon us, we find ourselves in Christ, we become a new creature: old things pass away, and all things become new (Ref. 2nd

Corinthians 5:17). Power for witnessing comes upon us along with, (Ref. Acts 1:8) the power to do all things through Him (2nd Thessalonians 4:13). Sins condemnation is gone, and I am free from the power of sin (Romans 8). Led into all truth (John 16:13; Acts 8:39). He controls our movements (Acts 10:19-20); and He imparts wisdom, hope, love, and eternal life (John 3:16, 14:26; Romans 15:13; Galatians 5:5; Romans 5:3-5; Acts 9:31). With all of these benefits, how can we not want to receive the same promises Samuel gave to Saul. Yes, brethren, we have these same promises. Jesus gave us the promise of the Holy Spirit dwelling within us (Luke 24:49: John 14:16-26: Acts 2:1-47)

Brethren, rest assured that as certainly as there is a call, there will be the equipment given to accomplish it. But we must ask and seek for it, and we must accept it, sometimes without feeling it; we must believe that it is ours, and step out on God's predestined path. It is in the act of obedience that we become suddenly and thankfully, aware of His anointing. Oh, that the Spirit of Christ may come mightily on all His servants, so that they may be equipped for the demands of this present age, and that the Master may say of each of them, "Behold! My Servant whom I uphold, My Elect One in whom My soul delights! I have put My Spirit upon Him; He will bring forth justice to all nations" (Isaiah 42:1 LITV).

After a short period, Samuel gathered all Israel to Mizpah. Samuel probably selected Mizpah (watchtower) because it was there that he had once before obtained for the people, by prayer, a great victory over the Philistines (1st Samuel 7:5). It was here that Samuel, charging the people with a rejection of God's institution, then proceeded to nominate a new monarch. Seeing that it was of utmost importance that the appointment was under the divine direction and control of God. The lot included tribes, families, and individuals where God chose Saul King of Israel, and as a result of the lot, Israel saw Saul's appointment as king a divine decision. Not only did God appoint Saul as king by this act in the sight of the whole nation, but Saul realized the certainty of his election. It was amid this national enthusiasm that the prophet Samuel's deep piety and genuine patriotism showed forth as a beckon light to all those lost in utter darkness. Samuel proceeded to explain "the manner of the kingdom," that is, the sovereign rights and privileges, together with the limitations to which they subjected themselves. These regulations the Lord laid out "before all Israel, along with the most sacred records of the nation.

1st Samuel 12:1-5 is perhaps the greatest testimony of Samuel's purity of life and ministry. No greater test of character can come than to ask all the people who you have lived among for 60+ years a question like this one;

> "Testify against me before Jehovah and before His anointed: Whose ox have I taken, and whose ass have I taken, and whom have I offended? Whom have I crushed, and from whose hand have I taken a bribe that I might hide my eyes with it, and I will give back to you?"
>
> 1st Samuel 12:3

No more significant proof of a life and ministry of purity can there be than to get such an answer as Samuel did. "You have not oppressed us, and you have not crushed us, and you have not taken from the hand of any man." (Ref 1st Samuel 12:4) What a way to resign an office than to have so much assurance of integrity, backed with the universal approval of the public? No man did He oppress under his government, no man defrauded! He had accumulated no riches for himself; he had procured nothing from his friends, nor had one needy dependent not find provision out of the public funds. Will this same thing represent you when it is your time to retire?

Samuel's next great lesson is that he was a man of unceasing prayer; he was a man who had God's ear. It was said of him, "Behold now, a man of God is in this city, and he is a man of honor. All that he speaks certainly come to pass." Samuel lived his entire life in the spirit of supplication. Samuel came into this world as a direct answer to prayer. He was born of a praying mother; whose heart was full of earnest desire for a son. He came into life surrounded by prayer, and his first years in this world were in direct contact with a woman who knew how to pray. It was a prayer accompanied by a solemn vow that he should be "lent unto the Lord all of his days," and true to that vow, this praying mother put him directly in touch with the minister of the sanctuary and under the influence of "the house of prayer." It was no wonder he developed into a man of prayer.

Samuel knew God as a boy, raised in the fear and admonition of the Lord, and as a significance, he knew God as a man. He recognized God in childhood, obeyed him, and prayed to him. The result was that he recognized God in manhood, followed him, and prayed to him. If more children were born of praying mothers, brought up in direct contact with "the house of prayer" and the Lord who ran the house. For it is under this type of upbringing that more children would hear the voice of God speaking to them, and would more quickly respond to the divine call to a religious life. Samuel's reputation of a man of prayer was so well known that future Biblical writers like David and Jeremiah mention him as chief among those that called on God's name and as having his prayers answered (Psalm 99:6). Jeremiah alludes to the wonderful power which he exercised in intercessory prayer when he pleaded for his people (Jeremiah 15:1).

All Israel, as well, knew of the long piercing cry of Samuel. In their perils, his petitions had been their deliverance, and in their battles, his prayers had secured the victory for them (1st Samuel 7:8; 8:6). They were all aware that there existed an open door between God and Samuel so that the thoughts of God were able to come into Samuel's heart, and Samuel's heartfelt prayers, that the Father would hear and answer.

Samuel is well aware that the eyes of the natural man ofttimes do not see the Divine workings of God, and too often, the natural man needs to know that God speaks by His servants. Samuel also knew that oft time's men do not recognize the still small voice of God, but only the hurricane, the fire, and a bolt of lightning from above. So, Samuel prays to God for a confirmation of his words. There is no sin in a man of God desiring evidence of his words so that the natural man can see God's glory, presence, and direction. So immediately after Samuel had surrendered his position and introduced his successor, he confronted his people with their sins and announced the heavy penalties that must follow them due to disobedience, he wanted them to experience and hear another voice, which would confirm his own. His hope was to deeply impress on their hearts the absolute need to follow the precepts of Jehovah. Notice what Samuel did to achieve that end:

> "Now, therefore, stand and see this great thing which the Lord will do before your eyes: (17) is today not the wheat harvest? I will call to the Lord, and He will send thunder and rain, that you may perceive and see that your wickedness is great, which you have done in the sight of the Lord, in asking a king for yourselves." (18) So, Samuel called to the Lord, and the Lord sent thunder and rain that day, and all the people greatly feared the Lord and Samuel."
>
> 1st Samuel 12:16-18

Samuel was indeed a man after God's own heart and who had God's ear!

Do we truly realize that the Holy Spirit is in the Church today, that He is prepared to bear witness to every true word spoken in the name of Jesus, but also, he is convicting us of sin, righteousness, and judgment? So that our faith should not stand in the wisdom of man, but in the power of God, God is bearing witness by giving them the Holy Spirit (Acts 15:8; 1st Corinthians 2:1-4). This writer does not believe we have a true understanding of this truth! We have mental acknowledgment but not a true realization of its reality. For we speak God's word in earnest and with all faith, but we do not with all our hearts expect divine co-witness; we do not understand or experience the communion and fellowship of the Comforter. The hearers do not hear His voice impacting their souls, as the thunder and lightning did in Samuel's day. How often do we pray, "Father glorify thy name," and we hear the voice from heaven declaring, "I have both glorified it and will glorify it again!" (Ref. John 12:28) Father, give us such power in prayer that when we pray you will answer and send the thunder and the rain, so that those around us will say "It thundered," and others will say that "an angel spoke" (John 12:28-29).

In concluding this section, we must notice one more lesson. The fear of the Lord came upon all Israel due to God's demonstration, and they earnestly entreated Samuel to pray for them. This request came because Samuel was known as a man of deep prayer. Samuel's heart was so pure and untouched by the past actions of his people that there request for prayer touched his very soul. He took their request before God with complete confidence that Jehovah would hear and corroborate his word and calm their fears. He then urged them never again to turn aside to idols, which could neither profit nor deliver. He then assured them that the Lord would not forsake them, and ended with these magnificent words: "Moreover, as for me, God forbid that I should sin against the Lord in ceasing to pray for you." What a pure and unselfish heart Samuel had. Samuel realized that prayer produced the action and the power of God. "The effective, fervent prayer of a righteous man avails much." It was when Epaphras could no longer help his brethren at Colossae by his words and deeds, he dedicated himself to prayer and labored fervently for them all (Colossians 4:12).

Samuel could no longer exert his energies for his people, as he had once done. The limitations imposed by his advancing years, and by the switch of the kingdom away from his judgeship, made it impossible that he should make his yearly rounds as before. However, he was then able to translate all his energy into another method of helpfulness; Prayer! Prayer is what the telescope is to the eye, the bicycle is to the foot, and the telephone is to the voice. They all enlarge and increase human power, that is what prayer is to the soul. Prayer links us with the all-mighty power of God, which breaks down every wall and frees up the captive. Mighty is he who is mighty in prayer and has learned to labor with the power of God.

To be a true man of prayer, we must look at it as Samuel saw it. Samuel viewed prayer as part of his divine nature, as much a part of his life as breathing, eating, or drinking. For Samuel, not to pray was nothing short of sin. "Far be it from me," Samuel said, "that I should sin against the Lord in ceasing to pray for you." Let us recognize one simple but profound truth, whether it is logical or not, men pray, they want to pray. The instinct to pray is a part of every man, woman, or child, and it is part of our very nature of faith, which all men possess (Ref. Romans 12:3). Granted, in many cases, it is not constant, and it is only the saints who remain in the spirit of prayer that pray consistently; but always when our spiritual nature stirs within us, we pray.

Charles G. Finney once said that all "Men ought always to pray because they always need the influence of prayer. Consider, what is prayer and what prayer does for you. Prayer bathes the soul in an atmosphere of God's divine presence. Prayer communes with God and brings the whole mind under the hallowed influence of such communion. Prayer goes to God to seek pardon and find mercy and grace to help in times of need. How obvious, then, that we always need its influence on our hearts and lives! Truly, there is no reason to wonder why God wants us to pray always" (c.f. 1st Thessalonians 5:17).

But that is not all that the prayers of holy men do! They appease God's wrath, drive away temptations, resist and overcome the devil, procure the ministry and service of angels, overturn the judgments of God. Prayer cures sickness and obtains pardon; it stops the sun in its course, stops the wheels of the chariot; it rules over all gods and opens and shuts the storehouses of heaven. Prayer unlocks the womb and quenches the violence of fire; it stops the mouths of lions and reconciles our suffering and weak faculties; it prevents the abuse of torment and persecution; it pleases God and supplies all our need.

The more praying that takes place, the better the world will be and the mightier the force against evil. In one phase of its operation, it is a disinfectant and a preventive. Prayer purifies the air and controls the contamination of sin. Prayer is not to be a sporadic or a short exercise. It is not a voice crying unheard and unheeded. It is a voice which goes into God's ear, and it lives as long as God's ear is open to holy pleas, and God's heart is alive to holy things. God shapes the world by prayer. Prayer is deathless. The saint's prayer may have ceased due to death, the heart that brought forth the plea may have ceased to beat, but those pleas are still alive before God, and God's heart is always set on them. They outlive a generation, an age, and will outlast the world. Through prayer, your life and world become revolutionized, and God's will become established as your prayers become more numerous and efficient.

The secret of success in Christ's kingdom is the ability to pray. The one who can wield its power is the strong one, the holy one in Christ's kingdom. The most important lesson we can learn is how to pray. Prayer is the keynote of a divine life and the holiest ministry. He does the most for God, who is the highest skilled in prayer. Jesus Christ fashioned and exercised His ministry after the order of prayer.

Samuel viewed prayer as a trust given to him by God and by his people. He could no longer physically act as judge, but he felt God entrusted him with the highest interests of the nation at the ultimate level. It would be treason, against God and man, to fail in his petitions. How often must he have gone aside, as Moses on the Mount, and as our Lord on the hills of Galilee, to pour out his soul in intense supplications and tears for his brethren, and in the service of God and God's promises? How often, had he with great heaviness and continual sorrow in his heart gone and cried out to God as he saw his newly appointed King go astray and sin against his God? Is this not the model that we must all emulate? The one question for the modern Church is whether she wants to see a new manifestation of the power of the Holy Spirit? Whether or not it is realized is entirely dependent on whether it is possible to bring today's Church to her knees?" If these words strike your heart, join with us in persevering in our appeal to God that He would bring forth a mighty spirit of prayer that would produce great things in this last day.

The next great lesson Samuel has to teach is that God would have obedience rather than sacrifice.

> "So, Samuel said, Has the Lord as great a delight in burnt offerings and sacrifices, as in obeying the voice of the Lord? Behold, to obey is better than sacrifice, and to heed than the fat of rams.
>
> 1st Samuel 15:22

Samuel did not reject sacrifices as worthless, for he did not say that God did not take pleasure in offerings; he compared sacrifices with obedience. He pronounced obedience of greater worth than that of any sacrifice. The sum and substance of divine worship consisted in obedience, and sacrifices were and still are simply appendages of obedient worship. It naturally follows, therefore, that sacrifices without obedience are utterly worthless; in fact, they are displeasing to God (Ref. Psalm 50:8; Isaiah 1:11, 66:3; Jeremiah 6:20).

Obedience to God is a moral duty, one that must be constant and crucial. Do not ignore it or overlook it in any way! A person's eternal destiny is determined by obedience; whereas sacrifice is but a ceremonial action, and sinful when offered in error. Any disobedience, therefore, to God's express commands needs no offering without true repentance and a change in attitude and a heartfelt change of thought. For if man had obeyed God and not sinned, there would have been no need for any sacrifice.

Obedience is the law of innocence but sacrifices are the result of sin coming into the world. Never is God more glorified and self, more denied then by obedience. It is much more comfortable and convenient to bring a bullock or lamb or a monitorial amount to a priest than to cast down "every high thing that exalts itself against the knowledge of God and bring every thought into captivity to the obedience of Christ (2nd Corinthians 10:5).

Obedience requires no special talent. It only requires character. Notice:

1. Obedience is following instructions.
2. Obedience is submitting to authority.
3. Obedience is the humbling of pride.
4. Obedience is the response of love.

Obedience is always the response of love. To love God is to obey God. When one disobeys God, he is saying, "I do not love God enough, and I love myself more." Anything less than obedience is sin! When we sin, it is because we willfully choose to disobey. Jesus put it this way:

> "He who has My commandments and keeps them, it is he who loves Me. And he who loves Me will be loved by My Father, and I will love him and manifest Myself to him…"If anyone loves Me, he will keep My word; and My Father will love him, and We will come to him and make Our home with him."
>
> John 14:21, 23

In 1st Samuel 15, we have an example of a man who refused to take responsibility for his disobedient actions by trying to blame others. Does this remind you of someone? Saul decided that it would be a shame to destroy the good along with the bad, despite the direct command of God. Accordingly, King Saul spared King Agag as a trophy of triumph. Then, he saved "the best of the sheep, and the oxen, and of the fatlings, and the lambs, and all that was good" (1st Samuel 15:9). Amazingly, when the prophet Samuel came to meet Saul on his triumphant return, Saul responded, "I have performed the commandment of Lord" (1st Samuel 15:13).

Do you think that Saul believed that he had obeyed God's commandment while destroying only part of the Amalekites? Very doubtful! It is much more probable that Saul was deceiving Himself by thinking partial obedience is acceptable to God. Is it possible that sometimes we trick ourselves into thinking the same thing? It is so easy for a man to explain away his sins as merely innocent mistakes, and to consider himself a loyal subject of God, even while living in violation of God's will.

> Samuel did not let Saul's statement go unchallenged. He asked, "What then is this bleating of the sheep in my ears, and the lowing of the oxen which I hear" (1st Samuel 15:14)? Saul explained he only saved the best of animals for sacrifice (here comes the shifting of blame) "at the will of the people" (verse 15). Notice that Saul knew whose will he was following, and it was not God's. It was at the climax of this conversation that Samuel declared, "Has the Lord as great delight in burnt offerings and sacrifices, as in obeying the voice of the Lord? Behold, to obey is better than sacrifice, and to heed than the fat of rams. (23) For rebellion is as the sin of witchcraft, and stubbornness is as iniquity and idolatry. Because you have rejected the word of the Lord, He also has rejected you from being king."
>
> (1st Samuel 15:22-23)

As we examine 1st Samuel 15, we discover some valuable lessons about the characteristics of disobedience.

- Disobedience is not a trivial thing (1st Samuel 15:23). God classifies disobedience as rebellion, witchcraft, stubbornness, iniquity, and idolatry!
- Disobedience is rebellion because it usurps the authority of God in one's life
- Disobedience is the same as witchcraft because it opens the heart to satanic control
- Disobedience is stubbornness because it refuses to yield to the will of God
- Disobedience is iniquity because it fails to recognize laws for Godly conduct
- Disobedience is idolatry because I worship myself above the worship of God

Any reading of the Old Testament, even a cursory one, clearly reveals the fundamental nature of this covenant between God and man. Whenever man has been willing to obey God's commandments, he receives a blessing. Whenever he has refused to follow God's directions, punishment comes. Blessings and punishments the unchanging truth about obedience and disobedience from the days of Adam and Eve on down through the annuals of time. Disobedience is the driving force behind the "cycle of sin" By disobedience, the first pair of humans started all the suffering and misery the human race has fallen heir to, all the tragic sufferings of individuals, as well as the sufferings of Israel and the world. "By one man's disobedience, many became sinners, so also by one Man's obedience, many will be made righteous (Romans 5:19). "Do you not know that to whom you present yourselves, slaves, to obey, you are

that one's slaves, whom you obey, whether of sin leading
to death or of obedience leading to righteousness?

Romans 6:16

God's system of working with His people was to establish a covenant between them. A set of commands designed to bless them as long as they remained true, thereby holding God to His covenant and all the blessings it contains. God is a covenant God, and those who are wise keep His covenant. In the opening chapter of Isaiah, there is an appealing paragraph,

> "Come now, and let us reason together," Says the Lord,
> "Though your sins are like scarlet, they shall be as white
> as snow; Though they are red like crimson, they shall be
> as wool. (19) If you are willing and obedient, you shall
> eat the good of the land; (20), but if you refuse and rebel,
> you shall be devoured by the sword"; for the mouth of
> the Lord has spoken."

Isaiah 1:18-20

The New Testament also places a strong emphasis on the importance of obedience. No fact indicates more clearly the vital importance of obedience than the fact that our Lord was consistently obedient to his heavenly Father. For example, the writer of Hebrews tells us,

"Though He as a Son, yet learned He obedience by the things which He suffered; and having been made perfect, He became unto all them that obey Him the author of eternal salvation" (Hebrews 5: 8-9).

To the Philippians, Paul said of Christ, "And being found in fashion as a man, He humbled Himself, becoming obedient even unto death, yea, the death of the cross" (Philippians 2:8).

It was through Jesus's perfect obedience to the will of God that Christ achieved His conquest over sin and the resulting way of salvation for mankind (Romans 5:19).

Many people think that they are obedient to God. They agree with God that a great many things commanded in the Bible are good, and therefore, accept them and live by them. When their thinking disagrees with God's commands; however, they go their own way. But, because they so often go the way that God directs in His word, they mistakenly think that they have obeyed God in "almost everything" and that partial obedience satisfies God. Here is the ultimate question, which is the proof of our commitment; do I go God's way no matter what? Let your obedience be your judge!

The final lesson we will cover in the life of Samuel comes from his last recorded words. The situation is this; Samuel had died and was buried in Ramah. The Spirit of God had departed from Saul and was now with David, and in its place, the Lord sent an evil spirit to oppress Saul. The Philistines were now gathering for war in Shunem. Shunem means (double resting-place) it is located 18 miles southwest of the southern tip of the Sea of Galilee. The armies of the Israelites gathered across from them, and Saul being afraid because he was not able to get any answers from the Lord regarding how to proceed against the Philistines (Ref. 1st Samuel 28:1). This is a perfect example of what happens to one's relationship with God do to disobedience. So, Saul decided to break his law and go to a woman that had a familiar spirit. His design was to have the medium at En-Dor bring Samuel up from the dead so Saul could get Godly direction from him, which she did (1st Samuel 28:7).

Saul, a once humble, courageous, and anointed King now, because of the absence of God's spirit due to recurring and unrepentant disobedience, trembled greatly. The heroic courage which faith might have brought him was now not available to him because he could not sense God's presence anymore.

> "Look, I go forward, but He is not there, and backward, but I cannot perceive Him; (9) when He works on the left hand, I cannot behold Him; when He turns to the right hand, I cannot see Him."
>
> Job 23:8-9

Though Saul was indeed attempting to hear from the Lord, probably for the first time in many years, and though this was a good thing, there was no repentance or confession of sin on his part; only hopelessness and frantic despair. Due to his disobedient and prideful heart, "the Lord did not answer him, either by dreams or by Urim or by the prophets (1st Samuel 28:6). "If I regard iniquity in my heart," David said, "the Lord will not hear me" (Ref. Psalm 66:18).

The witch at En Dor did raise Samuel from the dead. Samuel appears to Saul and does speak to him. Herein is the lesson we must learn. That is that there is an absolute certainty of a world beyond this one. Though the spirit of Samuel had passed from this world, the spirit of Samuel was in a real place, living. We need to live every moment with the understanding and realization of the reality of a spiritual eternity. Much of this life, especially how it relates to God's word, will only make sense in light of that knowledge. By the way, whether you believe it was actually Samuel or an evil spirit conjured up by the witch masquerading as Samuel does not matter for this particular lesson, I am, therefore, choosing to refer to this spirit as Samuel simply because verse 16 calls this spirit "Samuel."

> "Then Samuel said: "So why do you ask me, seeing the Lord has departed from you and has become your enemy? (17) And the Lord has done for Himself as He spoke by me. For the Lord has torn the kingdom out of your hand and given it to your neighbor, David. (18) Because you did not obey the voice of the Lord nor execute His fierce wrath upon Amalek, therefore the Lord has done this thing to you this day. (19) Moreover, the Lord will also deliver Israel with you into the hand of the Philistines. And tomorrow you and your sons will be with me. The Lord will also deliver the army of Israel into the hand of the Philistines."
>
> 1st Samuel 28:16-19

Now let us examine in much more detail the last words of Samuel. What sense is there in asking a servant of God for help, once God has denied His assistance? The multiplied misfortunes which had befallen Saul and his realm were due to his direct disobedience regarding the war with Amalek (Ref. 1st Samuel 15). The sin of going to the witch at En Dor was the finishing touch on Saul's life of disobedience. Destruction was at hand, and God had determined it, nothing or no-one at this point could stop it or change it. As Saul had sown, he must also now reap; as he had fallen, so he must lie. It was, therefore, revealed that the Lord would deliver Israel into the hand of the Philistines. Saul and his sons would die and be with Samuel in the realm of the spirit world.

At this point, we must ask ourselves, "what brought Saul to this point?" I propose four faults.

1. Saul ignored the silence of God brought upon him by his disobedience and rebellion. When you do not hear God's voice, you must find out why and repent.
2. Saul turned to witchcraft and divination for direction when he heard nothing from God. Which is another example of disobedience (Ref. Leviticus 19:31; Deuteronomy 18:10-12).
3. Saul abandoned the word of God for his desires – "Not thy will Oh Lord, but mine!"
4. The sum and substance of divine worship consisted in obedience – Saul disobeyed the clear commands of God with no real repentance or change.

The lesson here is that God's people ought to trust in the Lord rather than in any other type of spiritual activity. We ought not to delve into horoscopes or fortune-telling or Ouija boards, for such activity is following in the footsteps of Saul. In the best of situations, such attempts lead us to swindlers and con artists who will say and do anything to swindle you out of your hard-earned money. In the worst case, it leads to demon oppression. In other words, anyone who seeks after soothsayers and the like will come face to face with a terrible reality that God is against them, leaving the devil an open door for control and attack.

Saul, when told the description of the man the witch saw coming up, knew that it was Samuel, and he stooped with his face to the ground (1st Samuel 28:14). The witch described this figure as old and "wrapped with a robe" (28:14). Saul remembered that robe! He could not help but remember how Samuel had predicted the loss of the kingdom, and when he had turned to go how he (Saul) had grabbed the robe of Samuel and tore it. God told him that in just such a manner, the kingdom would be torn from his grasp. Samuel did not wait to question. He stopped Saul and directly asked him, "Why have you disturbed me by bringing me up?" Saul's response was one of despair and a need for guidance and hope. But from the lips of the prophet came no words of comfort or hope. Just words that all of us need desperately to heed when we are left without feeling God's presence and in deep despair. "Why do you ask me, seeing the Lord has departed from you and has become your enemy?" It was a very logical question for Samuel to ask. Samuel was on the Lord's side, so if the Lord would not tell Saul what he wanted, there was no reason for Saul to believe that Samuel would or that he could.

Notice Saul's answer; "I am greatly distressed; for the Philistines are waging war against me and God has departed from me and answers me no more, either through prophets or by dreams; therefore, I have called you, that you make known to me what I should do." (1st Samuel 28:15). Saul's statement reveals not only the absolute state of turmoil, despair, and desperation of Saul. Brethren, do you understand that God never departs from a man unless man demands God to withdraw from him by direct disobedience (Ref. Exodus 33:3; Joshua 7:11-12; Psalm 66:18; Isaiah 59:2, 64:7; Hosea 5:6; 2nd Corinthians 6:17; Hebrews 13:5). Samuel knowing that Saul was keenly aware of this truth, intentionally asks Saul that question designed as a reproof;

Saul has consistently ignored the word from the Lord. So, why should another word come from the Lord? What lesson do we see in this? It is that no second word will come from the Lord until we obey the first word. What was God's first word to Saul? It was that he should repent and humble himself before the Lord. It is the same word that God gives to all who are in sin. Samuel continues by saying that "the Lord has departed from you and has become your adversary (enemy)? The Lord has done as He spoke through me. The Lord has torn the kingdom out of your hand and given it to your neighbor, David." Here we see the why again stated! "As you did not obey the Lord and did not execute His fierce wrath on Amalek, so the Lord has done this thing to you this day" (1st Samuel 28:18). The message of the Lord to Saul is disturbingly consistent with the history of God's dealing with His people; obedience brings blessings; disobedience brings curses (cf. Deuteronomy 28).

There is an important principle also demonstrated here. Leaders have an impact upon those whom they lead; when leaders sin, their followers suffer consequences. Adam and Eve dramatically illustrated this point. They were the leaders and the representatives of the human race, and their sin had an impact upon all mankind (Ref. Romans 5:12). This same principle also applies to fathers or heads of families, the heads of churches, or the heads of governments. "Righteousness exalts a nation, but sin is a reproach to any people. The king's favor is toward a wise servant, but his wrath is against him who causes shame" (Proverbs14:34-35).

It is also important to notice what Samuel said in 1st Samuel 28:16. "God has become Saul's adversary." God becoming man's adversary is a statement we must not ignore. In our day, man believes God is everyone's friend, how striking is it to find out that God is the enemy of those people who disobey Him! So, before we think that we are safe from such a situation, we ought to remember that in two different passages of Scripture, God opposes the proud, but gives grace to the humble (James 4:6; 1st Peter 5:5). That was Saul's problem. Saul's pride had caused God to oppose him, even though he still considered God his friend who would never leave him. Wrong beliefs stemming from ignorance, arrogance and pride causes many to purposely take too much for granted when considering their relationship with God.

Then immediately upon hearing the words of Samuel, Saul fell full length on the ground and was dreadfully afraid because of the words of Samuel. It wasn't just that Samuel told him that he would fall in battle before the Philistines. It was far worse than that. It was the knowledge that the Lord was his adversary; that not only was the Philistines set against him but so was the Lord. Does this not bring to your mind the words of Cain in Genesis 4:13-14? "And Cain said to the Lord, "My punishment is greater than I can bear! (14) Surely You have driven me out this day from the face of the ground; I shall be hidden from Your face; I shall be a fugitive and a vagabond on the earth, and it will happen that anyone who finds me will kill me." Knowing this is more than Saul could bear. There is significance in the fact that he is lying prostrate on the floor. Saul was the man who had once stood head and shoulders above everyone in Israel. But now God stripped him of strength, ability, and all dignity. There is death in him, and 24 hours from now, he will again lay full length on the ground, his life ended, and the word of God fulfilled. Remember, "Pride goes before destruction, and a haughty spirit before a fall" (Proverbs 16:18). When God in his word speaks terror to sinners, he opens to them, at the same time, a door of hope if they repent; but those that apply to the gates of hell for comfort must only expect bondage with no hope of freedom and darkness without a glimpse of light.

One final question before closing this chapter on Samuel. What do you suppose was the purpose God had in bringing Samuel back, or allowing it to appear that way? Could there be three reasons for it?

1. To make Saul's crimes instruments, we can learn from
2. To show the heathen world God's righteous way of dispensing judgment and blessing
3. To confirm the fact that there is life after death. That there is a reality beyond this world.

Surely the thoughtful reader could find additional reasons, for the word of God is living, and it contains within its pages an innumerable amount of life-giving truths.

Samuel was a man of prayer. He was a man who heard from God and one God hears. Samuel represented a man who was able to live in the divine will of God. He understood the precepts of the covenant God had made with man and lived by them. This characteristic is one that we should all strive to achieve and never settle for anything else.

The high place which Samuel occupies in the thoughts and esteem of the people is manifest throughout history. All historical evidence regarding this man, agree that he is the last and most significant of the judges, the first of the prophets, and the man who God used to establish the Israelite kingdom and the Davidic kingdom and line. It is not without reason that with dignity and importance, Israel respected Samuel and considered to be equal in position and respect as that of Moses.

His exhortations and warnings remind us of the Mosaic discourse. Samuel is the man God used to deliver the nation of Israel from the hand of their oppressors; the Philistines, in the same way as Moses, deliver Israel from the bondage and oppression of the Egyptians. Thus, like Moses, he closes the door on the old era and establishes a new way of life with brighter prospects based upon a permanent indestructible and glorious foundation, one whose builder and maker was God. This foundation, when in place and built upon, brings national prosperity and greatness.

Samuel's nobility of character, his righteous life, his pure and holy words, and in his faithfulness to the Lord, are in every way equal with the lawgiver of Israel; Moses. Samuel's pure and holy life came visible in every act and word of his life. And all future Biblical and non-Biblical references to him shows just how high his life aspired to (Ref. Psalm 99:6; Jeremiah 15:1; 1st Chronicles 6:28, 9:22, 11:3, 26:28, 29:29; 2nd Chronicles 35:18).

Oh Lord, let the lessons and lifestyle that Samuel has brought us come alive in our hearts and become a reality in our lives; Amen!

THE UNSUNG HEROES — PREPARED, POISED AND PLEASED TO SERVE THE MINOR JUDGES SHAMGAR, TOLA, JAIR, IBZAN, ELON, ABDON

This chapter focuses on six men who altogether have only 14 verses written about them. If fact in some cases, there was only one short comment recorded. For example, between Shamgar, Tola, and Elon, there are only five verses. The Bible says nothing about their life, judgeship and except for Shamgar there are no details regarding any significant accomplishments

We have just finished looking at the main characters in the book of Judges and 1st Samuel; the classification of these six men is "minor judges," not "major" judges. This classification is not indicative of the impact they made on their country or people. For recorded details of their actions do not appear. This classification is based solely on the amount of historical content recorded in the Biblical record. In much the same way as the classification of the Prophets. But these men, as obscure and mysterious as they are, have much to teach us. Though in scripture, few details appear, about then, they ring loud and clear to anyone who has a heart to hear what they are teaching us.

Now let us take a look at what we do know about each of these judges.

1. Shamgar (Judges 3). his name means stranger, he was the son of Anath, and the third judge of Israel after the death of Joshua; He spectacularly delivered Israel from the Philistines via an ox-goad (Judges 3:31).

2. Tola – his name means scarlet, the son of Puah of the tribe of Issachar. Tola was the second of the six minor Judges and judged Israel for twenty-three years. He lived and died at Shamir, a place in the hill country of Ephraim (Ref. Judge 10:1, 2).

3. Jair – his name means Jehovah enlightens or arouses, or one who diffuses light. He was a Gileadite who succeeded Tola as a judge (Ref. Judges 10:1-2). He judged Israel for twenty-three years,

4. Ibzan – his name means splendid or active – He succeeded Jephthah, and judged Israel seven years and buried in Bethlehem. He had thirty sons and thirty daughters whose marriages he arranged. His sixty children testified to his multitude of wives and his social importance. Jewish tradition identifies Ibzan as Boaz (Judges 12:8, 10), the great grandfather of David (Ref. Ruth 4:21-22).

5. Elon – his name means an Oak tree or strong – he was a Zebulunite, and he judged Israel 10 years.

6. Abdon – his name means service or "Cloud of Judgment" – He was the son of Hillel, the Pirathonite, who judged Israel eight years, he had forty sons and thirty grandsons (some translations say nephews), who rode seventy young donkeys (Judges 12:13-15). Abdon rests in Pirathon in the land of Ephraim, in the mountains of the Amalekites.

As you can see, we don't know much about these men? That is precisely the point! At first glance, the casual Bible reader would recognize their insignificant reference and dismiss them as secondary characters with nothing to say, especially when compared to such giant characters as Samson, Gideon, and Samuel. But brethren, this could not be further from the truth. Ask yourself a question. Is there anything in God's word insignificant or irrelevant? No! These men have plenty to say. The lives and actions of these unsung heroes have plenty to teach us, not only about their cause, attitudes, desires, and their commitment to God but also about God and His actions, love, and disciplines toward His children.

We have seen the lessons that Shamgar has for us in chapter five. Let me list some of them for you:

1. He was a man who was ready to serve God whenever the need arose
2. unlikely instruments God can use. "What is that in thy hand?" In Shamgar's hand was an ox-goad with which he slew six hundred Philistines
3. He was a common man, not one of upbringing, wealth, or military training
4. He was a man of faith and boldness
5. He was a man sold out to God who had complete compassion for his people and country

Now let us look at what these other six men have to teach us.

▸ *If you think that you are nobody – Serve Him anyway!* God can and will use anyone. The Bible records many men and women who God used, who were of low education, wealth, position, or charisma; people who were simply available and responsive to God's commands. People we know little or nothing about, just like these men. People with menial jobs or no jobs at all. Men, women, and children who understood that their talents and possessions ultimately belong to the Lord and were not for self-promotion, pride, or greed. (Ref. Galatians 3:28; Colossians 3:11, 17, 22-25). These available and willing vessels achieved greatness and changed the world in which they lived. These individuals who are in the world's mind, weak-minded nobodies, God chose to use and raise to the amazement of the wise (Ref. 1st Corinthians 1:27). You can be that vessel!

> "For it is written: "I will destroy the wisdom of the wise and bring to nothing the understanding of the prudent." (20) Where is the wise? Where is the scribe? Where is the disputer of this age? Has not God made foolish the wisdom of this world...? (25) Because the foolishness

of God is wiser than men, and the weakness of God is stronger than men. (26) For you see your calling, brethren, that not many wise according to the flesh, not many mighty, not many noble, are called. (27) But God has chosen the foolish things of the world to put to shame the wise, and God has chosen the weak things of the world to put to shame the mighty things."

1st Corinthians 1:19-20, 25-27

▸ *God is no respecter of person – God shows no partiality* (Acts 10:34). Luke 20:21 combines the two words, "respecter and partiality" into one compound word "favoritism." The idea is not to consider one's looks, stature, wealth, or circumstance, but instead, God sees their intrinsic character. The Jews were God's chosen, and inherent sons of the kingdom because they were descendants of Abraham (cf. Matthew 3:9; Luke 3:8; John 8:39; Romans 9:6-7) and that knowledge went to their heads and causing them rebuke and replacement. Peter in Acts 20 says that he had learned the error of this belief and that all man God accepts no matter who or what they are. Everyone receives God's love; God will save and will use anyone that comes to Him, not because of external privileges, rank, or birth but according to their faith, for His boundless love extends equally to all.

The doctrine of equality is everywhere in the New Testament, for example, Romans 2:11; Ephesians 6:9; Colossians 3:25. These verses affirm that God will not save or use a man because he is a Jew, or rich, learned, or of high stature, or because of external privileges such as nationality or hereditary appointment. Neither will He exclude a man because he does not possess any of these privileges. If you look through the Bible, you will find this to be true. God used the rich, poor, non- educated, old, young, men, women, children, Jews, and non-Jews, animals, inanimate objects, the saved and the unsaved to achieve His goals. You have, therefore, no excuse, no argument, and no reason other than your stubbornness for God not to use in effecting your world. Die to your own will and live totally for Christ – see what wonders He can accomplish through you (Refer Galatians 2:20).

▶ *Serving God does not require specialized training or equipment –* God uses what is in your hands and what you are willing to give Him. Shamgar's only reference is in Deborah's victory song (Judges 5:6), and the fact that she mentions him indicates that he held high esteem in the land. The Bible records only two verses on His behalf. Judges 3:31, which says, "And after him (Ehud) was Shamgar the son of Anath, which slew six hundred Philistines with an ox goad: and he also delivered Israel;" and in Judges 5:6 referred to above.

Do you notice what his weapon was? An ox-goad! The weapon was a farming tool! Generally, it was about eight feet long with a half-moon sharp metal blade at one end, used to clean the blades of a plow and a point on the other, used to prod animals to move. Shamgar standing alone with this simple agricultural implement battled against trained and weaponized Philistine warriors and killed six hundred of them and won a great victory.

As we consider Shamgar and his humble weapon, let us allow the lesson of his ox-goad "prod" us to acknowledge the fact that there is room in God's kingdom for the "small things" that we can do (Ref. Luke 16:10; Matthew 25:21). Sometimes, we may feel that unless we are young, energetic, educated, economically situated, physically pleasing to the eye, or possessing a charismatic personality, God sets us aside for a better time and only uses those that possess such benefits. In the end, we may very well find that the most significant deeds man accomplished were quietly and unassuming, far distant from the limelight (Ref. the lesson of the widow's two mites in Luke 21:1-4). Moses' rod (Exodus 4:1-5) both were small and simple tools, but what great things God accomplished through them! And what about Peter's shadow that healed whoever it touched (Ref. Acts 5:15). Also, God used handkerchiefs to heal believers through Paul (Acts 19:11-12). All God is asking for brethren is, "What is that in your hand? "What is nearby and available that God can use if you are willing. You must discover the answer to this vital question, "who do you say I am? "It isn't what you would do tomorrow; if a million should be your lot; but what you're doing now with the dollar and a quarter you have got!" 1

▸ *Serving God requires one to be a volunteer, one of desire and bravery.* Tola, "arose" to save Israel; he was a volunteer who offered his talents in willing service. Nowhere in the Biblical record is it recorded that God summoned or called him to service. Neither did he wait for them to gather around him and beg him to do what was necessary. Tola saw the need, arose, and with God's help, saved Israel, end of story! God is looking for this kind of man; men He can make into champions! Should I mention Shamgar again, he faced 600 armed soldiers with a lowly farm tool. His bravery and courage are legendary.

God is looking for more people like Tola and Shamgar; men who will arise and stand against evil. God is looking for righteous volunteers (cf. Jude 3). Remember, there are no draftees in God's church (Psalm 110:3). The word found in Psalm 110:3 translated willing is *"ned-aw-baw"* which appears 26 times in the Old Testament; fifteen of them it means "free will" as in giving a freewill offering and ten times as "free," "willing" or "volunteer." It simply means to give without request or requiring reimbursement.

Often what the Lord requires looks at least through the natural eye, impossible or unlikely at best. How hard was it for Shamgar to face an army of well-armed Philistine warriors, with only a farm tool (Ref. Judges 3:31)? How hard was it for Moses to stand before Pharaoh carrying only his shepherd's rod and demand of Pharaoh, the immediate release of his people (Ref. Exodus 5:1)? How difficult was it for Elijah to face 850 occult priests with nothing but a word from God and his faith (Ref. 1st Kings 18:18-19)? How popular was it for Elisha and Jeremiah to proclaim the coming judgment of God against His people and their upcoming Babylonian captivity (Ref. 2nd Kings 13:17-19; Jeremiah 21:2-4)? How popular was Micaiah who stood before Ahab, King of Israel, Jehoshaphat King of Judah, and 400 false prophets and alone proclaim the word of the Lord which stood in opposition to what all the others were proclaiming (Ref. 1st Kings 22:14-17)? How improbable was it for Peter to step out of the boat and walk on water (Ref. Matthew 14:29)? And how daring was it for Paul to stand in front of a city outraged against him, crying for his death and still preach the Gospel. Let's not forget to include Paul's determination to preach Jesus and Him crucified even after suffering whippings and scourging's five times with thirty-nine stipes each (Ref. 2nd Corinthians 11:24; c.f. Acts 16; Acts 23).

It is not always popular or easy to stand against ungodliness, to stand alone against impossible odds, or to carry on in the face of impossibilities. It is frequently very tempting to "go with the flow" and look for the easy way out and compromise. The easy way is rarely the right way; however, we must be constant and true in our service to God and refuse to waiver in our convictions (Ref. 2nd Timothy 1:7-8a; 1st Corinthians 16:13). Is your service to God timid and hesitant, or is it compromising or non-existent? Should it not be: willing, courageous, and voluntary? If your spiritual service to God is truly willing, courageous, and voluntary, then you are, in God's eyes, on the same level as these unsung heroes of the book of Judges.

▶ *Our full-fledged service to God brings full-fledged blessings.* Hold your horses, everyone. Take a step back before reading another word. Do not for a moment think that the meaning of "full-fledged blessings" means monitorial, exaltation, status, or prestige. Do not get this writer wrong, for it might mean just that (please note that the word "might"). However, when we look at these unsung heroes, we see no such thing received. What their lives do show us is that recognition and reward are not necessary for their work. If God takes note and is pleased, is it not enough! The world may look upon our lives of service and laugh us to scorn, Oh, but God; acknowledged their lives by recording these men's names and legacy forever in the world's best known and most-read book. Their reward was that their names God recorded in heaven "where neither moth nor rust destroys and where thieves do not break in and steal" (Ref. Matthew 6:20). We are not to strive after worldly fame and acclaim (Ref. Galatians 1:10). We live by every word that proceeds from the mouth of God (Ref. Matthew 4:4), and our innermost desire is to hear His thrilling invitation: "Well done, my good and faithful servant...Enter into the joy of the Lord" (Ref. Matthew 25:21, 23; Luke19:17) or "Come, inherit the kingdom prepared for you from the foundation of the world." (Ref. Matthew 25:34; Hebrews 11:16). If you have an ear, let him hear.

▸ ***Actions speak louder than words.*** Throughout history, there have been unsung heroes who came and went without so much a whisper of recognition. They lived their lives in obscurity, but their actions changed the face of history and time. These men and women even today are not known by name or reputation, they are known only by the lives they touched and by memorials built in the name of their actions (e.g., the tomb of the Unknown Soldier, U.S. War Memorials, Twin Tower memorial, etc.) It is too often that we see leaders either in the political arena or the world stage who are great orators but are sadly lacking in service and results. What God requires are people who are not after the accolades of man and who excel in service and results.

The Bible emphasizes that; "whoever has the world's goods and beholds his brother in need and closes his heart against him, how does the love of God abide in him? Little children, let us not love with word or with tongue, but in truth and deed" (Ref. 1st John 3:17, 18). If we say we love our brothers but let him go on suffering when we can relieve his suffering, we do not love him at all. If our actions contradict our words, then plainly, our actions speak louder than our words. We are known by what we do – not by what we say no matter how often we say it! Jesus gave a command like this when he said;

> "Then the King will say to those on His right hand, 'Come, you blessed of My Father, inherit the kingdom prepared for you from the foundation of the world: (35) for I was hungry, and you gave Me food; I was thirsty, and you gave Me drink; I was a stranger, and you took Me in; (36) I was naked and you clothed Me; I was sick, and you visited Me; I was in prison, and you came to Me.' (37) "Then the righteous will answer Him, saying, 'Lord, when did we see You hungry and feed You, or thirsty and give You drink? (38) When did we see You a stranger and take You in, or naked and clothe You? (39)

Or when did we see You sick, or in prison, and come to
You?' (40) And the King will answer and say to them,
'Assuredly, I say to you, inasmuch as you did it to one of
the least of these My brethren, you did it to Me."

Matthew 25: 34-40

Christians let our manner of life back up what we say with our
mouths, and do it with the humility or gentleness of Christ using His
wisdom. We must do it unto the Lord with brotherly love. A gentle
friendliness and without selfishness toward others. When James
described the true wisdom that comes from God (James 3:17), he said
it is "without hypocrisy." One way to characterize people whose actions
are "hypocritical" is that they are inconsistent, professing something by
their words that is not in their hearts. The faithful and wise Christian
needs to act in a manner consistent with one's words.

These men of unheralded fame came from every tribe and were of
no particular class. They gave no great oratory, did not get involved in
heroic speeches or enthusiastic repartee to encourage and entice others
to join them. These men saw the needs of their fellow brethren and
without any hesitation or fanfare and only possessing what they had
in their hand, volunteered their service to God in whatever capacity
He wanted. With courage, determination, and faith, they proceeded
obediently into action conquering all and everything that stood before
them. They saw, they had compassion, they acted, and they conquered!
These actions are the definition of real heroes; unknown, unheralded,
unremarkable, unnoticed, whose actions were unrecorded.

These chosen men of God just gave without a desire for fame or
fortune; these men's attitudes and actions can teach us more than all
the major Judges combined.

Moses was one of these men. Moses was the humblest man who ever
lived (Ref. Numbers 12:3). How did he come to be that way? The life of
Moses divides into three parts:

1. Moses thought he was somebody – His years in Egypt –
    Pharaoh's adopted grandson

2. Moses learned the he was a nobody – His years in the desert – a mere shepherd

3. Moses understood his weaknesses and inabilities and learned what God could do with a nobody – despite his shortcomings and excuses. He was the savior and deliverer of God's people.

Brethren, no matter who you are or what state you are in, we absolutely must learn what Moses learned; God can still use us. These six men and yes, all the men mentioned and studied in this book were just nobodies, that God took, due to their availability, not their abilities, and used them to change the times in which they lived, and the state of their lives, their nation, and world. In the New Testament, we have more of the same examples. Remember the twelve. They were fisherman, one a tax collector, they were men of low estate and education, despised and rejected of men who Jesus called as worthy vessels. They gave Him they're all and followed him. Their work "turned the world upside down (Ref. Acts 17:6)." Does that declare your work for God today; if not - why not?

Today's world offers little in the way of security, encouragement, hope, and contentment. It too often beats us down with despair, hopelessness, discontentment, and inadequacies' which push us farther and farther down the road of sin. Oft times, we look for pleasure, peace, and love in places far away from God and by the very things that will give us a sense of purpose, contentment, hope, and love. God warns us that there is pleasure in sin (Ref. Hebrews 11:25). To many, follow that road of pleasure into what this writer calls the "Cycle of Sin." Here is the rub, the wages, of sin, is death [eternal death] (Ref. Romans 6:23) in a place "where their worm does not die, and the fire is not quenched." (c.f. Isaiah 66:24; Mark 9:48).

It is this writer's hope and prayer that the lessons gleaned for this book will help you to break the "Cycle of Sin" and will challenge the concerned Christian to seek new heights in your walk with the Lord. Romans 6:23a quoted earlier, has a significant second part, it says: "but the gift of God is eternal life in Christ Jesus our Lord." (Ref Romans 6:23b) God understands our human weaknesses and has made a provision for them, immediately repent when an error occurs and accept His gift of eternal life in His son (Ref. 1ˢᵗ John 1:9).

"The LORD bless you and keep you; (25) The Lord make His face shine upon you, and be gracious to you; (26) the LORD lifts His countenance upon you, and give you peace." (Numbers 6:24-26).

In His love and service
Your Brother in Christ
Rev. Mario A. Bruni D.D.
1ˢᵗ Corinthians 10:13

BIOGRAPHY

I would like to acknowledge the wonderful authors and their works referenced in the preparation of this book.

Their materials have been a source of much wisdom and understanding which has blessed me and helped change my life in more ways than I could have asked. This biography was written as a way of giving these men their just due in acknowledgment of their splendid work.

All scripture quoted in this book are taken from the Thompson Chain Reference Study Bible New King James version unless otherwise initialed.

1. *Unger's Bible Dictionary,* Moody Press, Chicago Illinois, 1987
2. *The New Lexicon Webster's Dictionary of the English Language,* Encyclopedic Edition, Lexicon Publications, Inc. 1998.
3. *The New Strong's Exhaustive Concordance of the Bible,* James Strong, LL.D., S.T.D., Thomas Nelson Publications, 1984.
4. *Young's Analytical Concordance of the Bible,* Robert Young, LL.D., Wm. B. Eerdmans Publishing Co., April 1977.
5. *Matthew Henry's Commentary,* Matthew Henry, MacDonald Publishing, 1706
6. *Jamison, Fausset, & Brown, a Commentary, Critical, Experimental, and Practical,* Wm. B. Eerdmans Publishing Co., 1973.
7. *Wesley's Explanatory Notes on the Whole Bible,* Baker Publishing Group (MI), December 1983.
8. *The New Schaff-Herzog Encyclopedia of Religious Knowledge* (13 Volumes), by Philip Schaff, J. J.Herzog, Albert Hauck, and Samuel Macauley Jackson, 1950.

9. *All the men of the Bible,* Herbert Lockyer, Zondervan Publishing, Grand Rapids, Michigan, 1958

10. *The Works of Flavius Josephus,* Baker Publishing House, Grand Rapids, Michigan, July 1974

11. *Keil and Delitzsch Commentary on the Old Testament,* C.F. Keil, F. Delitzsch, Hendrickson Publishers, 1996

12. *Conquest to Crisis,* John J. Davis, Baker Publishing House, Grand Rapids, Michigan, August 1969

13. *Old Testament History,* Charles F. Pfeiffer, Baker Publishing House, Grand Rapids, Michigan, July 1973

14. *Survey of Israel's History,* Leon Wood, Zondervan Publishing House, Grand Rapids, Michigan, 1970

15. *Hitchcock Bible Names Dictionary,* e-book, Roswell Hitchcock, Packard Technologies, December 2002

16. *Webster's Gold Encyclopedia,* Topics Entertainment, 1997

17. *People of the Past Babylonians,* Saggs, H.W.F., University of California Press, 2000.

18. *All the women of the Bible,* Herbert Lockyer, D.D., D.Lrrr., Zondervan Publishing House, 1958

19. *The Way of Lao-tzu,* Lao-tzu, Chinese philosopher (604 BC - 531 BC)

20. *Reason in Common Sense,* volume 1 of The Life of Reason, . Santayana, George, 1905

21. *Easton's Bible Dictionary,* M.G. Easton M.A., D.D, Thomas Nelson Publishing, London, England, 1897

22. *Major lessons from the "Minor Judges",* By Craig Meyer www. bible.ca, from Expository Files 4.5; May 1997

23. *Ryrie Study Bible,* Charles Ryrie, Moody Publishers, Chicago Illinois, October 1994

END NOTES

Introduction

Illustration #1 Ryre Study Bible
Illustration #2. *Webster's Gold Encyclopedia*, Topics Entertainment, 1997

Othniel

1. *People of the Past Babylonians*, Saggs, H.W.F., University of California Press, 2000.

Deborah

1. http://www.ancient-hebrew.org/27_wilderness.html
2. *All the women of the Bible*, Herbert Lockyer, D.D., D.Lrrr., Zondervan Publishing House, 1958

Gideon – Part One

1. *The Works of Flavius Josephus*, Antiqu. l. 5. c. 6. sect. J.Baker Publishing House, Grand Rapids, Michigan, July 1974

Gideon – Part Two

1. *The Way of Lao-tzu, Chinese Philosopher* (604 BC - 531 BC), Wing-tsit Chan., Prentice Hall Publishing, Upper Saddle River, New Jersey, January 1963

Jephthah

1. *Reason in Common Sense*, Santayana George, volume 1 of The Life of Reason, 1905
2. *Easton's Bible Dictionary*, M.G. Easton M.A., D.D, Thomas Nelson Publishing, 1897

Samson

1. *All the Men of the Bible*, Lockyer, Herbert, D.D., Zondervan Books, Grand Rapids, Michigan, 1958

Eli

1. Our earliest sighting of the item comes from a 2001 issue of "Smilers." It in turn gave as its source "Our Daily Bread," a publication of RBC Ministries.

The Unsung Heroes

1. www.bible.ca., Craig Meyer, from Expository Files 4.5; May 1997

1 **Shamgar** - Neal A. Maxwell
2 Urmila Matondkar

www.ingramcontent.com/pod-product-compliance
Lightning Source LLC
Chambersburg PA
CBHW051004140626
46546CB00016B/241